BRAVO!

BRAV!

Recipes, Legends & Lore

A Cookbook

Celebrating

120 Years

of the

University

Musical

Society,

Ann Arbor

Copyright© 1999
University Musical Society
881 North University Avenue
Ann Arbor, Michigan 48109-1011

Library of Congress Number: 99-071087
ISBN: 0-9670787-0-9

Favorite Recipes® Press
an imprint of

FRP

P.O. Box 305142
Nashville, Tennessee 37203
1-800-358-0560

Manufactured in the United States of America
First Printing: 1999
25,000 copies

There is a natural affinity between the performing arts and the culinary arts. Through 120 years, fine food has occupied a place of honor in the life of the University Musical Society and its audience, evidenced today by our pre-concert Camerata Dinners, the Delicious Experience events hosted by our supporters in their homes, the many receptions held for artists every year, and the gala dinners that begin and end our concert seasons.

The idea of a University Musical Society cookbook has been simmering for years. Finally, a dedicated volunteer group took on the project, with several objectives: to celebrate the remarkable 120-year history of UMS; to showcase some of the beautiful venues that have hosted performances over the decades; to capture some of the memories of the artists who have performed under UMS auspices and the audiences who have enjoyed them; and to recognize the special relationship between the University of Michigan and the city of Ann Arbor, which has nurtured the University Musical Society.

The team of volunteer cooks, writers, and artists collectively spent more than 10,000 hours gathering, testing, and re-testing recipes, conducting interviews, exploring the archives of the Bentley Historical Library, poring over photos old and new, writing the stories, and conferring often to compare and share ideas.

Cooks of all abilities and interests will appreciate the recipes, some of them from performing artists—including perfect gnocchi from Cecilia Bartoli and Irish Colcannon from James Galway—some from distinguished chefs, and others from the community's many accomplished hostesses and cooks. Lovers of music, theater, and dance will be delighted by the photos and the essays, and by the memories drawn from performers, audiences, and the rich record of the years. University of Michigan alumni and friends will find themselves revisiting their own memories of time spent in such beautiful campus buildings as Hill and Rackham Auditoriums and the Power Center for the Performing Arts.

The University Musical Society is proud of *Bravo!* It is a celebration—of the arts, of food, and of the riches they give our lives. We hope that you will come to associate it with life's best moments—whether in a kitchen, around a table with family and friends, or in a concert hall.

Kenneth C. Fischer
President,
University Musical Society

". . . Music is like earth, air, fire and water,
a great basic element that belongs everywhere;
like bread and compassion, mankind cannot live without it."

—Yehudi Menuhin

The words of violinist Yehudi Menuhin about music, community, and sustenance define the mission of the University Musical Society in Ann Arbor. As it has throughout its 120-year history, UMS provides the music that enriches the cultural and economic life of southeast Michigan. The community provides the "bread," the sustenance, in the form of hospitality, audience, and financial support. With this book of recipes, history, and stories, we share our lively, ongoing musical feast in hopes of helping to ensure that our community's future, like its past, will include glorious music.

The University Musical Society is one of a small group of institutions in the United States that bring internationally renowned performing artists to their communities year after year. Artists on the UMS roster appear in performing arts series in New York, Boston, Toronto, Washington, and Chicago, all of them major urban centers. By contrast, Ann Arbor, home to the University of Michigan since 1837, is a mid-sized mid-American community of about 120,000 people.

Many of the town's early residents were German immigrants, who arrived with a rich musical heritage. In 1879, several university faculty and townspeople gathered to study and sing Handel's "Messiah." Led by Professor Henry Frieze, an accomplished organist and a classical scholar, and Professor Calvin Cady, the "Messiah Club" soon became the Choral Union, performing regularly at local churches. Performances of "Messiah" have continued annually to this day. The University Musical Society was formed in 1881. Ever since, UMS has continued its founders' mission: "to provide for students and citizens the opportunity to listen to much music of a high order."

Today, UMS is internationally known as a presenter of new and established artists. It attracts orchestral, choral, chamber, and solo performances of classical, jazz, contemporary, world, and early music, plus dance, theater, and performance-art presentations. More than eighty events during the concert season bring thousands of people from as far as 200 miles away, and some performances have attracted national and international attendance.

Over the last two decades, as the community has become more global, UMS has kept pace. Through 150 educational events each year it reaches all age groups; through diversified programming it has built relationships with many cultural, ethnic, and faith-based communities from a widening area.

While UMS is affiliated with the university and housed on campus, it is a separate, not-for-profit organization, supported through ticket sales, corporate and individual contributions, and foundation and government grants. The earliest UMS concerts were in University Hall, built on the central campus in 1871. In 1913, most concerts moved to Hill Auditorium, an acoustical masterpiece designed by Albert Kahn that seats more than 4,000 people.

This book, a product of many volunteers' efforts, celebrates the rich past of the University Musical Society and salutes its future. Each section begins with a description of one or two historic performances from among the thousands of concerts presented over 120 years. The memories, anecdotes, and stories gathered from performers and audiences past and present are seasoning for the most important part: the recipes, gathered from performing artists, renowned chefs, and community cooks, tested with care, and presented with pride. *Bravo!* also celebrates a community and its musical history, and thus the music, the bread, and the compassion that "mankind cannot live without."

CONTENTS

Appetizers

1894

Saturday, May 19, 1894, 7:30 p.m.

University Hall

First Annual May Festival

The Choral Union and
The Boston Festival Orchestra
Albert A. Stanley   *Conductor*

"Manzoni" Requiem, Verdi

Soloists
Miss Emma Juch   *Soprano*
Miss Gertrude May Stein   *Mezzo-Soprano*
Mr. Edward C. Towne   *Tenor*
Mr. Max Heinrich   *Baritone*

1. *Requiem e Kyrie, "Grant Them Rest"*

2. *Dies Qiae, "Day of Anger"*
   a. *Dies Irae, "Day of Anger"*
   b. *Tuba Mirum, "Hark! The Trumpet"*
   c. *Liber Scriptus, "Now the Record"*
   d. *Quid Sum Miser, "What Affliction"*
   e. *Rex Tremendae, "King of Glories"*
   f. *Recordare, "Ah! Remember"*
   g. *Ingemisco, "Sadly Groaning"*
   h. *Confutatis (From the Accursed)*
   i. *Lacrymosa, "Ah! What Weeping"*

3. *Domine Jesu, "Oh, Lord, God"*

4. *Sanctus, "Holy"*

5. *Agnus Dei, "Lamb of God"*

6. *Lux Aeterna, "Light Eternal"*

7. *Libera Me, "Lord, Deliver My Soul"*

University Hall in 1894

"VISITORS have arrived in Ann Arbor on every train for the past 24 hours and more will arrive this afternoon," reported the local paper on the first day of the first May Festival in 1894. "Judging from the number of visitors in town and the number of tickets out before this week, standing room will be scarce tonight and tomorrow night in University Hall."

The Boston Festival Orchestra, a small touring orchestra, had been engaged to replace the Boston Symphony Orchestra, which had canceled its scheduled appearance. Charles Sink, who was with the University Musical Society from 1904 to 1968, said later: "But just one concert meant tremendous expense. Some enthusiasts said, 'Let's have them for three concerts. The travel won't cost any more.' That took like fire." So before it ever occurred, the University Musical Society board of directors boldly christened the event "the first annual May Festival."

Their courage was justified: not only did the festival sell out that first year, but it lasted through 102 seasons, until 1995, growing from three concerts to as many as six presented over four days.

Dr. Arthur "Dad" Stanley, head of both UMS and the University School of Music, established the format for this and every May Festival to follow: a mixture of orchestral and choral works, with soloists of the first rank. He chose the music to be performed by the visiting orchestra and by the Choral Union—the chorus of university students and townspeople that he directed and that was founded before UMS itself—and engaged the soloists.

Verdi's "Manzoni" requiem was performed during that first May Festival. Nineteen years later, on Thursday, May 15, 1913, at 8:00 p.m., the "Manzoni" was performed again, to celebrate the composer's centenary and the inauguration by the May Festival of the beautiful new Hill Auditorium. By then the Chicago Symphony Orchestra under Frederick Stock had taken over from the Boston Festival Orchestra—an association that would last until 1935—and the festival was so popular that it sold almost twice as many tickets that first year at Hill.

Another tradition began in 1913: a choir of 400 local school-children joined a concert of the festival. The Festival Youth Chorus lasted for forty-five years, and generations of kids had the thrill of singing with a full orchestra on Hill's huge stage before an audience of thousands. Of their first festival performance, the newspaper wrote: "The youngsters were magnificently drilled . . . .Their fresh young voices rang out confidently and the tone was always excellent."

The 1913 May Festival also honored Arthur Hill, the university regent whose bequest had helped to fund the auditorium named for him. At the final concert, as the orchestra played the funeral march from Richard Wagner's "Götterdämmerung" in Hill's memory, the audience stood, afterward refraining from applause and filing out in silence.

What was cooking?

Chef Auguste Escoffier created Peach Melba in honor of soprano Nellie Melba.

❖

The W. Atlee Burpee Company brought iceberg lettuce to market.

❖

In 1896, Fannie Merritt Farmer's Boston Cooking School Cookbook standardized measurements and oven temperatures, which allowed even a cook unfamiliar with a dish to make it by following a recipe.

Zesty Bruschetta

1 baguette French bread, cut into
    1-inch slices
1 cup chopped fresh or canned plum
    tomatoes, drained
2/3 cup chopped green onions
4 ounces feta cheese, crumbled
1/4 cup chopped black olives
2 tablespoons finely chopped fresh basil
1 teaspoon olive oil
1/2 teaspoon hot pepper sauce
Salt to taste

Place the bread slices in a broiling pan. Broil each side until lightly toasted.

Combine the tomatoes, green onions, cheese, olives, basil, olive oil, hot pepper sauce and salt in a bowl and mix with a fork. Top each toast slice with a generous mound of the tomato mixture. Broil briefly to reheat if desired.

Serve on a platter garnished with a large sprig of fresh basil.

YIELD: 20 TO 24 SLICES

Caramelized Onion Quesadillas

3 tablespoons olive oil
1 large onion, chopped
2 tablespoons balsamic vinegar
1 teaspoon sugar
12 flour tortillas
6 ounces fontina cheese, shredded
4 ounces goat cheese, crumbled
Olive oil

To caramelize the onion, heat the olive oil in a large skillet and add the onion. Cook for 10 minutes or until tender. Add the vinegar and sugar. Cook for 3 minutes or until the sugar is dissolved and the mixture is light brown. Remove from the heat.

Place 3 tortillas on a baking sheet. Cover each tortilla with fontina cheese, caramelized onion and goat cheese. Top each with a second tortilla. Brush the tops with additional olive oil.

Bake at 350 degrees for 8 to 10 minutes or until the tops are golden brown and the cheese is melted. Repeat with remaining ingredients.

Cut each quesadilla into 4 wedges. Serve hot.

YIELD: 24 PIECES

Miniature Quesadillas with Mango Salsa

2 cups cooked black beans, puréed
2 teaspoons chipotle chile purée, or to taste
1 scallion, minced
1 tablespoon fresh lime juice
2 tablespoons sour cream
Kosher salt to taste
12 (6-inch) flour tortillas
12 thin slices smoked Cheddar cheese (about 3x5 inches each)
Mango Salsa

For the filling, combine the black beans, chile purée, scallion, lime juice, sour cream and kosher salt in a bowl. Mix well and set aside.

Spray 1 side of 6 tortillas with nonstick cooking spray. Place the tortillas sprayed side down on a large baking sheet. Place 1 slice of cheese in the center of each tortilla. Spoon 3 tablespoons of the filling onto each cheese slice. Spread the filling to the edges with a spatula, leaving a 1-inch margin. Place 1 cheese slice in the center of the filling (the cheese will burn if it overlaps the edges of the tortilla). Cover each with 1 tortilla.

Bake at 400 degrees until golden brown. Cut each quesadilla into wedges and arrange on a serving dish. Place a spoonful of Mango Salsa on the center of each wedge. Garnish each with a cilantro sprig.

YIELD: 36 PIECES

Mango Salsa

1 firm mango, peeled, cut into ¼-inch cubes
½ small red bell pepper, cut into ¼-inch pieces
1 tablespoon minced cilantro

Combine the mango, red pepper and cilantro in a bowl and mix well.

YIELD: ABOUT 1¼ CUPS

Frieze Memorial Organ

The gold-stenciled organ pipes gracing the back wall of the Hill Auditorium stage are the re-created ornamental facade of an organ built for the 1893 Columbian Exposition in Chicago and afterward installed in the old University Hall in Ann Arbor. When Hill Auditorium was completed in 1913, the organ was moved there and dedicated to Henry S. Frieze, organist, scholar, founder of the University Musical Society, and twice acting president of the University of Michigan. The Frieze Memorial Organ was rebuilt in 1928, overhauled in 1955, and renovated from 1984 through 1988; it is continually repaired and tuned. Its 7,599 pipes (amazingly, eight ranks remain from the original organ) range in height from ¾ inch to thirty-five feet. Many distinguished artists have played the Frieze organ, which is a superb example of the type known as American Classic.

Black Bean Tortilla Swirls

2 cups black beans
8 cups cold water
1 cup chopped onion
1 garlic clove
1 carrot
1 rib celery
1 tablespoon salt
1 bay leaf
1 jalapeño chile, minced (optional)
2 garlic cloves, chopped
2 teaspoons cumin
1 small onion, chopped
Leaves only of ½ bunch fresh cilantro
2 tablespoons salsa
Salt and pepper to taste
8 flour tortillas

Rinse and sort the beans. Combine with the water, 1 cup onion, 1 garlic clove, carrot, celery, 1 tablespoon salt and bay leaf in a stockpot. Cook for 2 to 3 hours or until tender; drain well, discarding everything except the beans. Purée the beans in a food processor. Add the jalapeño, 2 garlic cloves, cumin, small onion, cilantro, salsa and salt and pepper to taste. Purée until smooth. Adjust seasonings. Chill in the refrigerator for 1 to 2 hours. Spread a thin layer of purée on each tortilla. Roll up each tortilla tightly. Chill, covered, for 1 to 2 hours.

Cut the rolls diagonally into 8 to 10 slices. Arrange on a serving platter. Serve with sour cream, additional salsa and/or guacamole. Garnish with cilantro sprigs and chopped scallions.

Variations: Spread a layer of cream cheese on the tortillas first; substitute refried beans for black beans; and/or add chopped tomatoes, green chiles, olives or chopped scallions to the filling.

YIELD: 8 SERVINGS

Focaccia Panini

1 loaf bakery-style focaccia bread (about
    12 ounces, 8 inches in diameter,
    1½ inches thick)
8 ounces Neufchâtel cheese or cream cheese
2 to 3 tablespoons low-fat milk
¼ cup oil-packed sun-dried tomatoes, patted
    dry, chopped
4 teaspoons chopped fresh basil, or
    1¼ teaspoons dried basil
1 teaspoon chopped fresh thyme, or
    1¼ teaspoons dried thyme
2 teaspoons chopped fresh oregano, or
    1 tablespoon dried oregano
1 small garlic clove, minced
1½ cups packed fresh spinach leaves, stems
    removed
8 ounces Italian salami, thinly sliced,
    chopped
½ cup sliced black olives

Split the bread into halves horizontally with a serrated knife and set aside. Process the cheese and milk in a food processor until smooth. Add the tomatoes, basil, thyme, oregano and garlic and mix well. Spread ¼ of the cheese mixture on the cut side of each bread half, spreading to the edges. Top with spinach, salami and olives. Spread with the remaining cheese mixture. Wrap each half securely in plastic wrap and chill for 1 hour to overnight. (The bread will slice more easily when thoroughly chilled.)

Cut each bread round lengthwise into 5 strips; cut each strip crosswise into 1½-inch pieces.

YIELD: 48 PIECES

Crab Salad Canapés

½ red bell pepper
½ green bell pepper
1 rib celery
3 tablespoons chopped
    pimiento-stuffed green
    olives

4 ounces lump crab meat, flaked
2 teaspoons light olive oil
1 tablespoon white balsamic
    vinegar
1 baguette French bread, cut
    into ¼-inch slices

Finely chop the bell peppers and celery. Combine the bell peppers, celery, olives and crab meat in a glass bowl. Add the olive oil and vinegar and marinate for 1 to 2 hours. Drain well.

Place the bread slices on a baking sheet. Brush lightly with additional olive oil or some of the marinade. Broil until lightly toasted. Spoon the crab meat mixture into a bowl. Arrange the bread slices around the bowl. Garnish with endive leaves.

YIELD: ENOUGH SPREAD FOR 10 TO 12 SLICES

Onion Confit Toasts

¼ cup olive oil
2 pounds Vidalia, Maui or
    other sweet onions,
    thinly sliced (about 8
    cups)
½ cup sugar

1 teaspoon salt
½ teaspoon pepper
1 cup dry red wine
6 tablespoons balsamic vinegar
2 tablespoons grenadine
36 (¼-inch) slices French bread

Heat the olive oil in a large heavy saucepan over medium heat. Add the onions, sugar, salt and pepper. Cook, covered, for 30 minutes or until the onions are very tender. Add the wine, vinegar and grenadine. Simmer, uncovered, for 25 minutes or until very thick, stirring frequently. Adjust the seasonings. Let stand until cool.

Arrange the bread slices on a baking sheet and brush with additional olive oil. Bake at 350 degrees for 5 minutes or until almost crisp. Spoon the onion confit onto the toast to serve.

Note: The confit can be prepared up to 2 days ahead and stored, tightly covered, in the refrigerator.

YIELD: 36 PIECES

Under construction

In the 1890s, University of Michigan President James B. Angell described his ideal performance hall. Hill Auditorium would not be built until 1913, but Angell was prophetic:

"The building should be monumental, . . . large enough to secure the best musical and dramatic effects, but not so large as to destroy the effect of shading in music or utterance. The seating capacity should be about five thousand. . . .

"All seats should command a favorable point of view of the stage. . . .

"The stage should be planned with great care . . . to provide seats for a chorus as large as may be consistent with the attainment of the highest art. . . .

"For unnumbered generations, the Auditorium will stand, consecrated to the genius of culture, and uplifting countless thousands to new levels of experience and inspiration."

15

Baked Pita Bread Appetizers

½ bunch parsley, finely chopped
A few stems fresh chives or green stems
*   from scallions, finely chopped*
½ cup (1 stick) butter, melted
2 cups sour cream
Juice and grated zest of ½ lemon
6 to 8 thin pita breads
*   (5 to 7 inches round)*
Grated Parmesan cheese to taste
Freshly ground sea salt and pepper to taste
Herbs of your choice to taste

Combine the parsley, chives, butter, sour cream, lemon juice and lemon zest in a bowl and mix well. (This mixture can be placed in an airtight container and stored in the refrigerator for several weeks if desired.)

Split the pita bread and cut into halves or quarters. Spread the sour cream mixture on the pita bread and sprinkle with cheese. Season with sea salt, pepper and any other herbs of your choice.

Place the bread on a baking sheet. Bake at 350 degrees for 15 minutes or until light brown and crisp. Serve immediately.

Note: The sour cream mixture makes an excellent spread or dip as it is, or it can be used as a base for others.

YIELD: 3 TO 4 DOZEN

Baked Brie

½ cup sifted flour
⅛ teaspoon salt
¼ cup cream cheese, softened
¼ cup (½ stick) butter, softened
1 (7-ounce) wheel of Brie
1 egg yolk
1 tablespoon water

Process the flour, salt, cream cheese and butter in a food processor until the mixture forms a ball. Chill for 1 hour to overnight.

Roll some of the dough into a ⅛-inch-thick circle large enough to cover the bottom and side of the cheese. Roll another circle large enough to cover the top of the cheese. Place the cheese in the center of the larger circle and fold the dough to enclose the cheese. Brush the edge of the smaller circle with some of the egg yolk. Place the dough on top of the cheese and seal. Decorate the top of the cheese with the remaining dough. Brush with a mixture of the remaining egg yolk and water. Chill for 1 hour.

Place the cheese on a baking sheet. Bake at 425 degrees for 20 minutes. Let stand for 30 minutes before serving.

YIELD: 8 TO 12 SERVINGS

16

Brio Trio

This dish is easy to make when fresh basil is plentiful, but it is also beautiful at holiday time when frozen pesto works wonderfully.

1 (2-pound) wheel of Brie
1½ cups oil-packed sun-dried tomatoes
1½ cups Pesto Italiano (page 186)

Two hours before serving time, place the cheese in the freezer for 10 to 20 minutes. Slice the rind off with a serrated knife. Place the cheese on a large platter.

Drain the tomatoes, reserving the oil. Mince the tomatoes in a food processor, adding just enough of the reserved oil to hold the mixture together. Spread the Pesto Italiano over the cheese and spread the tomatoes over the pesto. Garnish with fresh basil, toasted pine nuts and slivers of red and green bell pepper. Serve with crackers.

YIELD: 18 TO 20 SERVINGS

Marinated Cheese

10 ounces goat cheese
2 bay leaves
2 teaspoons black peppercorns
2 sprigs of fresh thyme
2 sprigs of fresh basil
A few dried red chiles (optional)
2 cups (or more) olive oil

Place the cheese in a large jar with a tight-fitting lid. Add the bay leaves, peppercorns, thyme, basil and dried chiles. Add enough olive oil to cover generously. Let stand, covered, at room temperature for 2 weeks or longer before using. (The cheese will keep for 6 to 8 weeks but will soften if kept too long.) Drain the cheese and serve with French bread or in salads.

Note: More cheese can be added to the olive oil as some of the cheese is used. Any leftover oil is excellent in salads.

YIELD: 2½ CUPS

The local press had a lot to say about the May Festival in its early years. In 1907, the Ann Arbor Argus *complained about latecomers: "All should come early so that ushers may seat the audience before the concert is to begin . . . so that those who so desire may leave on the late trains. The placing of chairs in the aisles or the carrying of chairs of any description is forbidden. The ladies are respectfully requested to remove their hats.*

"Only two other things need to be added: do not take children who are too young to appreciate the concerts and who annoy others, and if you cannot appreciate the concerts enough to stop talking yourself, then go out on the campus to talk instead of the Hall."

17

Pesto Bombe with Goat Cheese

2 cups loosely packed arugula leaves
2 tablespoons minced garlic
1/4 cup pine nuts, toasted
1/4 cup grated Parmesan cheese
2 tablespoons olive oil
Salt and pepper to taste
1 to 2 tablespoons chicken consommé
    or broth
8 ounces Neufchâtel cheese or cream cheese,
    softened
4 ounces goat cheese with herbs
Milk
1/4 cup oil-packed sun-dried tomatoes,
    drained, chopped
1/4 cup pine nuts, toasted

To prepare the pesto, combine the arugula, garlic, 1/4 cup pine nuts and Parmesan cheese in a food processor container. Add the olive oil gradually with the food processor running and process until smooth. Season with salt and pepper. Add some of or all the chicken consommé if the pesto is too dry.

Line a small bowl with plastic wrap, leaving an overhang. Mix the Neufchâtel cheese and goat cheese in a bowl until smooth, adding a small amount of milk if needed. Spread 1/3 of the cheese mixture in the prepared bowl. Spread half the pesto over the cheese mixture. Sprinkle with half the remaining 1/4 cup pine nuts and top with half the tomatoes. Repeat the layers once. Spread the remaining 1/3 of the cheese mixture over the top. Fold the plastic over the cheese and press gently. Chill until serving time.

To unmold, unfold the plastic and invert the bowl onto a serving plate. Remove the plastic. Let stand for 30 minutes before serving. Serve with crackers or sliced bread.

YIELD: 8 TO 10 SERVINGS

Pâté with Olives, Pine Nuts and Prosciutto

1/4 cup fresh bread crumbs
2 tablespoons brandy
1 pound ground pork
8 ounces ground veal
1/4 cup (1/2 stick) butter
1/3 cup black olives, pitted, chopped
1/4 cup pine nuts, lightly toasted
1/4 cup chopped prosciutto
1 1/2 teaspoons fresh basil
1/2 teaspoon dried thyme
1/4 teaspoon pepper
1 small garlic clove, minced
1/2 teaspoon salt
1 egg, lightly beaten
8 ounces lean bacon

Moisten the bread crumbs with the brandy and set aside. Combine the ground pork, veal and butter in a food processor container and process until well mixed. Combine with the bread crumbs, olives, pine nuts, prosciutto, basil, thyme and pepper in a large bowl and mix well. Press the garlic with the salt. Add to the meat mixture and mix well. Add the egg and mix well.

Line the bottom of a 10-inch loaf pan with half the bacon. Press the meat mixture firmly into the pan. Cover with the remaining bacon.

Bake at 350 degrees for 1 1/2 hours. Weight down the pâté and let stand until cool. Chill for 12 hours.

Unmold the pâté onto a serving dish. Remove and discard the bacon or reserve for another use. Serve the pâté at room temperature with gherkins, spicy mustard and sliced dark bread or French bread.

YIELD: 18 TO 20 SERVINGS

Calypso Black Bean Hummus with Grilled Sweet Potato Chips

4 cups undrained cooked black beans or undrained
    canned beans
½ cup tahini (sesame paste)
¼ cup lemon juice
2 tablespoons chopped garlic, or to taste
⅛ teaspoon cumin
1 to 2 drops of green hot pepper sauce or hot sauce
Salt to taste

Drain the beans, reserving the liquid. Combine the beans, tahini, lemon juice, garlic, cumin and hot pepper sauce in a food processor container and process until smooth. Thin with a small amount of the reserved liquid if needed.

Serve with Grilled Sweet Potato Chips (below); tomato salsa, sour cream and corn chips; or baked flour tortillas.

YIELD: 1 QUART

Grilled Sweet Potato Chips

2 medium sweet potatoes
1 teaspoon olive oil or olive oil cooking spray
Salt to taste

Peel the sweet potatoes and cut into ¼- to ½-inch slices. Brush lightly with olive oil. Place the slices on the center of the grill rack. Grill for 7 to 10 minutes or until tender-crisp, turning once. Remove from the grill and sprinkle with salt. Serve immediately. These chips are also good with roast pork.

Variation: Arrange thin sweet potato slices in a single layer on a baking sheet and drizzle with olive oil. Bake at 350 degrees or until light brown, stirring occasionally. Sprinkle with equal parts chopped parsley, lemon strips and chopped garlic.

YIELD: 4 SERVINGS

The cultural smugness that Ann Arbor is often accused of goes way back. In the 1890s, Lewis H. Clement, a local piano dealer, musician, conductor, and self-appointed cultural critic, wrote a weekly column called "Musical Musings" for the local paper. His earliest columns were signed "The Musician," anonymity that perhaps encouraged this overwrought praise of "the Athens of the West" (May 7, 1896):

"I wonder how many people in Ann Arbor realize how prominent a position the city occupies among the musical centers of America. The fact that our second May Festival was the largest in point of attendance of any similar festival in the United States, with but one exception, shows how all eyes are turned toward Ann Arbor in musical matters."

Stilton Shortbread "Cookies"

½ cup (1 stick) unsalted butter
2½ cups flour
8 ounces Stilton cheese, crumbled
4 ounces walnuts, ground
1 teaspoon pepper
2 eggs, beaten

Cut the butter into the flour in a bowl or food processor. Add the cheese, walnuts and pepper and mix well. Add the eggs and knead for 1 minute.

Roll the dough into a 1-inch-diameter log. Chill thoroughly.

Cut the dough into ¼-inch slices and place on a parchment paper-lined baking sheet. Bake at 350 degrees for 10 minutes.

YIELD: 4 DOZEN

Grilled Asian Shrimp

1 cup minced red onion
4 teaspoons grated lemon zest
2 teaspoons minced garlic
2 teaspoons coriander
1 teaspoon cumin
1 teaspoon turmeric
½ teaspoon crushed red pepper flakes
1 tablespoon lemon juice
1 tablespoon soy sauce
⅓ cup peanut oil
1 pound medium shrimp

Soak wooden skewers in water for 30 minutes. Combine the onion, lemon zest, garlic, coriander, cumin, turmeric, red pepper flakes, lemon juice, soy sauce and peanut oil in a shallow dish or bowl and mix well. Peel the shrimp, leaving the tails on. Butterfly the shrimp, thread onto the skewers and place in the marinade. Marinate, covered, in the refrigerator for 1 hour. Remove the shrimp from the marinade, discarding the remaining marinade.

Grill or broil for 3 minutes without turning. Serve hot.

YIELD: 6 TO 8 SERVINGS

Zubin Mehta's Chicken Fritters

¼ pound chick-pea flour
   (see Note)
¼ cup all-purpose flour
1 teaspoon salt
½ teaspoon freshly ground
   black pepper
¼ teaspoon chili powder or
   cayenne pepper

¼ teaspoon baking powder
2 teaspoons lemon juice
2 eggs, lightly beaten
3 pounds chicken breasts,
   boned, skinned, cut into
   finger-size strips
Vegetable oil for deep-frying

Combine the chick-pea flour, all-purpose flour, salt, black pepper, chili powder, baking powder, lemon juice and eggs in a bowl and mix well. Add enough water to make a batter the consistency of catsup. Add the chicken, turning to coat well.

Heat 2 inches of vegetable oil to 375 degrees in a wok or heavy skillet. Drop the chicken strips carefully into the hot oil. Deep-fry for 5 minutes or until golden brown. Serve with Lemon Pesto Butter (below); spicy tomato sauce; or sweet-and-sour mustard sauce.

Note: Chick-pea flour is available in Indian and Middle Eastern markets and in some supermarkets.

YIELD: 8 TO 10 SERVINGS

Lemon Pesto Butter

⅔ cup firmly packed fresh
   basil
¼ cup olive oil
3 to 4 teaspoons grated
   lemon zest
2 to 3 garlic cloves, chopped

¼ cup pine nuts, toasted
1 to 1½ cups (2 to 3 sticks)
   butter
Freshly ground black pepper
Red pepper flakes (optional)

Process the basil, olive oil, lemon zest, garlic and pine nuts in a food processor until mixed. Pour into a small heavy saucepan. Add the butter, black pepper and red pepper flakes. Cook over low heat until the butter is melted. Adjust the seasonings.

Note: If the sauce separates while being kept warm, add 1 to 2 pats of butter and stir constantly until blended.

YIELD: 2 TO 2½ CUPS

Very early in Ann Arbor's musical life, there was only one grand piano. It was a Steinway Style 2 with eighty-five keys, owned by Reuben and Pauline Kempf, well-known local music teachers. When it was needed for a concert, the piano was transported, probably by horse-drawn cart, from the Kempfs' home studio on Division Street to University Hall a few blocks away. Ignace Paderewski and Ernst von Dohnanyi were among the notable pianists who used it.

Madame Ernestine Schumann-Heink was accompanied on the Kempfs' piano. Taken to their home to inspect it before her recital, the great mezzo pronounced it "excellent." Then, admiring the large plate-glass mirror hanging on the parlor wall nearby, she requested that it be installed in her dressing room. It was.

Kempf House, now a city museum, still displays the historic piano.

Fragrant Lemon Chicken

Invite guests to use lettuce leaves for scooping and wrapping this chicken. It's a little messy, but delicious.

1 pound boneless chicken
    breast or boneless thighs,
    cut into bite-size pieces
1 medium onion, chopped
Celery leaves
1 to 2 tablespoons
    vegetable oil

Lemon Sauce (below)
1½ tablespoons dark soy sauce
Boston lettuce or red leaf lettuce,
    rinsed, patted dry
Finely chopped cilantro

Combine the chicken, onion, celery leaves and 1 to 2 tablespoons oil in a skillet or wok. Cook over medium-high heat until the chicken is cooked through, stirring constantly. Remove from the heat. Let stand, covered, for 30 minutes.

Combine the Lemon Sauce and soy sauce in a bowl and pour over the chicken. Marinate for 45 to 60 minutes.

Arrange lettuce leaves on a large platter. Remove the chicken to the platter with a slotted spoon, reserving the remaining marinade to serve with the chicken. Sprinkle with cilantro. Garnish with thin lemon slices.

YIELD: 8 TO 10 SERVINGS

Lemon Sauce

¾ cup chicken stock
1 tablespoon cornstarch
6 tablespoons orange juice
6 tablespoons lemon juice
2 tablespoons sugar, or
    to taste

Salt to taste
1 garlic clove, minced (optional)
1 tablespoon vegetable oil
    (optional)

Combine the chicken stock, cornstarch, orange juice, lemon juice, sugar and salt in a saucepan. Cook over medium heat until the sauce is thickened and glossy, stirring frequently. Sauté the garlic in the oil in a saucepan or deep skillet. Add the sauce and mix gently.

YIELD: 1¾ CUPS

Wild Mushrooms in Phyllo

3 tablespoons olive oil
1 tablespoon minced garlic
1 tablespoon chopped fresh thyme, or 1 teaspoon dried thyme
2 tablespoons minced onion
2 pounds mixed wild mushrooms, sliced
½ cup dry white wine
1 teaspoon paprika
1 cup grated Parmesan cheese
1 teaspoon salt
½ teaspoon freshly ground pepper
1 cup sliced green onions
1 egg
Olive oil
28 to 30 sheets phyllo dough (see Note)

For the filling, heat 3 tablespoons olive oil in a large saucepan over low heat. Add the garlic, thyme and onion. Cook until the garlic is tender. Add the mushrooms and increase the heat. Sauté for 8 to 10 minutes or until the mushrooms are tender. Add the wine and paprika. Cook until most of the liquid has evaporated. Remove to a large bowl. Mix in the cheese, salt, pepper, green onions and egg.

For the pastry, lightly oil 2 baking sheets. Cut the phyllo dough into 8x12-inch rectangles. Brush 1 sheet of dough lightly with olive oil. Cover with a second sheet and brush lightly with olive oil. Place 2 tablespoons of the filling 2 inches from 1 short edge in the center of the sheet. Fold each long edge toward the center, overlapping slightly to enclose the filling. Fold up completely from the top short edge. Repeat the process with the remaining filling and phyllo dough.

Place the pastry packets seam side down on the prepared baking sheets. Brush lightly with olive oil. Bake at 375 degrees until the pastry is golden brown and crisp. Serve warm or at room temperature.

Note: If using frozen phyllo dough, thaw the dough, unopened, in the refrigerator overnight. It dries out very quickly, so do not open the package until the filling has been prepared. Unroll the phyllo and cover it with waxed paper topped with a damp towel. Keep the unused portion covered until needed.

YIELD: 14 TO 15 PACKETS

Ernestine Schumann-Heink

Ernestine Schumann-Heink gave twelve concerts in Ann Arbor during the early years of the century. Her imposing size was matched by her warmth and humor. At the old University Hall, she looked at the tiny paneled door that led onto the stage and wondered aloud, "How do I get through that door?" To the suggestion that she try going through sideways, she replied, "Mein Gott, I haf no sideways!"

Vegetarian Sushi
(Nori Maki)

2 large dried shiitake
   mushrooms
1/4 cup water
1 tablespoon soy sauce
1/4 cup chopped fresh
   coriander
1/2 teaspoon minced garlic
1/4 cup rice vinegar
3 to 4 tablespoons sake,
   mirin or dry sherry
3 tablespoons sugar
1 tablespoon salt
1 1/2 cups short grain rice

3 cups cold water
1/8 teaspoon salt, or to taste
Rice vinegar
6 sheets of nori (dried seaweed),
   about 6x6 inches
1 medium cucumber, peeled,
   seeded, cut lengthwise
   into eighths
2 scallions, trimmed, cut
   lengthwise into thirds
Pickled ginger
Wasabi (see Note, page 95)
Soy sauce

Bring the mushrooms and 1/4 cup water to a boil in a saucepan. Remove from heat; let stand for 30 minutes. Squeeze the mushrooms dry; cut into thin strips. Marinate in a mixture of 1 tablespoon soy sauce, coriander and garlic.

Heat 1/4 cup rice vinegar, sake, sugar and 1 tablespoon salt in a small saucepan until the sugar and salt are dissolved. Turn off heat; let stand until cool.

Rinse the rice in several changes of water; drain. Combine rice and 3 cups water in a saucepan with a tight-fitting lid. Let stand for 30 minutes or longer. Bring the rice, water and 1/8 teaspoon salt to a boil. Simmer, covered, for 15 minutes; do not remove the lid. Turn off the heat; let stand, covered, for 10 minutes. Place rice in a large shallow bowl. Pour the sake mixture over the rice and toss to mix.

Have a bamboo mat and a small bowl of rice vinegar at hand. Toast 1 sheet of nori lightly by waving it over a warm stove burner. The nori should be warm and more flexible but not burned or shriveled. Place the sheet on the mat; spread a thin layer of rice over 2/3 of the sheet, extending the rice to the edges. Place mushroom strips, cucumber, scallions and/or pickled ginger in a line across the center of the rice. Dab uncovered edge of the nori with rice vinegar; use the mat to roll as for a jelly roll. Let stand for 1 minute. Repeat the process with remaining ingredients. Cut each roll into 6 slices; place cut side up on platter. Mix the wasabi and additional soy sauce for a dipping sauce. Serve with additional pickled ginger.

YIELD: 36 ROLLS

Spiced Almonds

2 teaspoons each salt and
    ginger
½ teaspoon cumin
1 teaspoon crushed red
    pepper flakes

¼ cup each sesame seeds and
    sugar
2 tablespoons vegetable oil
3 cups blanched almonds
½ cup sugar

Mix the salt, ginger, cumin, red pepper, sesame seeds and ¼ cup sugar in a large bowl. Heat the oil in a heavy sauté pan over medium heat. Add the almonds. Cook for 2 minutes or until the almonds become fragrant, stirring constantly. Sprinkle in ½ cup sugar, shaking the pan occasionally to prevent burning. Cook until the almonds are a dark golden brown and smoking slightly, stirring only after the sugar has begun to dissolve and caramelize.

Add the almonds to the spice mixture, tossing quickly to coat well. Spread the almonds on a nonstick baking sheet. Separate the hot almonds with 2 forks. Finish separating by hand once the almonds are cool enough to handle. This must be done quickly; if the almonds become cool and the caramel hardens, they are difficult to separate. Store in an airtight container for up to 2 to 3 weeks.

YIELD: 3½ CUPS

Orange Candied Nuts

1½ cups sugar
½ cup corn syrup
2 tablespoons (¼ stick)
    butter or margarine

4 cups walnuts, pecans and/or
    whole almonds
1 teaspoon orange extract

Combine the sugar, corn syrup and butter in a large shallow pan. Cook over medium-high heat until the sugar is dissolved and the butter is melted. Add the nuts. Cook for 15 minutes or until the sugar mixture is amber colored, stirring constantly. Stir in the orange extract.

Spread the nuts evenly on a greased baking sheet, separating into small clusters. Cool completely.

YIELD: 4 CUPS

The Flonzaley String Quartet performed in 1907 during the first American tour of their successful twenty-five-year existence. (They would return many times.) That winter, heavy blizzards had delayed and canceled trains around the country. On concert day, the four musicians were still unaccounted for, and a worried Charles Sink, having met every train, called hotels in Ann Arbor and Detroit. Finally, at a local "workingman's hotel," he found them. "You mean those fiddlers? Yes, they have been here three or four days, and they do nothing but fiddle and fiddle. We'll be glad when they're gone." As Sink wrote later, they had arrived early, "and perfect as they were in their performances," had spent their time practicing. "So absorbed were they in their work" that they neglected to tell anyone they were in town.

Soups

1919

Monday, March 3, 1919, 8:30 p.m.

Hill Auditorium

Enrico Caruso in Concert

Enrico Caruso   *Tenor*
Nina Morgana   *Soprano*
Elias Breeskin   *Violinist*

Souvenir de Moscow   **Wieniawski**
Elias Breeskin

Cavatina, "Come per me sereno"
from **"Sonnambula"**   **Bellini**
Nina Morgana

Aria, "Celeste Aïda" from **"Aïda"**   **Verdi**
Enrico Caruso

Caprice Espagnole   **Chaminade**
Zapateado   **Sarasate**
Elias Breeskin

Songs, **"He Loves Me"**   **Chadwick**
"The Wee Butterfly"   **Mana Zucca**
"Summer"   **Chaminade**
Nina Morgana

Aria, "Una Furtiva Lagrima"
from **"L'Elisir d'Amore"**   **Donizetti**
Enrico Caruso

Gypsy Airs   **Sarasate**
Elias Breeskin

Shadow Dance, from **"Dinorah"**   **Meyerbeer**
Nina Morgana

Aria, "Vesti La Giubba" from
"Pagliacci"   **Leoncavallo**
Enrico Caruso

"The Star-Spangled Banner"
Francis Scott Key
Enrico Caruso and Nina Morgana

Enrico Caruso being met at the train

CHARLES Sink had been with the University Musical Society for fifteen years when it faced a deepening problem. Concert attendance had fallen during the "Great War," and unless UMS could find a way to bring back its audience, not only was the organization in jeopardy, but the community stood to lose one of its defining pleasures. Sink knew he needed a legend, a spectacular performer who could sell out a house—even one as large as Hill Auditorium—on the strength of his name alone. Who else but the Great Caruso, the most celebrated singer of his time?

Sink had observed the effects of wartime hysteria upon the musical landscape. The Metropolitan Opera had fired the great soprano Frieda Hempel and other "enemy aliens" and cleansed its repertoire of all operas by Mozart and Wagner. Throughout the country, symphony orchestras had dismissed German conductors.

Fritz Kreisler, a resident alien, had been ostracized. He was not only an Austrian but a dedicated pacifist who refused to buy or sell Liberty Bonds. Cutting out German and Austrian performers and their literature, all the way back to Bach, cut the heart out of musical programming.

But there was Caruso. In an age with neither radio nor talking pictures, when artists rolled by rail to their concerts, Caruso had an enormous following, built almost entirely upon his recordings. Never mind that reviewers were beginning to notice a "darkening" of his voice. (He smoked incessantly and performed through exhaustion and sickness. He would die three years later, at the age of forty-eight.) Dark voice or not, he was a matchless draw.

Sink took the train to New York to approach Caruso's managers. He offered them the huge size and acoustics of Hill Auditorium and—after a trip back to Ann Arbor for consultation—he guaranteed the fee of $13,850, a sum eight to ten times higher than customary fees. His idea was to recoup this expense by requiring Caruso ticket-buyers to buy season tickets for the next three years of Choral Union concerts—artists to be announced.

The concert, set for October 19, 1918, had to be postponed because of the influenza pandemic, but it took place at last on March 3, 1919. Caruso electrified the audience with "Vesti la giubba" and two other well-known tenor arias. His companions on the bill, a violinist and a soprano, offered selections by Wieniawski, Sarasate, and Chaminade, and the final number was "The Star-Spangled Banner," performed by the two singers. Sink's bold plan had worked: with this concert, UMS was on the way back to recapturing its audience and its vitality.

During the concert, Sink had a final bit of luck. Still without a star for that year's May Festival, he was handed a telegram announcing that the sensational young soprano Rosa Ponselle had signed. It would be her first concert outside New York after her Metropolitan Opera debut.

What was cooking?

In 1919, Congress passed the Prohibition Enforcement Act, the "Great Experiment," which some food writers believe set back the development of American cuisine.

❖

Ice cream and soda sales soared, though, as bars were replaced by soda fountains and bartenders by "soda jerks."

Cold Beet Soup

1 pound fresh beets
1 quart buttermilk
½ cup chopped chives
1 teaspoon salt
White pepper to taste

Combine the beets with water to cover in a saucepan. Cook over medium heat until tender; drain well. Peel the beets and cut into thin slices.

Combine the beets and buttermilk in a food processor or blender container. Process until puréed. Stir in the chives, salt and white pepper. Cover and chill until serving time.

YIELD: 4 TO 6 SERVINGS

Easy Chilled Borscht

1 medium cucumber, cut into small pieces
Salt to taste
1 (16-ounce) can beets
1 bunch scallions, thinly sliced
1 cup sour cream
1 teaspoon dillweed

Place the cucumber pieces in a bowl. Sprinkle lightly with salt. Let stand for 30 minutes; drain well. Drain the beets, reserving the liquid. Cut the beets into strips.

Combine the cucumber, beets and scallions in a large bowl. Stir in the sour cream. Stir in the reserved liquid gradually. Mix well. Stir in the dillweed. Chill until serving time.

YIELD: 4 SERVINGS

Carrot Vichyssoise

4 cups chopped potatoes
3 cups chopped carrots
2 cups chopped leeks
6 cups chicken broth
2 chicken bouillon cubes, or 1 tablespoon
  chicken bouillon granules
2 cups milk
Salt and white pepper to taste

Combine the potatoes, carrots, leeks, chicken broth and bouillon cubes in a large saucepan. Bring to a boil and reduce the heat. Simmer, covered, for 10 minutes or until the vegetables are very tender.

Purée the vegetables and cooking liquid in batches in a blender or food processor until very smooth. Combine the puréed batches in the blender container. Add 1 cup of the milk, salt and pepper and process until blended. Add enough of the remaining milk to bring the soup to the desired consistency and mix well. Chill until serving time.

Check the consistency of the soup, adding additional milk if needed. Adjust the seasonings.

Ladle into chilled bowls to serve. Garnish with snipped chives.

YIELD: 6 TO 8 SERVINGS

Chilled Cantaloupe Soup

½ cup chablis or other dry
    white wine
1 large cantaloupe, peeled,
    coarsely chopped
Juice of 1 lime
Juice of ½ orange

1 cup crème frâiche or light
    cream
1 tablespoon honey
½ cup Champagne
1 tablespoon grenadine

Simmer the chablis in a saucepan over medium heat until reduced by ½. Remove from the heat and let stand until cool.

Process the cantaloupe, lime juice and orange juice in a blender or food processor until finely puréed. Add the crème frâiche, honey, chablis, Champagne and grenadine and mix well. Chill until serving time.

Ladle into chilled cups. Garnish each serving with a thick slice of lime.

This soup is refreshing as a first course or as a dessert served with Champagne.

YIELD: 2 TO 4 SERVINGS

Peach Soup

4 cups chopped peeled
    peaches
2 cups sauternes
2 cups water

⅓ cup sugar
1 (3-inch) cinnamon stick
1½ teaspoons lemon juice
⅛ teaspoon almond extract

Combine the peaches, wine, water, sugar and cinnamon stick in a 3-quart saucepan. Bring to a boil and reduce the heat. Simmer, covered, for 30 minutes, stirring occasionally. Remove from the heat and discard the cinnamon stick. Stir in the lemon juice and almond extract. Process half the soup in a blender or food processor until smooth. Pour into a bowl or pitcher. Repeat with the remaining soup. Chill, covered, until serving time.

Ladle the soup into bowls or wide-bowled wine glasses. Garnish with lemon slices and mint sprigs.

YIELD: 4 TO 6 SERVINGS

Before his Ann Arbor concert in 1919, Enrico Caruso had a midday dinner with Charles Sink at the Michigan Union. Then they went to the home of Francis W. Kelsey, archaeologist, classicist, and longtime director of the University Musical Society. Kelsey's splendid house on Oxford Street at Hill, Bavarian in style, had a high-ceilinged living room with a balcony at one end that must have beckoned to Caruso like a familiar stage set.

He climbed to it and delighted his host and the assembled guests with an impromptu aria. The story survives in the history of the Sigma Nu fraternity, longtime owner of the house.

Easy White Gazpacho

2 cucumbers, peeled, seeded
1½ cups chicken broth
2 teaspoons (or more) rice vinegar
Chopped green onions to taste
1½ cups sour cream or nonfat sour cream
1 teaspoon salt, or to taste
⅛ teaspoon white pepper, or to taste
Chopped cucumber
Chopped tomato
Pumpkin seeds

Combine the cucumbers, chicken broth, vinegar, green onions, sour cream, salt and white pepper in a blender or food processor container. Process until the mixture is blended and smooth. Chill until serving time.

Ladle the gazpacho into bowls. Serve chopped cucumber, chopped tomato and pumpkin seeds on the side or use to top each serving of gazpacho.

YIELD: 4 SERVINGS

Mangozpacho

3 large ripe mangoes, finely chopped
(about 6 cups)
¼ cup rice vinegar, or to taste
¼ cup light olive oil
1 cup (about) water
Salt and pepper to taste
¼ cup finely chopped red onion
1 cucumber, peeled, seeded, finely chopped
¼ cup finely chopped cilantro
2 tablespoons finely chopped chives
1 to 2 tablespoons sugar, or to taste

Combine half the mangoes, vinegar, olive oil, water, salt and pepper in a food processor container. Process until puréed. Add additional water if the purée is too thick.

Pour the puréed mixture into a bowl. Add the onion, cucumber, cilantro, chives and remaining mangoes and mix well. Adjust the seasonings, adding the sugar if the soup is too tart. Chill for 1 hour or longer before serving.

YIELD: 4 TO 6 SERVINGS

Potato and Roquefort Swirl Soup

3 medium onions, thinly sliced
2 tablespoons (¼ stick) butter
4 cups thinly sliced potatoes
½ cup thinly sliced leeks
3 cups chicken broth
1 cup freshly chopped watercress
¼ cup freshly chopped parsley
¼ cup freshly chopped dill
½ cup water
8 ounces Roquefort or Stilton cheese, crumbled
1 cup heavy cream
Salt and white pepper to taste

Sauté the onions in the butter in a saucepan until translucent. Add the potatoes, leeks and chicken broth. Simmer, covered, for 25 minutes or until the vegetables are tender. Purée the mixture in a blender or food processor or press through a food mill.

Combine 1 cup of the puréed mixture, watercress, parsley, dill and water in a saucepan. Simmer, covered, for 15 minutes. Remove from the heat and stir in the cheese. Purée in a blender or food processor or press through a food mill.

Add ¾ cup of the cream to the remaining puréed potato mixture. Add the remaining ¼ cup cream to the cheese mixture. Season each with salt and white pepper. Cover and chill for several hours.

Pour the potato mixture into a tureen. Add the cheese mixture and swirl into an attractive pattern with a spoon or thin spatula.

YIELD: 6 TO 8 SERVINGS

Ignace Paderewski

From the minutes of the
University Musical Society
board meeting of
October 15, 1922:

. . . Engagements for the
Choral Union Series have
been completed as follows:

October 24, Mischa Elman,
Violinist, $1,750.00
December 5, Mary Garden,
Soprano, $3,000.00
January 8, Ignace
Paderewski,
Pianist, $4,000.00
January 24, Impresario
Opera Company, $750.00
February 15, Ukranian
National Chorus, $1,200.00
March 9, Guy
Maier & Lee Pattison,
Two-Piano Recital, $800.00

Tuscan Bean Soup

3 (15-ounce) cans Great
　　Northern or cannellini
　　beans, drained, rinsed
8 cups cold water
1 sprig of rosemary
2 sage leaves
1 bay leaf
2 tablespoons olive oil
1 onion, chopped
　　(about 1½ cups)
5 garlic cloves, minced

½ teaspoon basil
1 teaspoon salt
¼ teaspoon pepper
¼ cup dry white wine
1 (15-ounce) can chopped
　　tomatoes
Salt and pepper to taste
4 ounces Parmesan cheese,
　　shaved
½ cup herb-flavored croutons

Combine the beans, water, rosemary, sage and bay leaf in a stockpot. Bring to a boil and reduce the heat. Simmer for 20 minutes or until the beans are very tender. Remove and discard the herbs.

Remove and reserve 1 cup of the beans. Press the remaining beans through a fine grater or a food mill, adding some of the cooking liquid if needed. (This can be done instead in batches in a food processor.)

Return the ground beans to the stockpot. Cook over low heat until the mixture reaches the consistency of heavy cream.

Heat the olive oil in a skillet over medium heat. Add the onion, garlic, basil, 1 teaspoon salt and ¼ teaspoon pepper. Sauté for 7 minutes or until the vegetables are tender. Add the wine and cook until most of the liquid has evaporated. Add the undrained tomatoes. Simmer over medium-low heat for 10 minutes.

Add the tomato mixture and the reserved beans to the stockpot. Cook, covered, over low heat for 30 minutes, thinning with a small amount of water if needed. Season with salt and pepper to taste. Ladle into bowls and top each serving with Parmesan cheese and croutons.

Note: This soup is best if kept in the refrigerator for 1 day before serving. To serve, reheat over low heat.

YIELD: 6 TO 8 SERVINGS

Smoky Black Bean Soup

1 pound black turtle beans
2 tablespoons olive oil
1 large Spanish onion, chopped
3 carrots, chopped
3 ribs celery with leaves, chopped
2 leeks, chopped
3 whole heads garlic, chopped
6 bay leaves
1 tablespoon chopped fresh thyme, or 1½ teaspoons
    dried thyme
1 tablespoon chopped fresh rosemary, or 1½ teaspoons
    dried rosemary
1 tablespoon coarsely ground black peppercorns
4 quarts water
Liquid smoke or fajita seasoning to taste

Rinse and sort the beans. Soak in cold water to cover overnight (use plenty of water, as the beans will absorb quite a bit). Drain well.

Heat the olive oil in a 6-quart stockpot. Add the onion, carrots, celery, leeks, garlic, bay leaves, thyme, rosemary and ground peppercorns. Sauté over low heat for 25 minutes or until the vegetables are tender. Add the beans and 4 quarts water. Partially cover the stockpot and bring the water to a boil. Reduce the heat. Simmer, preferably on a heat diffuser, for 2 to 3 hours or until the beans are tender, stirring occasionally.

Strain through a sieve, reserving the cooking liquid. Purée the vegetables in a food processor or blender and return to the stockpot. Add the reserved cooking liquid and liquid smoke.

This soup makes a good main course served as it is or served over rice and garnished with chopped onion seasoned with olive oil and white vinegar.

YIELD: 8 TO 10 SERVINGS

Madame Ernestine Schumann-Heink, a great audience favorite, loved the students who packed her Ann Arbor concerts. In an appearance shortly after World War I, the great mezzo sang "Trees," a musical setting of the poem by Joyce Kilmer, who had lost his life in the war. Afterward, a young man came backstage to meet her. He was Kilmer's son, and they exchanged "a tender and affectionate greeting."

Carrot and Candied Ginger Soup

¼ cup minced onion
2 tablespoons (¼ stick) butter
1 pound carrots, peeled, sliced
1 teaspoon brown sugar
½ teaspoon salt
Freshly ground pepper to taste
2 cups chicken stock or vegetable stock
1 cup (or more) heavy cream or
    evaporated milk
¼ teaspoon nutmeg, or to taste
1 teaspoon (or more) garam masala or curry
    powder (optional)
¼ cup chopped candied ginger

Sauté the onion in the butter in a stockpot until translucent. Add the carrots, brown sugar, salt, pepper and chicken stock. Bring to a boil and simmer until the carrots are tender. Add the cream, nutmeg and garam masala. Let stand for 20 minutes.

Purée the soup in a food processor, adding additional chicken stock or cream if needed to achieve the desired consistency. Stir in the ginger.

Ladle the soup into bowls and garnish each serving with chopped parsley. Serve hot or cold.

Note: The candied ginger may be used as a garnish instead of being added to the soup.

YIELD: 4 TO 6 SERVINGS

Spicy Corn Chowder

1 (16-ounce) can whole kernel corn
¼ cup (½ stick) margarine or butter
1 small onion, minced
½ cup chopped red bell pepper
½ cup chopped green bell pepper
½ teaspoon cumin
¼ teaspoon cayenne pepper
¼ cup flour
Juice of ½ lemon
¼ cup white wine
1 cup chicken broth
1 cup milk
1 teaspoon hot sauce

Drain the corn, reserving the liquid. Melt the margarine in a heavy saucepan over medium heat. Add the onion, bell peppers, cumin and cayenne pepper. Sauté for 3 minutes or until the vegetables are tender. Add the flour and sauté for 1 minute. Add the lemon juice, wine, chicken broth, milk, hot sauce and reserved corn liquid.

Bring the soup to a simmer, whisking constantly until smooth. Add the corn and simmer until cooked through.

Ladle into bowls. Garnish with minced cilantro or parsley.

YIELD: 4 TO 6 SERVINGS

Mediterranean Fish Soup

2 tablespoons olive oil
8 garlic cloves, finely chopped
1 teaspoon fennel seeds
Bay leaf
1 sprig of thyme
1 sprig of rosemary
2 teaspoons salt
2 tablespoons tomato paste
2 tablespoons pastis, ouzo or anisette liqueur
6 medium tomatoes, peeled, cut into quarters
6 cups water
1/4 teaspoon cayenne pepper, or to taste
1 (14-ounce) can tomatoes
4 small fennel bulbs (about 1 1/2 pounds), cut into
    bite-size pieces
1/4 teaspoon saffron
2 1/2 to 3 pounds fresh fish, such as sea bass, halibut,
    cod and/or monkfish, boned, cut into pieces

Heat the olive oil in a large stockpot. Add the garlic, fennel seeds, bay leaf, thyme, rosemary and salt. Cook for 10 minutes; do not brown. Add the tomato paste, pastis, fresh tomatoes, water and cayenne pepper and mix well. Cover and bring to a boil over high heat. Reduce the heat and simmer for 45 minutes. Remove and discard the herbs.

Purée the undrained canned tomatoes in a blender or food processor. Add the puréed tomatoes and fennel to the stockpot. Simmer, covered, for 15 to 20 minutes or until the soup is heated through and the flavors have blended.

Stir in the saffron and fish. Reduce the heat. Cook for 10 minutes or until the fish is done to taste.

Spoon the soup into a large tureen. Serve with bowls of freshly grated Parmesan cheese, rounds of dry French bread rubbed with garlic, or Aïoli (page 187).

YIELD: 6 TO 8 SERVINGS

Jascha Heifetz

Russian violinist Jascha Heifetz first performed in Ann Arbor in 1919, at age eighteen. He was already a sensation. He was also, as Charles Sink remembered, "a normal boy interested in everything about him." Touring the campus before his concert, Heifetz wanted to see the medical school, asking, "Do they cut up bodies, and can one see them?" Sink arranged to take him to an anatomy lab, where Heifetz watched intently, asking many questions. To Sink's relief, the medical students "refrained from their usual practice of dropping stray toes" or other body parts into the pockets of an unwary visitor. Heifetz returned for many concerts, and he always mentioned his Michigan "medical course."

Evgeny Kissin's Mushroom Soup

1/4 ounce dried mushrooms
1 cup hot water
1 tablespoon unsalted butter
1 tablespoon vegetable oil
5 ounces fresh mushrooms, chopped
1 small leek, white part only, chopped
1 medium rib celery, diced
1 small carrot, diced
2 garlic cloves, minced
1/2 cup pearl barley
4 cups beef stock
Salt and pepper to taste
Chopped dill to taste

Soak the dried mushrooms in the hot water for 20 minutes; drain well. Heat the butter and oil in a stockpot. Add the fresh mushrooms, leek, celery, carrot, garlic and barley. Cook for 5 minutes or until lightly toasted.

Stir in the reconstituted dried mushrooms and the beef stock. Bring to a boil. Simmer for 40 minutes or until the vegetables are tender. Season with salt, pepper and dill.

YIELD: 4 SERVINGS

Consommé with Mushrooms

4 ounces dried shiitake mushrooms
6 cups rich chicken stock
4 cups clam broth or clam juice
2 tablespoons minced shallots
1 tablespoon mushroom soy sauce or
  other soy sauce
Grated peel of 1/2 lemon or thin lemon slices

Soak the mushrooms in boiling water to cover for 20 minutes. Strain the liquid and reserve 1 cup. Thinly slice the mushrooms.

Combine the chicken stock, clam broth, shallots, soy sauce and mushrooms in a large stockpot. Bring to a boil and reduce the heat. Simmer for 20 minutes.

Strain the soup into a tureen. Add the reserved liquid. Remove 12 to 16 of the mushroom slices with a slotted spoon and set aside. Serve the soup from the tureen or ladle into bowls. Top each serving with 2 mushroom slices and lemon peel or lemon slices.

YIELD: 6 TO 8 SERVINGS

Roasted Yellow Pepper Soup

6 yellow bell peppers
2 tablespoons extra-virgin olive oil
2 ribs celery with leaves, minced
2 carrots, peeled, minced
1 Spanish onion or sweet onion, minced
2 leeks, white part only, chopped
4 to 5 large potatoes, peeled, coarsely chopped
6 cups chicken stock or water
Salt and freshly ground pepper to taste

To roast the peppers, place the whole peppers directly over the flame of a gas burner, turning frequently until the entire pepper is charcoal black. Remove the peppers from the flame and place in a paper bag for 5 to 10 minutes or until cool enough to handle. Hold the peppers under cold running water and rub off the peel. Remove and discard the seeds and stems. Drain in a colander over a bowl, reserving the liquid to add to the soup if desired. (To roast peppers in an electric oven, cut the peppers in half and remove and discard the seeds and stems. Flatten the peppers slightly and place in a shallow baking pan. Broil briefly until completely blackened. Peel with a sharp knife. If the peel does not come off easily, hold under running water to peel.)

Heat the olive oil in a 6-quart stockpot. Add the celery, carrots, onion and leeks. Sauté for 5 minutes or until tender. Add the peppers and potatoes and sauté for 5 minutes. Add the chicken stock and bring to a boil. Reduce the heat. Simmer, partially covered, for 30 to 40 minutes or until the potatoes are tender.

Strain the liquid into a large saucepan. Purée the solids in a food processor. Combine the puréed mixture with the liquid in the saucepan (the soup should be thick). Bring to a simmer. Season with salt and pepper to taste.

YIELD: 6 TO 8 SERVINGS

Evgeny Kissin

Ann Arbor realtor Ed Surovell has bought season tickets for the Choral Union Series at Hill Auditorium for years—the same two seats, Section 4, Row K. "It feels like home," he says. "I can't imagine sitting anywhere else."

In April 1998, young Russian piano prodigy Evgeny Kissin appeared in recital. Surovell, taking his usual place beforehand, noticed a stranger next to him, in the seat long held by a friend. "Hello," he said, extending his hand. "You're not Lois!"

"I'm Mr. Kissin's mother," the woman replied.

Watching the pride and pleasure she took in her son's performance made an "absolutely spectacular" concert even better, Surovell recalls. "She knew every note, and you could feel her moving with each note, feeling the music."

Pumpkin Soup

6 small cooking pumpkins (5 to 6 inches
    in diameter)
1 large or 2 medium cooking pumpkins
6 cups chicken broth
¼ to ½ teaspoon nutmeg
⅛ teaspoon mace (optional)
Salt and pepper to taste
2 cups heavy cream
12 croutons, toasted (see Note)
2 cups shredded Swiss cheese and/or
    Emmenthaler cheese

Cut the tops from the small pumpkins and set
aside. Remove and discard the seeds.

Cut the pulp from the large pumpkin into
cubes. Combine the pumpkin cubes and chicken
broth in a saucepan. Cook for 20 minutes or until
tender. Stir in the nutmeg, mace, salt and pepper.
Drain well.

Mash the pumpkin cubes in a bowl until
almost smooth. Add the cream and mix well.

Place 1 crouton in each of the small pumpkins.
Divide half the cheese among the pumpkins.
Season with additional pepper. Ladle the soup
into the pumpkins and top each with 1 crouton.
Sprinkle the remaining cheese over the top
croutons. Place the pumpkins in a baking pan and
replace the tops.

Bake at 400 degrees for 20 minutes. Decrease
the oven temperature to 350 degrees. Bake for
20 minutes. Serve hot.

Note: To make the croutons, cut a baguette of
French bread into thick slices. Remove the crust
and trim the bread slices to fit into the bottom of
each small pumpkin.

YIELD: 6 SERVINGS

Scallop Chowder

2 medium potatoes, peeled, diced
1 small carrot, peeled, diced
1 large rib celery, chopped
1 medium onion, peeled, chopped
2 cups chicken stock
½ teaspoon salt
¼ teaspoon white pepper
1 bay leaf
½ teaspoon thyme
8 ounces fresh mushrooms, sliced
1½ tablespoons butter
1 pound fresh bay scallops (cut into halves or
    quarters if large)
½ cup dry white wine
1 cup heavy cream
1 egg yolk, lightly beaten (optional)

Combine the potatoes, carrot, celery, onion
and enough chicken stock to cover in a stockpot.
Bring to a boil. Add the salt, pepper, bay leaf and
thyme. Reduce the heat. Simmer, covered, until
the vegetables are tender. Remove and discard the
bay leaf. Let stand to cool slightly.

Process the mixture in batches in a food
processor or blender until blended and smooth.
Return to the stockpot.

Sauté the mushrooms in the butter in a skillet
until tender. Add the scallops and wine and sauté
for 1 minute. Stir in a mixture of the cream and
egg yolk. Add to the mixture in the stockpot. Cook
over low heat until very hot; do not boil.

Ladle the chowder into bowls. Garnish each
serving with chopped fresh parsley. Serve hot.

YIELD: 10 SERVINGS

Boozy Squash Soup

3 to 4 small squash (any
  combination of Hubbard,
  Glory Girl, butternut and
  acorn)
2 cups chicken stock
2 tablespoons chopped fresh
  parsley
Salt to taste

Green hot pepper sauce
  to taste
1 cup (or more) milk
2 tablespoons molasses
2 tablespoons bourbon
  (optional)
½ teaspoon cinnamon
¼ teaspoon nutmeg

Place the squash in a baking pan. Bake at 350 degrees for
40 minutes. Let stand until cool enough to handle. Cut the squash
into halves and remove and discard the seeds. Scoop out the pulp.

Process the pulp, chicken stock, parsley, salt and hot pepper
sauce in a blender or food processor until blended and smooth.

Pour the squash mixture into a stockpot. Add the milk, molasses,
bourbon, cinnamon and nutmeg and mix well. Simmer for 10
minutes, stirring occasionally. Adjust the seasonings. Ladle into wide
bowls. Garnish with sour cream and parsley sprigs.

YIELD: 6 TO 8 SERVINGS

Sweet Potato and Pear Soup

2 teaspoons unsalted butter
1 red onion, chopped
3 sweet potatoes, peeled,
  cut into 1-inch pieces
2 Bartlett pears, peeled,
  cut into 1-inch pieces

5 cups vegetable stock
⅛ teaspoon allspice, or to taste
Kosher salt and freshly ground
  pepper to taste
Pear brandy (optional)
Crème frâiche (optional)

Melt the butter in a heavy saucepan. Add the onion and sauté for
5 minutes. Add the sweet potatoes, pears and vegetable stock. Bring
to a boil over medium heat. Reduce the heat and simmer for 40
minutes or until the sweet potatoes are tender. Add the allspice.

Purée the soup in a food processor. Season with kosher salt,
pepper and pear brandy. Spoon into bowls. Swirl a bit of crème
frâiche into each serving.

YIELD: 6 SERVINGS

Rosa Ponselle

Charlotte McGeoch is a rare
source of local musical
history. She sang in the
Children's Festival Chorus in
1922 and later was a member
of the Choral Union. She has
attended hundreds of concerts
in Hill Auditorium, many
with her late husband, Glenn
McGeoch, a beloved music
school professor. She recalls
the time soprano Rosa
Ponselle inadvertently
demonstrated Hill
Auditorium's remarkable
acoustics. "For an encore, she
was singing a little song—
something like 'He loves me,
he loves me not,'" McGeoch
remembers. "After one line,
she put her head down and
under her breath she said,
'God help him if he doesn't!'
The whole second balcony
burst into laughter."

Broiled Fresh Tomato Soup
in Bread Bowls

2 pounds fully ripe tomatoes, cored, cut into halves
3 medium onions, cut into halves
6 garlic cloves
2 tablespoons olive oil
1 tablespoon red wine vinegar
1 teaspoon sugar
1 teaspoon salt
½ teaspoon pepper
1 (14-ounce) can chicken broth
4 (5-inch) Kaiser rolls
¼ cup cubed Muenster or Monterey Jack cheese

Place the tomato and onion halves cut side down in a shallow baking pan. Place the garlic around the vegetables. Mix the olive oil, vinegar, sugar, salt and pepper in a cup. Brush over the vegetables, coating them completely. Broil 3 to 4 inches from the heat source for 7 to 10 minutes or until lightly charred. Remove the garlic cloves as they brown and soften and turn the pan for even cooking. Broil for 7 to 10 minutes longer or until the vegetables are lightly charred and tender. Remove from the oven and let cool, reserving the pan juices.

Peel the tomato halves. Process the tomatoes, onions, garlic and pan juices in a food processor or blender until almost smooth. Pour into a medium saucepan. Stir in the chicken broth. Bring to a boil and reduce the heat to medium-low. Simmer, covered, for 10 minutes or until the flavors have blended. Remove from the heat and keep warm.

For the bread bowls, cut the top off each roll with a sharp knife; set aside. Remove and discard the doughy center, leaving a ½-inch shell. Place the bowls and tops on a baking sheet. Bake at 350 degrees for 5 to 8 minutes or until crisp, turning once.

To serve, place the bread bowls on soup plates. Ladle the soup into and around the bread bowls. Top each serving with cheese. Garnish with chopped basil or parsley. Place the tops on the bread bowls and serve immediately.

YIELD: 4 SERVINGS

Herbed Tomato Rice Soup

1 large Spanish onion, diced
1 green bell pepper, diced
1 rib celery, chopped
3 garlic cloves, minced
3 tablespoons olive oil
1 teaspoon dried basil
1 teaspoon dried oregano
1 teaspoon dried thyme

6 cups chicken stock
4 cups chopped peeled
    tomatoes, canned puréed
    tomatoes or canned whole
    plum tomatoes
3 cups cooked white rice
Salt and freshly ground pepper
    to taste

Sauté the onion, green pepper, celery and garlic in the olive oil in a skillet until tender. Add the basil, oregano and thyme and sauté for 30 seconds to remove the dried taste of the herbs.

Combine the sautéed mixture, chicken stock, tomatoes and rice in a stockpot. Season with salt and pepper. Add more herbs if desired. Cook until heated through.

YIELD: 6 TO 8 SERVINGS

Basil Zucchini Soup

1½ cups fresh basil leaves
3 garlic cloves
2 tablespoons pine nuts
¼ cup grated Parmesan
    cheese
Olive oil

8 cups chicken stock
1½ cups broken vermicelli or
    other thin pasta
3 small zucchini, cut into
    ¼-inch slices
Salt and pepper to taste

Purée the basil, garlic, pine nuts and cheese in a food processor. Add olive oil in a thin stream with the food processor running, using just enough oil to make a smooth thick paste.

Heat the chicken stock in a large saucepan. Add the pasta and cook, covered, until tender. Add the zucchini and cook until tender. Season with salt and pepper. Whisk in the basil paste. Serve hot or cold.

YIELD: 8 SERVINGS

When Charles Sink, University Musical Society president, died in December 1972, the Ann Arbor News recalled "the famed hospitality of Dr. Sink and his wife, Alva." Because of them, "a side street in the Burns Park area probably was known to more musical artists than many concert halls."

The Sinks lived in the house at 1325 Olivia Avenue, near the university campus, from the day of their marriage in 1923, and their guest book was filled with the names of artists from fifty years of concerts. Alva Sink remained a lively presence there until her own death in 1998. Every year, when Choral Union carolers came to her home, she invited them in for a delicious spread that included Swedish meatballs and ice cream punch, both standbys from her decades of post-concert suppers.

Salads

1933

Wednesday, February 8, 1933, 8:15 p.m.

Hill Auditorium

Budapest String Quartet

José Roismann *First Violinist*
Alexander Schneider *Second Violinist*
Stephan Ipolyi *Violist*
Mischa Schneider *Cellist*

String Quartet in G minor, Op. 10
Debussy
I. Animé et très décidé
II. Assez vif et bien rythme
III. Andantino doucement expressif
IV. Très modéré

String Quartet in A major, Op. 41
Schumann
I. Andante expressivo—
Allegro molto moderato
II. Assai agitato
III. Adagio molto
IV. Finale (Allegro molto vivace)

String Quartet in A minor, Op. 29
Schubert
I. Allegro ma non troppo
II. Andante
III. Menuetto (Allegretto)
IV. Allegro moderato

Guarneri String Quartet

THIS was the first of many concerts the Budapest String Quartet would give under UMS auspices over the next thirty-two years. Other quartets had performed here repeatedly, most notably the Flonzaley early in the century, and others appear through the years. But with the Budapest, UMS audiences entered a golden era of chamber music.

Despite its name, the group was hardly a "Budapest" quartet. Of the original all-Hungarian ensemble formed in 1917, three players had been replaced by Russians by the time of this concert. The fourth was replaced by a Russian a few years later. But whatever the nationalities of its players, the Budapest in its time was the definitive string quartet, through its nationwide broadcasts from the Library of Congress, its residencies at the Marlboro Festival, its extraordinary recordings, and its continual touring across the country.

When Rackham Auditorium opened in 1938, it was quickly recognized as ideal for chamber music. In 1941, the Chamber Music Festival began: three concerts in three days. The auditorium became one of the Budapest's favorite venues. Designed as a lecture hall, it is perfect for chamber music: wide plush seats arranged in a semi-circle, allowing every audience member an unobstructed view, and an acoustical environment so clear that no detail is lost, yet so warm that every tone seems as richly upholstered as the seats.

And part of Rackham's appeal is an enthusiastic audience that appreciates chamber music as a music of intellectual, emotional, and spiritual depth, despite its lack of opera's spectacle, the virtuoso's fireworks, or the orchestra's opulent tonal spectrum. For many composers and performers, its technically challenging repertoire—originally created for the salon after a sumptuous meal—is the measure of musical mastery.

In the 1963–1964 season, the Chamber Arts Series—seven or eight concerts throughout the season—replaced the Chamber Music Festival. That series, now well into its fourth decade, offers traditional chamber ensembles in both classical and contemporary repertoire.

The Budapest Quartet's last performance was in 1965, and the local audience waited for a quartet that would take up its mantle. No one knew that the first appearance of the Guarneri String Quartet, on February 25, 1971, would inaugurate a second golden age of chamber music for the city. But the audience that evening recognized that they were hearing the equal of the Budapest's lush, romantic sound world. Like the Budapest, the Guarneri is a group of profoundly individualistic players who through aural alchemy become a unified ensemble.

The Guarneri has appeared in Ann Arbor twenty-eight times over twenty-seven years, approaching the Budapest's glorious thirty-two-year reign. Arnold Steinhardt, for twenty years first violinist of the Guarneri, summed up the secret of a great string quartet: "...the uncharted process in which four people let their individual personalities shine while [creating] that almost mystical amalgam of the four players that hovers somewhere in between the music stands."

Black Bean and Corn Salad

¼ to ½ cup balsamic vinegar, or to taste
½ to ¾ cup olive oil, or to taste
2 teaspoons cumin
2 teaspoons coriander
2 tablespoons fresh lime juice
Grated zest of 1 lime
Salt and pepper to taste
2 to 3 ears fresh corn, cooked
3 medium tomatoes, chopped
2 (15-ounce) cans black beans, drained
1 green bell pepper, chopped
1 red bell pepper, chopped
1 bunch scallions, chopped
1 cup chopped cilantro

For the dressing, combine the vinegar, olive oil, cumin, coriander, lime juice and lime zest in a bowl and whisk until mixed. Season with salt and pepper.

For the salad, remove the kernels from the corn with a sharp knife. Combine the corn kernels, tomatoes, beans, bell peppers and scallions in a large bowl. Add the dressing and toss to coat. Add the cilantro and toss well.

Note: Be sure to use a high-quality vinegar in this salad.

YIELD: 6 TO 8 SERVINGS

Itzhak Perlman's Bean Sprout Salad with Ginger

2 pounds bean sprouts
3 scallions, chopped
¾ cup soy sauce
¾ cup water
2 tablespoons chopped fresh gingerroot
1 teaspoon sesame oil

Rinse the bean sprouts with cold water and drain well. Combine the sprouts and scallions in a serving bowl.

Combine the soy sauce, water, gingerroot and sesame oil in a small saucepan. Cook over low heat until heated through; do not boil.

Pour the soy sauce mixture over the bean sprout mixture. Chill, covered, for 2 to 3 hours.

For a bit more color, blanch and julienne 1 cup pea pods. Add to the bean sprouts and scallions and mix well.

YIELD: 4 SERVINGS

Asparagus Citrus Salad

1 cup pine nuts
2 pounds fresh asparagus, trimmed
1 pound fresh pea pods
1 English cucumber
Honey Vinaigrette (below)
1 head Bibb lettuce, separated into leaves
4 navel oranges, peeled, cut into sections
1 small red onion, cut into thin rings

Place the pine nuts on a baking sheet. Bake at 350 degrees for 5 to 10 minutes or until toasted. Set aside.

Cut the asparagus into 2-inch pieces and drop into a large saucepan of boiling water. Boil for 1 to 2 minutes or just until tender. Remove from the boiling water and plunge immediately into cold water. Drain on paper towels and pat dry. Repeat the procedure with the pea pods. Peel the cucumber and cut into halves lengthwise. Remove any seeds. Cut the cucumber halves into ⅛-inch slices.

Toss the asparagus, pea pods and cucumber with the Honey Vinaigrette in a large bowl. Line a serving platter with lettuce leaves. Spoon the salad onto the lettuce. Top with the orange sections, pine nuts and onion rings.

YIELD: 16 SERVINGS

Honey Vinaigrette

1 cup vegetable oil
⅓ cup rice vinegar
2 tablespoons walnut oil
1 teaspoon honey
Salt and pepper to taste

Combine the vegetable oil, vinegar, walnut oil and honey in a bowl and whisk until mixed. Season with salt and pepper.

YIELD: 1⅓ CUPS

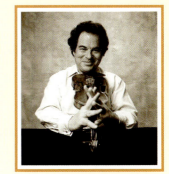

Itzhak Perlman

Itzhak Perlman was sure he could negotiate the few steps down to stage level at the back of Hill. But when staffer Carol Wargelin showed him a small elevator back there, he said, "I'll try that," and disappeared into it.

Wargelin took the stairs, then waited. And waited. She listened as the elevator went up and down, up and down. Then, from inside came a full, rich baritone singing, singing. Finally the door opened and Perlman emerged, smiling like a child with a new toy.

Eggplant Antipasto

1/3 cup olive oil
3 cups cubed peeled eggplant
1/2 cup chopped green bell pepper (optional)
1 medium to large onion, coarsely chopped
3/4 cup sliced fresh mushrooms
    (about 4 ounces)
2 (or more) garlic cloves, minced
1 (8-ounce) can tomato paste
1/4 cup water
2 to 3 tablespoons red wine vinegar
1/2 cup whole or sliced pimiento-stuffed
    green olives
2 teaspoons sugar
1 teaspoon oregano
1 teaspoon salt
Freshly ground pepper to taste

Heat the olive oil in a skillet. Add the eggplant, green pepper, onion, mushrooms and garlic. Cook, covered, over low to medium heat for 10 minutes, stirring occasionally.

Add the tomato paste, water, vinegar, olives, sugar, oregano, salt and pepper and mix well. Simmer, covered, for 30 minutes or until the eggplant is tender. Cover and chill in the refrigerator.

Serve at room temperature with crackers or French bread rounds; over cream cheese; as a salad on lettuce leaves; or folded into an omelet; or serve warm over rice.

YIELD: 6 TO 8 SERVINGS AS A SALAD
10 TO 12 SERVINGS AS AN APPETIZER

Fennel Salad

3 medium fennel bulbs
8 ounces mushrooms
12 kumquats
3 tablespoons fresh lemon juice
Salt and freshly ground white pepper to taste
Parmesan cheese

Trim away the tough stems and the fronds of the fennel bulbs. Cut each bulb into halves and remove the core. Cut the fennel into very thin slices. Trim the ends of the mushrooms and wash the caps. Cut the mushrooms into very thin slices. Cut each kumquat into thin rounds, removing the seeds and discarding the stem ends.

Arrange some of the fennel slices on individual plates or a platter. Top with some of the mushrooms and kumquats. Sprinkle with some of the lemon juice and salt and white pepper to taste. Shave cheese over the top. Repeat the layers until all the ingredients are used, ending with shaved cheese.

This salad is especially good with fish.

Note: Do not prepare this salad too far ahead. It is best to prepare each of the parts and keep them refrigerated until ready to assemble and serve the salad.

YIELD: 4 SERVINGS

Couscous and Chick-pea Salad

4 cups chicken broth
¼ cup olive oil
¼ teaspoon turmeric
¼ teaspoon cinnamon
¼ teaspoon ginger
2 cups couscous
½ cup raisins or currants
½ cup chopped dates, or
    ½ cup chopped dried
    apricots, or ½ cup
    dried cherries (use 1 or
    2 of these)

2 cups chopped zucchini
1 cup chopped carrots
½ cup chopped red onion
1 large tomato, seeded, chopped
1 (15-ounce) can chick-peas,
    drained
2 tablespoons olive oil
1½ tablespoons lemon juice
½ teaspoon salt
½ cup slivered almonds, toasted

Combine the chicken broth, ¼ cup olive oil, turmeric, cinnamon and ginger in a large saucepan and bring to a boil. Stir in the couscous gradually. Boil for 1 to 2 minutes or until all the liquid has been absorbed. Remove from the heat. Stir in the raisins and dried fruit. Let stand, tightly covered, for 15 minutes. Remove the couscous to a large bowl and let stand to bring to room temperature.

Stir the zucchini, carrots, onion, tomato and chick-peas into the couscous. Mix 2 tablespoons olive oil, lemon juice and salt in a small bowl. Pour over the salad and toss to mix well. Chill, covered, for 4 hours to overnight. Adjust the seasonings. Sprinkle with the almonds.

Serve with broiled chicken, pork tenderloin or fish.

YIELD: 8 TO 10 SERVINGS

Fritz Kreisler, Charles Sink, and Fritz Crisler

Fritz Kreisler, the great violinist and composer, was occasionally confused with University of Michigan football coach "Fritz" Crisler, particularly by people more familiar with athletics than with music. In fact, the coach's nickname came as a direct result of the artist's fame.

As a student, Herbert Orin Crisler played football at the University of Chicago. After he had bungled the same play three times, the Chicago coach, Amos Alonzo Stagg, asked him his name, then whether he was related to the renowned violinist. "Kreisler is a gifted, talented artist," Stagg told Crisler. "I'm going to call you 'Fritz' for reasons of contrast, not likeness."

Arugula Salad with Apples and Pears

1 cup walnuts, toasted
3 Granny Smith apples
2 firm pears
2 tablespoons walnut oil
Freshly ground pepper to taste
2 teaspoons Dijon mustard
4 teaspoons sherry vinegar
½ tablespoon walnut oil
2 teaspoons olive oil
Salt to taste
12 (¼-inch) slices French bread
½ tablespoon walnut oil
¼ to ½ cup crumbled Stilton cheese
6 cups arugula

Coarsely chop half the walnuts. Grind the remaining walnuts and set aside. Peel the apples and cut into halves lengthwise. Cut crosswise into ¼-inch slices. Cut the unpeeled pears into halves lengthwise; cut crosswise into ¼-inch slices. Brush the apple and pear slices with 2 tablespoons walnut oil. Arrange in a single layer on a baking sheet. Sprinkle with pepper. Bake at 225 degrees for 2 hours or until the slices are reduced to ¾ of their original size. Set aside.

For the dressing, whisk the Dijon mustard and vinegar in a bowl. Whisk in ½ tablespoon walnut oil and the olive oil gradually. Season with salt and additional pepper.

Place the bread slices on a baking sheet. Brush with ½ tablespoon walnut oil. Sprinkle with the ground walnuts. Top with the cheese. Bake at 350 degrees for 3 minutes or until the cheese is melted.

Toss the arugula, dressing and chopped walnuts in a large bowl. Divide among 6 plates. Arrange apple and pear slices around the edge of each plate. Place 2 of the toasted bread slices on top of each salad. Serve immediately.

YIELD: 6 SERVINGS

French Farm Salad

¼ cup minced shallots
1 garlic clove, minced
¼ cup Grand Marnier
2 tablespoons balsamic vinegar
3 tablespoons fresh orange juice
1 tablespoon fresh lemon juice
2 to 3 teaspoons Dijon mustard
1 teaspoon grated orange zest
Salt and pepper to taste
½ cup olive oil
2 to 3 tablespoons walnut oil
12 ounces mixed baby greens
½ cup chopped walnuts, toasted
8 ounces Roquefort, Gruyère or chèvre cheese
8 slices French bread, buttered, lightly toasted
¼ cup chopped walnuts

For the dressing, bring the shallots, garlic, Grand Marnier and vinegar to a boil in a small heavy saucepan. Boil until the liquid is reduced to 2 tablespoons. Combine with the orange juice, lemon juice, Dijon mustard, orange zest, salt and pepper in a medium bowl and mix well. Add the olive oil and walnut oil gradually, whisking constantly until the mixture is thick and smooth.

Toss the greens, ½ cup walnuts and dressing in a large bowl. Spread the cheese on the toast and sprinkle with ¼ cup chopped walnuts. Broil 6 inches from the heat source for 1 minute or until the cheese is heated through.

Arrange the salad on individual plates and top with the cheese toast.

YIELD: 4 SERVINGS

Romaine Salad with Spiced Pecans

½ cup balsamic vinegar
2 garlic cloves, mashed
1 cup olive oil
¼ teaspoon cumin
¼ teaspoon thyme
Salt and pepper to taste
3 heads romaine lettuce, torn into pieces
6 ounces Gorgonzola cheese, crumbled
Spiced Pecans (below)

For the dressing, combine the vinegar and garlic in a bowl and mix well. Add the olive oil gradually, whisking constantly. Season with cumin, thyme, salt and pepper.

Toss the lettuce with the cheese and dressing in a large bowl. Divide among 6 plates. Top with Spiced Pecans.

YIELD: 6 SERVINGS

Spiced Pecans

2 teaspoons butter
1 tablespoon sugar
½ teaspoon kosher salt or sea salt
½ teaspoon black pepper
⅛ teaspoon cayenne pepper
1 teaspoon water
⅔ cup pecan halves

Melt the butter in a heavy saucepan. Add the sugar, salt, black pepper, cayenne pepper and water. Cook until the mixture bubbles. Add the pecans. Cook for 5 minutes or until the sugar begins to caramelize, stirring until the pecans are coated.

These pecans can be prepared 1 day ahead and stored in an airtight container.

YIELD: ⅔ CUP

"We take a positive attitude," explained Alva Gordon Sink of her numerous parties. "Instead of saying it can't be done because of remodeling in process or because we are about to leave town, we proceed anyway. We never fuss or hover over our guests, and the buffet allows for real informality and congeniality."

A warm, efficient, and charming hostess, Mrs. Sink kept meticulous guest lists and menus from the hundreds of dinners, post-concert suppers, and receptions that she and her husband, Charles, longtime University Musical Society president, gave for visiting musicians. She shrewdly repeated what went over well. Among the dishes she served for decades: maple mousse (recipe on page 206), Swedish meatballs, a fruit salad, and scalloped oysters. The Sinks never served alcoholic beverages. Offered at every party: Vernor's ginger ale, a Michigan product.

Marinated Fresh Vegetable Salad

2 cups fresh green beans, cut into 2-inch
  pieces
½ cup olive oil or canola oil
¼ cup red wine vinegar
2 garlic cloves, minced
⅛ teaspoon oregano, or to taste
Salt and pepper to taste
1 to 1½ cups fresh or frozen peas
1 pint cherry tomatoes, cut into halves
Flowerets of 1 head cauliflower
1 cup coarsely chopped celery, cut into
  ½-inch pieces
1 small bunch green onions, cut into
  ½-inch pieces
2 cups julienned carrots
8 ounces kalamata or other brine-cured black
  olives, pitted (see Note with next recipe)
1 cup chopped fresh parsley
½ cup chopped fresh basil

Blanch the green beans in boiling water in a saucepan for 1 minute. Plunge immediately into cold water. When cool, drain well and set aside.

For the marinade, combine the olive oil, vinegar, garlic, oregano, salt and pepper in a medium bowl and mix well.

Combine the green beans, peas, tomatoes, cauliflower, celery, green onions, carrots, olives, parsley, basil and marinade in a large bowl and toss to mix well.

Cover and store in the refrigerator overnight, stirring occasionally. This salad improves with age and will keep for up to 1 week. It complements grilled foods very nicely.

YIELD: 10 TO 12 SERVINGS

White Bean and Goat Cheese Salad

1 pound dried small navy beans
6 cups chicken stock, chicken broth or water
3 carrots, peeled, chopped
4 pieces sun-dried tomatoes
2 bay leaves
2 garlic cloves, minced
1½ tablespoons Dijon mustard
⅓ cup fresh lemon juice
½ cup olive oil
Salt and pepper to taste
1 medium red onion, chopped
8 ounces goat cheese, crumbled
½ cup kalamata olives, pitted, cut into halves
  (see Note)
½ cup pine nuts, toasted
1 bunch parsley, chopped

Rinse and sort the beans. Soak the beans in cold water to cover overnight; drain well. Combine the beans, chicken stock, carrots, tomatoes and bay leaves in a large saucepan. Bring to a boil and skim off any foam. Simmer for 30 to 40 minutes or just until tender. Drain well, reserving the cooking liquid for soup or risotto if desired.

Mix the garlic, Dijon mustard and lemon juice in a small bowl. Whisk in the olive oil and season with salt and pepper. Combine with the beans in a large bowl. Add the onion, cheese, olives, pine nuts and parsley and toss to mix well. Serve at room temperature.

Note: An easy way to pit olives is to place them on a paper towel or waxed paper and roll gently with a rolling pin. Press with the heel of the hand to push the pit out.

YIELD: 8 TO 10 SERVINGS

Broiled Chicken Breast Salad with Curry Dressing

2 teaspoons olive oil

2 tablespoons fresh lemon juice

2 tablespoons chopped fresh rosemary, or 1 teaspoon dried

2 teaspoons minced garlic

Salt and freshly ground pepper to taste

4 boneless skinless chicken breasts (about 1¼ pounds)

1 head radicchio, separated into leaves

2 heads Bibb lettuce, separated into leaves

4 ounces arugula, cut into pieces

Curry Dressing (below)

¼ cup coarsely chopped fresh basil or chervil

Mix the olive oil, lemon juice, rosemary, garlic, salt and pepper in a bowl. Add the chicken, turning to coat. Marinate, covered, in the refrigerator for 1 to 6 hours. Remove the chicken from the marinade; discard remaining marinade. Place the chicken over medium-hot coals; close the grill. Cook for 3 to 5 minutes or until cooked through, turning occasionally. Remove chicken from grill and cut diagonally into ¼-inch slices. Toss the greens in a large bowl. Add half the warm Curry Dressing and toss again. Place the chicken on top. Sprinkle with the remaining Curry Dressing and basil.

YIELD: 4 SERVINGS

Curry Dressing

2 teaspoons Dijon mustard

1 teaspoon curry powder

2 tablespoons (or more) balsamic vinegar

¼ cup chopped scallions

⅓ cup olive oil or vegetable oil

Salt and freshly ground pepper to taste

¼ cup coarsely chopped fresh basil or chervil

Heat the Dijon mustard, curry powder, vinegar and scallions in a saucepan over low heat, whisking constantly. Whisk in the olive oil. Remove from the heat. Season with salt and pepper. Stir in the basil. Keep warm.

YIELD: 1 CUP

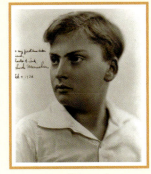

Yehudi Menuhin

When he first performed in Ann Arbor in 1932, Yehudi Menuhin was a young boy making his first appearance in long trousers. Charles Sink recalled showing Menuhin and his father around town before the concert. At the father's request, the group went into a grocery to buy some fruit. Back in the car, Sink and his wife watched with surprise as Menuhin produced a lime from his pocket, "which in true boy's style he had surreptitiously picked up in the store," and began to cut into it with a jackknife. "And he, the world's most famous boy violinist, with a concert to be played that night!" Mrs. Sink, who was driving, stopped the car while the elder Menuhin carefully "took possession of the knife."

Menuhin returned to Ann Arbor for more than a dozen concerts over the years, several of them with his sister, Hephzibah.

Crunchy Chicken Salad

2½ cups torn spinach
2 cups small broccoli florets
1 (8-ounce) can sliced water chestnuts,
    drained
2 cups chopped cooked chicken breast
1 large tomato, cut into small wedges
1 tablespoon grated Parmesan cheese
2 tablespoons reduced-sodium soy sauce
2 tablespoons red wine vinegar
2 tablespoons grated Parmesan cheese
2 tablespoons vegetable oil
1 tablespoon minced onion
¼ teaspoon sugar
⅛ teaspoon pepper, or to taste
1 teaspoon sesame seeds, toasted

Layer the spinach, broccoli, water chestnuts
and chicken on a large serving platter. Arrange the
tomato wedges around the layers. Sprinkle with
1 tablespoon Parmesan cheese. Cover and chill
thoroughly.

For the dressing, combine the soy sauce,
vinegar, 2 tablespoons Parmesan cheese, vegetable
oil, onion, sugar, pepper and sesame seeds in a
small bowl and mix well. Pour over the salad just
before serving.

YIELD: 4 SERVINGS

Curried Duck Salad

1 cup mayonnaise
⅔ cup chutney, puréed
8 teaspoons curry powder
2½ teaspoons fresh lemon juice
8 teaspoons honey
1 teaspoon white vinegar
4 cups chopped roast duck (about 2 whole
    ducks or 2 duck breasts)
2 large ribs celery, peeled, finely chopped
1 small onion, finely chopped
2 apples, chopped
¼ cup sliced almonds, toasted
Salt and pepper to taste
Boston lettuce leaves or shredded romaine
    lettuce

Combine the mayonnaise, chutney, curry
powder, lemon juice, honey and vinegar in a large
bowl and mix well.

Add the duck, celery, onion, apples and almonds
and toss well. Season with salt and pepper.

Chill, covered, for 2 hours or longer. Serve
over the lettuce.

**YIELD: 6 TO 8 SERVINGS AS A SALAD
4 TO 6 SERVINGS AS AN ENTRÉE**

Shrimp Salad alla Cremona

1 cup each dry white wine
    and water
10 to 15 peppercorns
1 or 2 bay leaves
50 large shrimp
1 cup whole hazelnuts or
    almonds
Olive oil
10 ounces broccoli florets

2 bunches green onions,
    chopped
2 red bell peppers, roasted
    (see page 39)
2 green bell peppers, roasted
10 ounces shell pasta, cooked
1½ cups freshly grated
    Parmesan cheese
Basil Vinaigrette (below)

Combine the wine, water, peppercorns and bay leaves in a heavy saucepan. Bring to a boil and add the shrimp. Cover and remove from the heat. Let stand until cool. (The shrimp will continue to cook in the poaching liquid.) Discard the poaching liquid or reserve for soup stock.

Spread the hazelnuts on a baking sheet and brush with olive oil. Bake at 350 degrees for 5 minutes or until brown. Let cool. Finely grind the hazelnuts in a food processor or blender.

Drop the broccoli into boiling water in a saucepan. Boil for 2 to 3 minutes. Remove from the saucepan and plunge immediately into cold water.

Combine the shrimp, hazelnuts, broccoli, green onions, bell peppers, pasta and cheese in a large bowl. Add the Basil Vinaigrette and toss to mix well.

YIELD: 10 SERVINGS

Basil Vinaigrette

¾ cup chopped fresh basil
3 tablespoons red wine vinegar
6 tablespoons minced garlic
1½ cups olive oil

Combine the basil, vinegar and garlic in a blender container. Add the olive oil in a steady stream, processing constantly until blended.

YIELD: 2 TO 2½ CUPS

A woman who was a teenager in the 1930s remembers that "everything about concert nights was glamorous. Turned out in satin or velvet or printed chiffon, ladies wore beaded head bands or velvet chokers, long drop earrings, and evening slippers with cut-steel buckles.

"At Hill Auditorium, her escort or driver sprang out of the car or the taxi, opened the door, and offered an arm to help her down from the running board. Shrugging cozily in her short seal fur cape, or clutching her black woolen cloak with its small chinchilla collar, she mounted the steps and entered the lobby. There she joined in the high-pitched 'Hellos,' elevated by the anticipatory excitement in an atmosphere of confidence and privilege."

Roasted Asparagus and Crab Meat Salad

1 pound fresh asparagus, trimmed,
  cut into 1-inch pieces
Salt to taste
2 tablespoons olive oil
Pepper to taste
1 pound lump crab meat
½ cup Aïoli (page 187) or your favorite
  vinaigrette
12 (¼-inch) slices beefsteak tomatoes
2 tablespoons capers, drained
1 medium Vidalia onion or other sweet onion,
  very thinly sliced

Cook the asparagus in boiling salted water
in a saucepan for 2 minutes. Remove from the
saucepan and plunge immediately into a bowl of
ice water. Let stand for 4 minutes. Remove and
pat dry.

Toss the asparagus with the olive oil in a
bowl. Season with salt and pepper. Spread on a
parchment paper-lined baking sheet. Bake at 400
degrees for 6 minutes. Remove from the oven and
let stand until cool.

Toss the crab meat with the Aïoli in a bowl.
Season with salt and pepper. Season both sides of
the tomatoes with salt and pepper.

Set aside a few of the asparagus tips for a
garnish. Layer the tomato slices, remaining
asparagus, capers and onion slices on a plate in
the order listed. Mound the crab meat mixture in
the center. Garnish with reserved asparagus tips.

YIELD: 6 SERVINGS

Asparagus, Shrimp and Pasta Salad

6 ounces fusilli, rotini or other curly pasta
1 pound fresh asparagus, trimmed
1 medium papaya, peeled, cut into halves
⅓ cup light sour cream
¼ cup papaya or mango nectar
1½ tablespoons mango chutney
Grated zest of ½ lemon
⅓ pound small shrimp, cooked, peeled,
  deveined
¼ cup sliced green onions
8 Boston or Bibb lettuce leaves

Cook the pasta in boiling water in a saucepan
until al dente. Rinse with cold water and drain
well. Cook the asparagus in boiling water in a
saucepan for 3 to 5 minutes or until tender-crisp.
Drain and rinse under cold water. Reserve and
chill 12 asparagus spears. Cut the remaining
asparagus into 1-inch pieces. Cut half the papaya
lengthwise into 8 to 12 thin slices. Chill
thoroughly. Cut the remaining papaya into bite-
size pieces.

Combine the sour cream, papaya nectar,
chutney and lemon zest in a large bowl. Add the
pasta and mix well. Stir in the cut asparagus,
papaya pieces, shrimp and green onions.
Chill briefly.

To serve, place 2 lettuce leaves on each of
4 plates. Spoon the pasta mixture onto the lettuce.
Arrange the reserved papaya slices and asparagus
spears over the top. Garnish with fresh mint and
lemon twists or lemon wedges.

YIELD: 4 SERVINGS

Salmon Salad Niçoise

2 cups vegetable broth or fish broth
¼ cup dry white wine
½ teaspoon lemon pepper
1 pound fresh salmon fillet, cut crosswise into halves
2 quarts mixed greens
½ cup fresh tarragon leaves
½ red onion, thinly sliced
2 medium-large tomatoes, cut into wedges, or
    1 pint cherry tomatoes
4 large hard-cooked eggs, cut lengthwise into quarters
¾ cup black French or Greek olives
1 cup feta cheese, cut into large pieces
½ to 1 cup vinaigrette
4 sprigs of fresh tarragon

Bring the vegetable broth, wine and lemon pepper to a boil in a saucepan. Add the salmon and simmer just until done. Remove the salmon to a plate and let cool. Discard the broth or reserve to use as a base for a sauce or chowder.

Combine the mixed greens and tarragon leaves in a large salad bowl or pasta bowl. Spread the onion slices evenly over the top. Arrange tomato wedges, egg quarters and some of the olives alternately in a circle around the edge of the salad. Arrange the cheese and remaining olives in a circle immediately inside the tomato wedge circle. At this point, the salad can be held in the refrigerator for 1 to 2 hours.

Remove and discard the salmon skin. Divide the salmon into 4 equal portions. Shake the vinaigrette well and drizzle ⅓ cup over the salad. Top with the salmon, separating small sections to form small fans. Top each with 1 tarragon sprig. Drizzle with a small amount of additional vinaigrette.

Serve with crusty French bread. Serve the remaining vinaigrette on the side.

Note: A good combination of greens for this salad is half romaine, the remainder a mixture of mesclun and a small amount of arugula.

YIELD: 4 SERVINGS

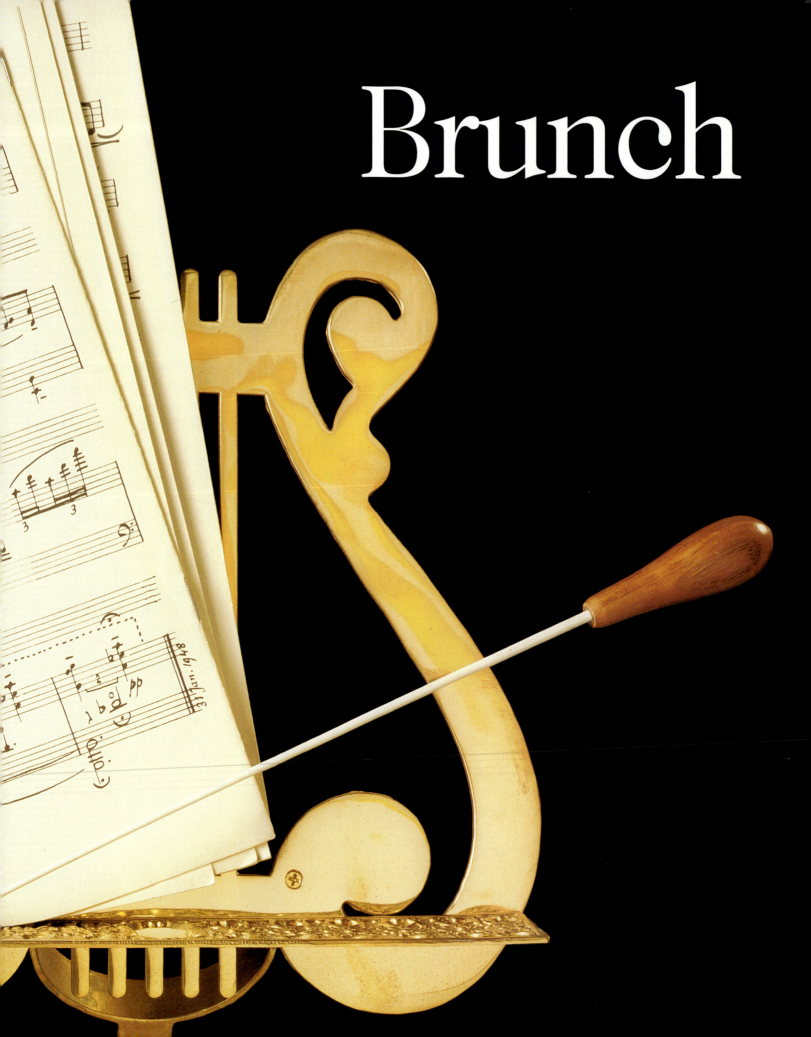

Brunch

Wednesday, May 12, 1937, 8:30 p.m.

Hill Auditorium

May Festival Concert

The Philadelphia Orchestra
Eugene Ormandy   *Conductor*
Soloist: Kirsten Flagstad   *Soprano*

Prelude and Fugue in F minor
Bach

Chorale Prelude,
"Jesu, Joy of Man's Desiring"
Bach

"La Mer"   Debussy
From Dawn to Noon at Sea
Gambols of the Waves
Dialogue Between the Wind and the Sea

Aria: "Leise, Leise," from
"Der Freischütz"   Weber
Kirsten Flagstad

"Pictures at an Exhibition"
Moussorgsky
Promenade—Gnome—The Old Castle—
Tuileries—Bydlo (Cattle)—Ballet of Chicks in
Their Shells—Samuel Goldenberg and
Schmuyle—Limoges—Catacombs—The Hut
on Fowls' Legs—The Gate
of the Bogatirs at Kiev

Brünnhilde's Immolation and
the Closing Scene from
"Götterdämmerung"   Wagner
Mme. Flagstad

Conductor Eugene Ormandy

"HE sounded marvelous. Every concert was good," says Allen Britton, dean emeritus of the University of Michigan School of Music, recalling Eugene Ormandy and the Philadelphia Orchestra. The 1937 May Festival was Ormandy's first appearance with the orchestra (which had played the preceding year under Leopold Stokowski); the Philadelphia returned every spring until 1984, with Ormandy conducting for all but the final two seasons.

Hungarian-born and -trained, Ormandy was known as a Romanticist. His affinity was so great for the works he loved—those of Beethoven, Schumann, and Richard Strauss—that he conducted them from memory. According to the *Ann Arbor News*, the audience at Ormandy's first concert, "after two hours and a half of glorious music," stayed "until near midnight demanding more encores."

Following the pattern established in 1894, the 1937 May Festival included both orchestral and choral works. Guest artists besides Kirsten Flagstad, who appeared in this opening concert, were two other Metropolitan Opera stars, tenor Lauritz Melchior and baritone Ezio Pinza, singing with the Choral Union and the Young People's Festival Chorus.

The annual May Festivals occasioned many parties—including a dinner reception for the maestro after the first performance. In the early years this was hosted by University Musical Society president Charles Sink and his wife, Alva, in their home. During the forty-eight years, Ormandy and members of the Philadelphia formed lasting friendships. Orchestra members played golf or tennis with local friends during the day and were entertained at many informal parties around town. Allen Britton, himself a trumpet player, always hosted the orchestra's trumpet section. Several Philadelphia Orchestra members, when they tired of touring, joined the university music school faculty, including Jacob Krachmalnick, Abe Torchinsky, Charles Owen, and Armando Ghitalla.

Ormandy continued conducting regularly into his seventies. After 1975, when he was seventy-six, he shared the May Festival duties with assistant or visiting conductors. Every year, in a gracious and witty gesture that delighted his audiences, he ended the final concert with "The Victors," the university fight song. In 1982, at what would be his last May Festival concert—the 149th—he led the traditional encore, "shaking the rafters of Hill Auditorium," according to the newspaper. "Emotions surfaced in vociferous clapping and cheering and Ormandy, with flushed and smiling face, took his bows, visibly moved. It was a moving farewell to a man felt to be here for the last time."

The Philadelphia Orchestra came for its last May Festival in 1984, under Aldo Ceccato and William Smith. The May Festival itself, after a glorious 102-year history, ended in 1995.

What was cooking?

The introduction in 1937 of the shopping cart, a wicker basket on wheels, foretold a shift in American shopping habits and the eventual dominance of supermarkets over neighborhood groceries.

❖

The next year, the first Trader Vic's introduced restaurant exotica: rum punch and Polynesian dishes.

❖

And Howard Johnson originated the concept of franchised restaurants.

Pumpkin Pancakes with Sautéed Apples

½ cup yellow cornmeal
1 cup boiling water
1 cup milk
½ cup canned pumpkin purée
1 large egg, lightly beaten
1 cup flour
1 tablespoon sugar
2½ teaspoons baking powder
1 teaspoon allspice
½ teaspoon cinnamon
¾ teaspoon salt

Combine the cornmeal and water in a large bowl. Let stand for 5 minutes. Add the milk, pumpkin purée and egg and mix well.

Sift the flour, sugar, baking powder, allspice, cinnamon and salt together. Add to the milk mixture, stirring just until mixed.

Bake the pancakes on a hot griddle. Serve with Sautéed Apples (below) and maple syrup.

YIELD: 24 (¼-CUP) PANCAKES

Sautéed Apples

2 tablespoons (¼ stick) butter
3 large McIntosh apples or other baking apples,
   peeled, cored, thinly sliced
1 tablespoon cinnamon sugar

Melt the butter in a skillet over medium heat. Add the apple slices and sauté until slightly softened. Sprinkle with cinnamon sugar and stir to mix well.

YIELD: 4 TO 6 SERVINGS

The Waverly Consort's Giant Pancake

3 eggs
¾ cup milk
¾ cup sifted flour

¼ teaspoon almond extract
¼ cup (½ stick) butter
Confectioners' sugar

Beat the eggs in a bowl until thick and pale yellow. Add the milk and flour alternately, beating well after each addition. Stir in the almond extract.

Heat the butter in an ovenproof skillet until melted and bubbly. Add the pancake batter. Bake at 425 degrees for 20 minutes or until puffed and brown.

Cut the pancake into wedges and sprinkle lightly with confectioners' sugar. Serve with lemon wedges and fresh fruit.

YIELD: 4 SERVINGS

Jessye Norman's Quick Tea Cake

Thinly slice this cake and serve with tea or for dessert with chopped fresh fruit, fruit or wine sorbet, or ice cream. Toast leftovers for a second-day treat.

2 cups flour
1 tablespoon baking powder
¾ teaspoon salt
3 eggs, beaten
¾ cup milk
¾ cup (1½ sticks) unsalted
  butter, softened

¾ cup packed brown sugar, or
  to taste
½ cup raisins
½ cup Grand Marnier or
  thawed orange juice
  concentrate
Confectioners' sugar (optional)

Sift the flour, baking powder and salt into a large mixer bowl. Add the eggs, milk, butter, brown sugar, raisins and liqueur. Beat at medium speed for 4 minutes. Let stand for 10 minutes. Beat at high speed for 2 to 3 minutes or until blended and smooth. Spoon into a buttered and floured 10-inch bundt pan or tube pan.

Bake at 350 degrees for 45 to 55 minutes or until the top is firm and the side has pulled away from the pan. Let stand for 5 minutes. Invert onto a wire rack to cool. Dust with confectioners' sugar.

YIELD: 8 TO 10 SERVINGS

Like many of us, Michael Jaffee, artistic director of the Waverly Consort, is a chocoholic. His favorite food? Chocolate. His favorite post-concert snack? "A satisfying dessert, especially if it's chocolate. Otherwise, apple pie is good—with chocolate ice cream, please."

Cinnamon Raisin French Toast

6 tablespoons milk
6 tablespoons buttermilk
2 eggs
3 tablespoons sugar
1 teaspoon vanilla extract
½ teaspoon cinnamon
⅛ teaspoon nutmeg, or to taste
8 slices cinnamon-raisin bread
¼ cup (½ stick) unsalted butter
Confectioners' sugar

Combine the milk, buttermilk, eggs, sugar, vanilla, cinnamon and nutmeg in a large shallow dish and beat until mixed. Add the bread slices and let stand until the bread is soaked through but still intact.

Melt 2 tablespoons of the butter in a large skillet over medium heat. Add 4 bread slices. Cook for 5 minutes or until crisp and golden-brown on both sides. Remove the toast and keep warm. Repeat with the remaining bread slices and butter.

Sprinkle each slice with confectioners' sugar. Serve with Date Nut Butter (below) or syrup.

YIELD: 4 SERVINGS

Date Nut Butter

¼ cup (½ stick) unsalted butter, softened
¼ cup finely chopped pitted dates
3 tablespoons chopped walnuts, toasted
1 teaspoon sugar
¼ teaspoon vanilla extract

Beat the butter in a small mixer bowl until smooth and creamy. Add the dates, walnuts, sugar and vanilla and mix well. Serve immediately or store in the refrigerator until serving time. Let stand at room temperature to soften.

YIELD: 2 CUPS

Lemon Bread

3¼ cups flour
1 teaspoon salt
2 teaspoons baking powder
2 cups sugar
1 cup (1 stick) butter or
   margarine, softened
4 egg yolks, beaten

1¼ cups milk
1 cup finely chopped pecans or
   walnuts
Grated zest and juice of
   2 lemons
4 egg whites, stiffly beaten
½ cup sugar

Mix the flour, salt and baking powder together. Cream 2 cups sugar and butter in a mixer bowl until light and fluffy. Beat in the egg yolks 1 at a time. Add the flour mixture and milk alternately, beating well after each addition. Stir in the pecans and lemon zest. Fold in the egg whites. Spoon the batter into 2 greased 4x8-inch loaf pans. Bake at 350 degrees for 50 to 60 minutes or until the loaves test done. Pour a mixture of the lemon juice and ½ cup sugar over the hot loaves. Let stand until cool before removing from the pans.

This bread freezes well.

YIELD: 2 LOAVES

Orange Date Nut Bread

½ cup chopped pecans
1 unpeeled orange, cut into
   wedges, seeded, chopped
1 cup chopped pitted dates
¾ cup water
1 egg
1 teaspoon vanilla extract

2 tablespoons (¼ stick) butter,
   melted
1 cup sugar
2 cups flour
1 teaspoon baking powder
1 teaspoon baking soda
¼ teaspoon salt

Spread the pecans on a waxed paper-lined or parchment paper-lined baking sheet. Bake at 350 degrees for 10 minutes or until light brown. Combine the orange wedges and dates in a bowl. Add the water, egg, vanilla and butter and mix well. Add the sugar and mix well. Add the flour, baking powder, baking soda and salt and mix well. Stir in the pecans. Spoon into a waxed paper-lined loaf pan. Bake at 350 degrees for 1 hour.

YIELD: 1 LOAF

67

Christopher Parkening's Buttermilk Coffee Cake

2 cups flour
1½ teaspoons baking powder
1 teaspoon cinnamon
¾ teaspoon nutmeg
½ teaspoon baking soda
1 cup buttermilk
½ cup (1 stick) butter, melted
1 egg
1 cup sugar
¼ teaspoon salt
½ cup chopped walnuts or pecans (optional)
½ cup packed brown sugar
¾ teaspoon cinnamon
Butter
¼ cup chopped walnuts or pecans (optional)

Sift the flour into a bowl. Add the baking powder, 1 teaspoon cinnamon and nutmeg and sift again. Dissolve the baking soda in the buttermilk in a cup.

Cream ½ cup butter, egg, sugar and salt in a mixer bowl until light and fluffy. Add the flour mixture and buttermilk alternately, beating well after each addition. Stir in ½ cup walnuts. Spoon into a lightly greased 9x9-inch baking pan.

Sprinkle a mixture of the brown sugar and ¾ teaspoon cinnamon over the top of the batter. Dot with butter and ¼ cup walnuts. Bake at 350 degrees for 45 minutes.

YIELD: 6 TO 8 SERVINGS

Sour Cream Coffee Cake

½ cup packed brown sugar
1 cup ground walnuts
1 teaspoon cinnamon
4 cups flour
½ teaspoon salt
1 teaspoon baking soda
1½ teaspoons baking powder
1 cup (2 sticks) butter, softened
2 cups sugar
2 cups sour cream
1 to 2 teaspoons vanilla extract
5 eggs, at room temperature
1½ cups fruit in season, such as cranberries, blueberries or dried cherries

Mix the brown sugar, walnuts and cinnamon in a small bowl. Sift the flour, salt, baking soda and baking powder together.

Cream the butter and sugar in a mixer bowl until light and fluffy. Add the sour cream and vanilla. Add the flour mixture and eggs alternately, beating well after each addition and beginning and ending with flour mixture.

Layer the batter, the fruit and the walnut mixture ⅓ at a time in a greased and floured bundt pan.

Bake at 350 degrees for 1¼ hours or until the coffee cake tests done. Let stand in the pan on a wire rack for 10 minutes. Invert onto a plate and let cool.

YIELD: 8 TO 10 SERVINGS

Buttery Apple Pound Cake

⅓ cup packed light brown sugar

⅓ cup chopped pecans, toasted

1 teaspoon cinnamon

1 teaspoon nutmeg

3 cups flour

1½ teaspoons baking powder

1½ teaspoons baking soda

½ teaspoon salt

¾ cup (1½ sticks) butter, softened

1½ cups sugar

3 eggs

1½ teaspoons vanilla extract

And + juice of 1 orange

1½ cups sour cream or reduced-fat sour cream *or yogurt*

1½ cups thinly sliced peeled apples

2 tablespoons (¼ stick) butter

⅓ cup packed light brown sugar

2 tablespoons milk

½ teaspoon vanilla extract

Mix ⅓ cup brown sugar, pecans, cinnamon and nutmeg together. Mix the flour, baking powder, baking soda and salt together.

Cream ¾ cup butter in a mixer bowl until smooth. Beat in the sugar gradually. Beat in the eggs and 1½ teaspoons vanilla. Add the flour mixture and sour cream alternately, beating well after each addition.

Spoon half the batter into a generously buttered and floured 12-cup bundt pan or 10-inch tube cake pan. Arrange the apple slices over the batter. Spoon half the brown sugar mixture over the apples and press lightly into the batter. Spoon the remaining batter over the top and sprinkle with the remaining brown sugar mixture.

Bake at 350 degrees for 60 to 70 minutes or until a wooden pick inserted near the center comes out clean. Let stand in the pan on a wire rack for 15 minutes. Loosen the cake gently from the side of the pan with a sharp knife. Invert onto a wire rack.

Heat 2 tablespoons butter in a small saucepan over medium heat until it begins to brown. Remove from the heat. Stir in ⅓ cup brown sugar, milk and ½ teaspoon vanilla. Drizzle over the warm cake.

YIELD: 16 SERVINGS

Christopher Parkening

Leopold Stokowski conducted the Philadelphia Orchestra at the 1936 May Festival, inaugurating the orchestra's decades-long association with the annual event. Perhaps the most famous conductor of his time, the middle-aged maestro charmed his hosts with his joie de vivre. He toured the Ford auto plant, where he met Henry Ford and bought a sparkling new Lincoln Zephyr. "He was as proud of it as a boy with a new bicycle," remembered Charles Sink, longtime president of the University Musical Society.

Stokowski capped his visit by skipping a fancy social gathering and going with a group of students to the Pretzel Bell, a student hangout. He autographed concert programs, then joined the merriment. Standing on his chair, and with the graceful hands that were a part of his legend, he led the student crowd in singing "The Victors."

Glazed Orange Currant Scones

½ cup currants
¼ cup orange juice
¼ to ½ cup skim milk
1 egg, lightly beaten
1¾ cups flour
⅔ cup wheat germ
½ cup sugar
1 tablespoon baking powder

2 teaspoons grated orange zest
5 tablespoons plus
   1 teaspoon 70% vegetable oil
   spread in stick form, chilled,
   cut into pieces
½ cup confectioners' sugar
1 to 1½ tablespoons orange
   juice

Combine the currants and ¼ cup orange juice in a small bowl. Let stand for 10 minutes. Remove the currants; set aside. Add enough milk to the orange juice to measure ½ cup. Stir in the egg. Mix the flour, wheat germ, sugar, baking powder and orange zest in a large bowl. Cut in the vegetable oil spread until crumbly. Add the egg mixture; stir with a fork just until dry ingredients are moistened. Fold in the currants. Turn the dough onto a lightly floured surface. Knead gently 8 to 10 times. Pat the dough into an 8-inch circle on a baking sheet lightly sprayed with nonstick cooking spray. Cut into 8 wedges; separate wedges slightly. Bake at 375 degrees for 18 minutes or until golden brown. Cool on a wire rack for 5 minutes. Blend confectioners' sugar with enough of the remaining 1 to 1½ tablespoons orange juice to make a glaze. Drizzle over the warm scones. Serve warm.

YIELD: 8 SCONES

A Perfect Pot of Tea

Water
Tea leaves or tea bags

Milk to taste
Sugar to taste

Bring a saucepan of water almost to a boil. Warm a teapot by swishing in a small amount of the hot water around inside; discard water. Add tea leaves to the teapot, 1 teaspoon per person plus 1 teaspoon for the teapot. Pour in boiling water. Let stand to brew for 5 minutes or to desired strength. Serve in elegant tea cups. Stir in milk and sugar.

YIELD: VARIABLE

Best-Ever Blueberry Muffins

1 cup whole wheat flour
1 cup all-purpose flour
1 tablespoon baking powder
¾ teaspoon salt
2 teaspoons cinnamon
¼ cup packed brown sugar
½ cup sugar

2 eggs
5 tablespoons vegetable oil
¾ cup milk
2 cups fresh or frozen
  blueberries
1 cup chopped walnuts
Cinnamon sugar to taste

Combine the whole wheat flour, all-purpose flour, baking powder, salt, cinnamon, brown sugar and sugar in a large bowl. Beat the eggs, oil and milk in a medium bowl.

Fold the egg mixture into the flour mixture. Stir in the blueberries and walnuts; do not overmix.

Spoon the batter into 12 greased muffin cups. Sprinkle with cinnamon sugar. Bake at 375 degrees for 20 minutes.

YIELD: 12 MUFFINS

Joshua Bell's Avi Eggs

As a young boy, Joshua Bell had a friend, Avi, who lived across the street. Avi's mother frequently made this dish for the neighborhood children, and it's been one of Joshua's favorites ever since.

1 tablespoon butter
4 slices bread
4 medium eggs

Salt and pepper to taste
Hot pepper sauce to taste

Melt the butter in a large skillet, tilting to coat the bottom of the skillet. Cut or tear a hole in the center of each bread slice. Place in the skillet in a single layer. Break 1 egg into the center of each bread slice. Cook until the bread begins to toast. Turn the bread over and brown the other side. Season with salt and pepper or hot sauce.

YIELD: 4 SERVINGS

Joshua Bell

Violinist Joshua Bell remembers his recital at Rackham Auditorium in 1994. He was playing John Corigliano's violin sonata, and a troublesome draft, probably from a stage door left ajar, riffled the score. "The music kept blowing off the stand," Bell says, but "somehow we were able to finish." The next selection was not on the printed program, and when he announced it from the stage, Bell began, "Due to the windy conditions . . ."

Twenty-Four Hour Wine and Cheese Omelet

1 large loaf dry French or Italian bread,
    broken into small pieces
6 tablespoons (¾ stick) unsalted butter,
    melted
12 ounces Swiss cheese, shredded
8 ounces Monterey Jack cheese, shredded
9 slices prosciutto, bacon, ham or Canadian
    bacon, coarsely chopped
16 eggs
3¼ cups milk
⅓ cup dry white wine
1 tablespoon Düsseldorf mustard
¼ teaspoon freshly ground black pepper
⅛ teaspoon red pepper flakes or Tabasco
    sauce
4 large green onions, minced
1½ cups sour cream
1 cup (or less) freshly grated Parmesan
    cheese or shredded Asiago cheese

Butter 2 shallow 3-quart baking dishes.
Arrange half the bread in a single layer in each of
the baking dishes. Drizzle with the melted butter.
Sprinkle the Swiss cheese and Monterey Jack
cheese over the bread. Top with the prosciutto.

Beat the eggs, milk, wine, mustard, black
pepper, red pepper and green onions in a bowl
until the eggs are foamy. Pour over the bread and
cheese in the baking dishes. Cover each baking
dish with foil, crimping the edges to seal. Chill,
covered, in the refrigerator for up to 24 hours.

Remove the baking dishes from the refrigerator
and let stand for 30 minutes. Bake, covered, at
325 degrees for 1 hour or until set. Uncover and
spread sour cream over the top. Sprinkle with the
Parmesan cheese. Bake, uncovered, for 10 minutes
or until crisp and light brown.

YIELD: 12 SERVINGS

Avalanche Egg White Omelet

1 tablespoon butter or margarine, softened
3 large egg whites, beaten
½ avocado, peeled, cut into ¼- to ⅜-inch
    slices
1 or 2 sun-dried tomatoes, julienned
Coarsely chopped fresh basil to taste
2½ ounces provolone cheese, shredded
4 ounces smoked chicken or smoked turkey,
    chopped (optional)
Salt and freshly ground pepper to taste
Fresh fruit (optional)

Brush a nonstick skillet with the butter. Add
the egg whites. Add most of the avocado slices,
sun-dried tomatoes, basil, cheese and chicken.

Cook until the omelet is set on 1 side. Flip the
omelet over and cook until the other side is set.
Roll onto a warm plate. Top with the remaining
avocado slices, sun-dried tomatoes, basil, cheese
and chicken. Season with salt and pepper. Arrange
fresh fruit over the top.

Note: You can use a broiler to set the top of the
omelet instead of flipping it.

YIELD: 1 TO 2 SERVINGS

Mushroom Terrine with Saffron Sauce

2 tablespoons clarified
   butter (see Note,
   page 190)
2 pounds mushrooms, thinly
   sliced
3 shallots, thinly sliced

2 garlic cloves, thinly sliced
6 large eggs, lightly beaten
1½ cups heavy cream
1 tablespoon minced parsley
Salt and pepper to taste
Saffron Sauce (below)

Heat the clarified butter in a heavy skillet over medium heat. Add the mushrooms, shallots and garlic. Cook for 10 minutes or until the vegetables are tender but not brown, stirring constantly. Spoon into a 1½-quart terrine or two 4x8-inch glass loaf pans.

Whisk the eggs, cream, parsley, salt and pepper in a bowl. Pour over the mushroom mixture. Tap the terrine gently on a hard surface. Cover with foil and place the terrine in a larger baking pan. Add enough warm water to the baking pan to come halfway up the sides of the terrine.

Bake at 325 degrees for 1 hour. Remove the terrine from the oven and let cool to room temperature. Chill in the refrigerator overnight.

To unmold, dip the terrine in hot water and run a knife around the edges. Invert onto a platter. Cut into 10 slices. Bake at 450 degrees for 5 minutes or just until heated. Serve topped with Saffron Sauce.

YIELD: 10 SERVINGS

Saffron Sauce

½ teaspoon saffron
1 cup dry white wine
2 tablespoons clam juice

1½ cups heavy cream
Salt and pepper to taste

Soak the saffron in the wine for 1 hour. Combine the wine mixture and clam juice in a heavy saucepan. Boil until the liquid is reduced to ¼ cup. Add the cream. Boil until the liquid is reduced to 1 cup. Season with salt and pepper.

YIELD: 10 SERVINGS

73

During his annual May Festival visits, Eugene Ormandy often found Hill Auditorium (which is not air-conditioned) uncomfortably warm. After rehearsal on a balmy day, he would return to his room at the Michigan League, just to the east of the auditorium, and call the Hill ticket office. The message, recalls Michael Gowing of the box office staff, was invariably, "This is Mr. Ormandy. The auditorium is too warm. I will not be able to perform."

Gowing would immediately open the doors on the auditorium's east side, "wide, in view of Mr. Ormandy's window. That would be that. Hill Auditorium would be 'air'-conditioned."

Broccoli Timbales with Michigan Morel Sauce

3 bunches fresh broccoli	1½ cups heavy cream
Salt to taste	Pepper and nutmeg to taste
8 eggs	Michigan Morel Sauce (below)

Chop the florets from the broccoli. Peel the stalks; cut tender portions into ¼-inch slices. Drop florets and stalks into boiling salted water in a 2-gallon stockpot. Boil for 5 to 8 minutes or until broccoli turns slightly olive green. Plunge broccoli immediately into ice water. Drain for 20 minutes; squeeze out excess moisture. Purée the broccoli in a food processor. Add 2 eggs and ½ cup of the cream; process for 1 minute. Pour into a large bowl. Add the remaining 6 eggs and 1 cup cream; mix well with a rubber spatula. Season with salt, pepper and nutmeg.

Brush 8 to 10 timbale molds lightly with corn oil. Fill with the broccoli mixture. Place molds in larger baking pan. Add enough warm water to baking pan to come halfway up the side of the molds. Bake at 325 degrees for 1 hour and 20 minutes or until firm. Let stand in the water for 1 hour; remove from the water. Chill for 2 hours or until set. Unmold timbales onto plates. Serve chilled, at room temperature or warm with Michigan Morel Sauce.

YIELD: 8 TO 10 SERVINGS

Michigan Morel Sauce

¼ cup finely chopped shallots	½ pound fresh Michigan morels, cleaned, or
1 tablespoon butter	equivalent reconstituted
1 teaspoon minced garlic	dried morels
¼ cup madeira	1 pint heavy cream
¼ cup brandy	Salt and pepper to taste

Sauté shallots in butter in a skillet until golden brown. Add garlic; sauté for 1 minute. Add wine and brandy. Simmer for several minutes, scraping up any browned bits. Add mushrooms and cream. Simmer, covered, for 15 minutes. Simmer, uncovered, for 30 minutes or until thick, stirring occasionally. Season with salt and pepper.

YIELD: 8 TO 10 SERVINGS

Fallen Crab Soufflé

1 cup grated Parmesan
   cheese
1 cup fine bread crumbs
1/4 cup (1/2 stick) butter,
   melted
1 teaspoon grapeseed oil
1/2 cup each minced green
   and red bell pepper

1/2 cup minced onion
2 teaspoons kosher salt
1/2 teaspoon white pepper
12 ounces cream cheese, softened
4 eggs
1/2 cup shredded Gouda cheese
1 pound lump crab meat, flaked
Jalapeño Garlic Sauce

Mix the Parmesan cheese, bread crumbs and butter in a bowl. Press onto the bottom of 6 greased 3-ounce ramekins. Heat the oil in a sauté pan. Add the bell peppers and onion. Season with salt and pepper. Sauté until wilted. Remove from heat; let cool.

Beat the cream cheese and eggs in a mixer bowl until thick. Add the Gouda cheese and sautéed vegetables; mix well. Fold in crab meat. Spoon into the ramekins. Place the ramekins in a larger baking pan. Add enough warm water to the baking pan to come halfway up the side of the ramekins. Bake at 350 degrees for 35 minutes or until set. Chill thoroughly. Unmold the ramekins onto a baking sheet. Bake at 400 degrees for 10 minutes or until heated through. Spoon Jalapeño Garlic Sauce onto each of 6 plates. Place 1 soufflé over the sauce on each plate. Garnish with baby lettuce.

YIELD: 6 SERVINGS

Jalapeño Garlic Sauce

1/2 cup chopped onion
1/2 cup each chopped green
   and red bell pepper
3 cups undrained chopped
   tomatoes
1 teaspoon minced garlic

1/4 cup whole capers, drained
1/4 cup sliced green olives
1 jalapeño chile, minced
2 tablespoons olive oil
1/4 cup chopped cilantro
Salt and pepper to taste

Sauté the onion, bell peppers, tomatoes, garlic, capers, olives and jalapeño in the olive oil in a skillet. Simmer for 15 minutes. Stir in the cilantro and season with salt and pepper.

YIELD: 6 SERVINGS

75

Marian Anderson

The great contralto Marian Anderson sang at least ten times in Hill Auditorium. Her first engagement was as a last-minute replacement for Nelson Eddy. Recalling that March 1937 concert in his memoirs, University Musical Society president Charles Sink said that the hugely popular Eddy had sold out the entire hall. Sink was certain, though, that "some of our regular patrons of the 'high and mighty' type, who were above listening to a movie star at a concert, had graciously given their tickets to friends, or more likely to their maids."

When the local press announced that Marian Anderson would appear instead of the ailing Eddy, "the sophisticates who had given up their Eddy tickets," wrote Sink, came "rushing back to the office" trying to replace them.

Spinach and Zucchini Tartlets in Whole Wheat Crust

2 cups whole wheat flour
¼ teaspoon salt
¼ cup corn oil or safflower oil
⅓ cup ice water
Corn oil for brushing pastry
3 to 4 small zucchini, shredded (about 2 cups)
Salt to taste
10 ounces fresh or thawed and drained frozen chopped spinach
2 tablespoons water
3 tablespoons butter
1 cup finely chopped onion
½ cup finely chopped celery
½ teaspoon finely chopped fresh garlic
1 teaspoon dried juniper berries, finely crushed
Pepper and nutmeg to taste
2 cups shredded Swiss cheese
2 cups light cream
4 extra-large eggs, beaten
1 cup grated Parmesan cheese
2 to 3 tablespoons butter, melted

For the crust, combine the flour and ¼ teaspoon salt in a bowl. Blend in ¼ cup corn oil. Add just enough ice water to gather the dough into a ball. Wrap in plastic wrap; shape into a ball. Chill for 1 hour. Press a walnut-size piece of dough into twelve 3¼-inch-diameter molds. Brush lightly with corn oil. Line each with waxed paper; add several pie weights or dried beans. Place on a baking sheet. Bake at 275 degrees for 20 minutes or until the edges begin to brown. Remove from the oven; remove pie weights and waxed paper. Let stand until cool.

Sprinkle the zucchini generously with salt. Weigh down for 30 minutes. Rinse; squeeze dry. Cook the spinach in 2 tablespoons water in a covered skillet over high heat until the water has evaporated.

Melt 3 tablespoons butter in a skillet. Add the onion and sauté briefly. Add the celery, garlic, zucchini and spinach. Cook until the liquid evaporates. Add the juniper berries. Season with salt, pepper and nutmeg. Sprinkle the Swiss cheese over the bottom of each crust. Spoon the spinach mixture over the cheese.

Beat the cream and eggs in a bowl. Season lightly with additional salt, pepper and nutmeg. Remove to a pitcher and fill each tartlet from the pitcher. Sprinkle with Parmesan cheese and drizzle with 2 to 3 tablespoons melted butter. Bake at 375 degrees for 25 to 30 minutes or until puffed and set. Serve immediately.

These tartlets can be frozen. To serve, place on a baking sheet. Bake at 325 degrees for 25 minutes or until heated through.

YIELD: 12 SERVINGS

Chicken Apple Hash

1 potato, peeled, cut into ¼-inch cubes
Salt to taste
2 tablespoons olive oil
1 onion, cut into ¼-inch cubes
½ cup cubed red bell pepper
½ cup cubed green bell pepper
1 tablespoon olive oil
1 whole boneless skinless chicken breast, cooked, cut into
    ¼-inch pieces
1¼ teaspoons fresh thyme, or ½ teaspoon dried thyme
Pepper to taste
1 cup cubed Golden Delicious or other cooking apples
¼ cup chopped fresh flat-leaf parsley
Chili sauce to taste
4 eggs, poached (optional)

Cook the potato in boiling salted water to cover in a small saucepan for 8 minutes or until tender; drain well.

Heat 2 tablespoons olive oil in a medium nonstick skillet over medium heat. Add the onion. Cook for 4 minutes or just until the onion is wilted, stirring constantly. Add the bell peppers. Cook for 5 minutes, shaking the skillet constantly.

Increase the heat to medium-high. Add 1 tablespoon olive oil. Add the chicken and potato and sprinkle with thyme, salt and pepper. Cook for 5 minutes, stirring constantly. Press down the hash with a heatproof plate or small skillet. Cook for 5 minutes or until brown. Turn the hash in sections with a spatula and weigh down again. Cook for 4 minutes or until brown on all sides.

Add the apple and parsley. Cook for 4 minutes or until the apple is tender, turning with the spatula occasionally.

Remove the hash to a platter. Season with chili sauce. Serve with the eggs.

YIELD: 4 SERVINGS

Foods
from the
Sea

1942

Saturday, May 9, 1942, 2:30 p.m.

Hill Auditorium

May Festival Concert

The Philadelphia Orchestra
Eugene Ormandy   *Conductor*
Sergei Rachmaninoff   *Pianist*

All-Rachmaninoff Program

**"The Isle of the Dead,"
Symphonic Poem,
after Böcklin, Op. 29**

Symphonic Dances, Op. 45
Non allegro
Andante con moto (Tempi di valse)
Lento assai; Allegro vivace

**Concerto for Piano No. 2
in C minor, Op. 18**
Moderato
Adagio sostenuto
Allegro scherzando
Sergei Rachmaninoff

Sergei Rachmaninoff

UNIVERSITY Musical Society president Charles Sink had tried for fifteen years to bring Sergei Rachmaninoff to a May Festival, but the artist's schedule had never allowed a visit in the spring. Internationally famous and familiar to local audiences (this concert was his eighth in Ann Arbor), he filled Hill Auditorium on his name alone. Charles Sink wrote that "he played like an inspired god." This wartime program, devoted exclusively to his own compositions, was exceptional musical bounty.

Rachmaninoff played with the Philadelphia Orchestra, under his good friend Eugene Ormandy. Indeed, the Symphonic Dances, Opus 45, written just two years earlier, were dedicated to Ormandy and the orchestra. The composer's last major work, it is considered a crowning achievement of his career.

Throughout his life, Rachmaninoff is said to have agonized over whether he should pursue a career primarily as a composer, a conductor, or a pianist. Certainly he was extraordinarily successful at all three, and all three gave him great satisfaction. Although at times he found these multiple gifts a burden, the fortunate people who saw him conduct or heard him play, and we who today are enriched by the recordings he made and by the music he wrote, are simply grateful.

He was sixty-nine years old at the time of this concert, but what people remember is his quiet vigor. A tall man, he walked onto the stage slowly, taking surprisingly short steps. He sat at the piano with his back straight, his feet above the pedals, his face expressionless. Once he began to play, his trunk remained nearly motionless, and he performed without broad gestures. Afterward, he left as he had entered, with an appealing air of shyness and humility.

The late Benning Dexter, professor of piano at the University of Michigan School of Music, described Rachmaninoff's compositions as "flowing, revealed, like a bolt of cloth unrolling colorfully and evenly without interruption."

Despite his quiet demeanor, Rachmaninoff was an artist of great passion. Born into the Russian gentry, he nevertheless sympathized with the cause of the peasants during the simmering unrest of the early 1900s. Russian folk music was part of his being, and he drew upon its melodies and rhythms to write music that expresses the most universal joys and sorrows. He once said, "Music cannot be only color and rhythm, but must be revealed emotion of the heart." In 1917, at age forty-four, Rachmaninoff left a Russia in turmoil, and he was never permitted to return. In 1931, he wrote a letter to the *New York Times* critical of Stalin and his regime, which resulted in a ban on the study or performance of his music in the Soviet Union. The ban was ineffectual: Rachmaninoff's music was never allowed to disappear from the country he loved.

This concert was Rachmaninoff's last in Ann Arbor. He died less than a year later, in March 1943.

What was cooking?

Gourmet *magazine, dedicated to intricate and international cooking, appeared in 1941. With World War II raging, perhaps M. F. K. Fisher's book* How To Cook a Wolf *better reflected the situation of most cooks. To limit the expensive use of the oven, she advised, "you can cook what the home economists love to call a 'one-dish meal,' 'a co-ordinated dinner,' or, less genteelly, a casserole."*

Crab Cakes and Avocado Butter

½ cup fresh bread crumbs
1 cup cooked corn kernels
8 ounces fresh crab meat
2 eggs, beaten
2 tablespoons chopped chives or scallions
1 teaspoon Old Bay seasoning
¼ teaspoon salt
⅛ teaspoon cayenne pepper
Paprika to taste
2 tablespoons (¼ stick) butter
2 tablespoons vegetable oil

Combine the bread crumbs, corn kernels, crab meat, eggs, chives, Old Bay seasoning, salt, cayenne pepper and paprika in a bowl.

Heat the butter and olive oil in a 12- or 14-inch skillet over medium heat. Shape the crab meat mixture into 6 to 8 cakes. Sauté until brown on both sides, turning once (use 2 spatulas if necessary).

Serve with Avocado Butter (below) or with rice or pasta.

YIELD: 4 SERVINGS

Avocado Butter

1 avocado, peeled, chopped
3½ teaspoons fresh lime juice
Salt and freshly ground pepper to taste

Process the avocado and lime juice in a food processor or blender until puréed and smooth. Season with salt and pepper.

YIELD: ABOUT ¾ CUP

Seafood Roulade

1 cup bread crumbs
¼ cup freshly grated
    Parmesan cheese
¼ teaspoon dry mustard
2 tablespoons (¼ stick)
    unsalted butter
¼ cup flour
¾ teaspoon Dijon mustard
Salt and red pepper flakes
    to taste
¾ cup milk
2 tablespoons heavy cream
6 sheets phyllo dough,
    thawed (see Note,
    page 23)

¾ cup (1½ sticks) unsalted
    butter, melted
½ cup shredded Swiss cheese
2 large eggs, hard-cooked,
    chopped
¾ cup sour cream
1 pound crab meat, shrimp,
    lobster or halibut, cooked,
    cut into bite-size pieces
¼ cup chopped parsley
¼ cup chopped shallots
2 tablespoons chopped chives
1 large garlic clove, minced

Combine the bread crumbs, Parmesan cheese and dry mustard in a small bowl and set aside. Melt 2 tablespoons butter in a small saucepan. Add the flour gradually, stirring to make a smooth paste. Cook until the mixture bubbles, stirring constantly. Remove from the heat. Add the Dijon mustard, salt and red pepper flakes. Stir in the milk gradually. Cook over medium heat until the mixture bubbles and thickens, stirring constantly. Stir in the cream. Adjust the seasonings. Chill, covered, for 2 hours.

Brush 1 sheet of phyllo dough with some of the ¾ cup melted butter. Fold into halves or thirds and brush again with butter. Sprinkle with ⅙ of the bread crumb mixture. Sprinkle with ⅙ of the Swiss cheese and ⅙ of the chopped eggs. Dot with ⅙ of the sour cream. Place ⅙ of the crab meat at 1 end of the phyllo dough. Sprinkle with ⅙ of the parsley, shallots, chives and garlic. Dot with ⅙ of the chilled whipped cream mixture. Tuck in the sides of the phyllo and roll up. Place seam side down on a buttered baking sheet. Brush with melted butter. Repeat the process until all the ingredients are used.

Bake at 375 degrees for 30 minutes or until the pastry is brown. Serve with additional sour cream, chopped eggs and parsley.

YIELD: 6 SERVINGS

On the morning after a concert in 1939, renowned cellist Gregor Piatagorsky married Jacqueline de Rothschild, of the banking family, at the home of Charles and Alva Sink. When Mrs. Sink, hospitable by temperament and experience, got word that the couple planned a City Hall ceremony, she said, "No such thing—you will be married in our home." She hired a florist and a caterer while Charles Sink helped Piatagorsky, an expatriate Russian, arrange permission to marry a French citizen. The local justice of the peace performed the ceremony wearing Sink's academic gown. Years later, the bride wrote, "I signed Jacqueline de Rothschild in [the Sinks'] guest book. The next morning . . . on the same page in the guest book I was proud to sign 'Jacqueline Piatagorsky.'"

Lobster Strudel

3 cups bread crumbs
1 cup grated Parmesan
   cheese
1 teaspoon dry mustard
1 cup shredded Swiss cheese
4 eggs, hard-cooked,
   chopped
¼ cup (½ stick) butter
Salt and pepper to taste
1 teaspoon Dijon mustard
¼ cup flour
1½ cups milk

¼ cup light cream
5 sheets phyllo dough, thawed
   (see Note, page 23)
1 cup (2 sticks) butter, melted
1 pound frozen lobster meat,
   thawed
1½ cups sour cream
½ cup chopped parsley
¼ cup chopped chives
½ cup minced shallots
2 teaspoons minced garlic
Béarnaise Sauce (page 190)

Mix the bread crumbs, Parmesan cheese and dry mustard together and set aside. Mix the Swiss cheese and eggs together and set aside.

For the cream sauce, melt ¼ cup butter in a saucepan. Stir in salt and pepper to taste and Dijon mustard. Add the flour gradually, stirring constantly until smooth. Stir in the milk and cream gradually. Cook until thickened and smooth, stirring constantly. Remove from the heat and let cool.

For the pastry, brush each phyllo sheet with some of the melted butter, stacking the phyllo sheets together. Sprinkle with the bread crumb mixture. Spread the lobster meat on top. Sprinkle the Swiss cheese mixture over the lobster. Dot with sour cream and sprinkle with the parsley, chives, shallots and garlic. Spread cooled cream sauce over the top. Fold over the long edges of the phyllo. Sprinkle with melted butter. Roll up loosely as for a jelly roll. Place on a buttered baking sheet with sides.

Bake at 375 degrees for 40 to 50 minutes or until the pastry is golden brown. Let cool briefly before serving. Serve with Spicy Béarnaise Sauce.

This dish can be prepared ahead and reheated to serve. Reduce the initial baking time by 10 minutes if the strudel is to be frozen.

YIELD: 4 TO 6 SERVINGS

Leaf-Wrapped Sea Scallops with Tarragon Cream Sauce

1 tablespoon butter
1 tablespoon olive oil
18 very large sea scallops (about 1½ pounds)
Fresh spinach, lettuce or Swiss chard, stems removed
Tarragon Cream Sauce (below)
6 tablespoons salmon caviar
6 tablespoons chopped black olives

Heat the butter and olive oil in a large sauté pan. Add the scallops and sear over high heat. Remove from the heat and let cool.

Cook the spinach briefly in boiling water in a saucepan. Plunge immediately into cold water. Drain well and blot dry on paper towels.

Wrap each scallop in a spinach leaf. Spoon a small amount of Tarragon Cream Sauce into a lightly oiled shallow baking pan. Add the scallop packets seam side down. Cover the pan with buttered parchment paper or foil. Bake at 450 degrees for 10 minutes.

Spoon a small amount of warm Tarragon Cream Sauce on each of 6 warm plates. Arrange 3 scallops in the center of the sauce. Arrange caviar and olives alternately around the outside edge of each plate.

YIELD: 6 SERVINGS

Tarragon Cream Sauce

2 shallots, minced
1 tablespoon butter
2 cups white wine
¼ cup tarragon vinegar
3 tablespoons chopped fresh tarragon
1 cup heavy cream
Salt and freshly ground pepper to taste

Sauté the shallots in the butter in a skillet. Add the wine, vinegar and tarragon. Simmer until the liquid is reduced by ½. Add the cream and mix gently. Simmer until the liquid is slightly thickened and somewhat reduced. Season with salt and pepper.

YIELD: 1½ TO 2 CUPS

Chicago Symphony with Christoph Eschenbach

Encores, the concert-goer's delight, are often diverting and sometimes piquantly revealing of an artist's lighter side. Conductors and performers have for years indulged Ann Arbor audiences with "The Victors," Louis Elbel's University of Michigan fight song. It was a tradition for Eugene Ormandy during his decades of annual May Festivals; in 1994 the Philadelphia Orchestra played it once again, under Wolfgang Sawallish. Leonard Bernstein led it in 1967, unrehearsed, after the music had been passed among the orchestra members. The Chicago Symphony has played it twice, under two different conductors. The Soviet Emigre Orchestra played it in 1983. And the National Symphony Orchestra played "The Victors" under the baton of Russian-born cellist Mstislav Rostropovich.

Smoked Scallops with Pink Grapefruit

2 tablespoons light soy sauce
2 tablespoons extra-virgin olive oil
½ teaspoon liquid smoke
3 tablespoons fajita sauce or red salsa
1 pound (about) large sea scallops
2 large pink grapefruit, peeled, cut into sections
Julienned arugula
12 ounces snow peas, blanched

Mix the soy sauce, olive oil, liquid smoke and fajita sauce in a shallow pan. Add the scallops and marinate for up to 1 hour. Remove the scallops from the marinade, discarding the remaining marinade.

Heat a grill or ridged sauté pan to 440 degrees. Brush lightly with oil. Reduce the heat to medium and add the scallops. Cook until the scallops are firm, turning once and stirring frequently.

Warm the grapefruit slices in a microwave or in a covered sauté pan with a small amount of grapefruit juice.

Spoon arugula onto the center of 6 plates. Arrange the scallops over the arugula. Arrange the grapefruit slices and snow peas spoke-fashion around the scallops.

YIELD: 6 SERVINGS

Leontyne Price's Shrimp Gumbo

Leontyne Price's father's eyes always had "an extra glow" when her mother served this gumbo after church on Sunday. It's rustic and hearty, with a blend of delicately balanced flavors. Serve it over hot rice followed by fruit or sorbet for dessert.

2 tablespoons butter	1 garlic clove, minced
½ cup chopped onion	2 bay leaves
½ cup (1 stick) butter	2 cups cooked okra
3 tablespoons flour	24 jumbo shrimp, peeled,
4½ cups chicken broth	deveined
2½ cups canned tomatoes	12 ounces frozen crab meat,
½ teaspoon salt, or to taste	thawed, flaked
2 teaspoons chopped parsley	1 teaspoon filé powder
½ teaspoon thyme	4½ cups hot cooked rice

Melt 2 tablespoons butter in a large saucepan. Add the onion and sauté for 5 minutes or until wilted but not brown. Add ½ cup butter and cook until melted. Blend in the flour gradually. Cook for 1 to 2 minutes, stirring constantly. Add the chicken broth gradually, stirring constantly until thickened and smooth. Add the tomatoes, salt, parsley, thyme, garlic and bay leaves. Simmer, covered, for 1 hour. Add the okra and shrimp and mix well. Simmer for 8 minutes. Add the crab meat. Simmer for 2 to 3 minutes or until heated through. Stir in the filé powder. Serve over the rice.

YIELD: 4 TO 6 SERVINGS

Brilliant, eccentric Canadian pianist Glenn Gould suffered from "dry hands" and wore an overcoat and mittens year-round. He traveled with his own piano stool, a folding chair with short legs, which put his chin close to the level of his hands.

For one of his local concert appearances, Gould forgot his dress tie. One was found for him, but, unlike his own, it didn't simply hook on—it had to be tied. Someone tied it for him, and he went onstage perfectly outfitted. During intermission, however, he wanted to replace his damp dress shirt with a clean one, and there was no one around to retie the borrowed tie. Gould managed to change his shirt without removing the tie.

Shrimp Istanbul

The recipe for this dish is presented as it was prepared for Maestro and Mrs. Eugene Ormandy on one of their many visits to Ann Arbor with the Philadelphia Orchestra.

4 to 6 tablespoons (about) butter
1½ to 1¾ pounds shrimp, cooked, peeled, deveined
½ cup sliced white mushrooms
¼ cup finely chopped green bell pepper
¼ cup sherry
2 tablespoons tomato paste
1 cup sour cream
Half-and-half
2 onions, sliced
Butter or vegetable oil

Heat 4 tablespoons butter in a large skillet until melted and no longer foaming. Add the shrimp and cook for 1 minute. Remove the shrimp and keep warm.

Add some or all of the remaining 2 tablespoons butter to the skillet if needed. Add the mushrooms and cook for 5 minutes. Add the green pepper and sherry and cook for 5 minutes longer. Stir in the tomato paste and sour cream. Add enough half-and-half to make of the desired consistency. If the sauce is too thin, thicken with a mixture of 1 tablespoon cornstarch and milk.

Sauté the onions in butter in a skillet until brown and crisp. Add the onions and shrimp to the mushroom mixture just before serving. Serve with rice pilaf or couscous.

YIELD: 4 TO 6 SERVINGS

Shrimp Veracruz

2 tablespoons olive oil
1 large green bell pepper, cut into thin strips
1 large yellow bell pepper, cut into thin strips
1 medium onion, chopped
2 garlic cloves, minced
1 pound large shrimp, peeled, deveined
1 (14-ounce) can stewed tomatoes
¼ cup sliced pimiento-stuffed olives
1 teaspoon capers, drained
2 tablespoons tequila
½ teaspoon salt
¼ teaspoon hot pepper sauce
2 cups yellow rice, cooked

Heat the olive oil in a 12-inch skillet over medium heat. Add the bell peppers and onion. Cook for 5 minutes or until tender-crisp. Add the garlic and cook for 2 minutes.

Add the shrimp and cook for 3 minutes or until the shrimp turn pink. Add the undrained tomatoes, olives, capers, tequila, salt and hot pepper sauce. Bring to a boil over high heat and reduce the heat to low. Simmer, covered, for 5 minutes, stirring occasionally.

Serve the shrimp mixture over the rice. Garnish with sprigs of parsley or cilantro.

YIELD: 4 SERVINGS

Marinated Shrimp with Artichokes

3 pounds shrimp, cooked,
    peeled, deveined
2 cups vegetable oil
1½ cups white vinegar
3 tablespoons Worcestershire
    sauce
2 teaspoons hot pepper
    sauce, or to taste
Salt and pepper to taste
2 (8-ounce) cans artichoke
    hearts, drained,
    cut into halves

¼ cup capers
1 pound small mushrooms,
    trimmed, cleaned
1 red onion, thinly sliced
½ cup Greek or black olives,
    drained, pitted
1 pint cherry tomatoes
Lettuce leaves

Place the shrimp in a large glass bowl. Mix the oil, vinegar, Worcestershire sauce, hot pepper sauce, salt and pepper in a bowl and pour over the shrimp. Marinate in the refrigerator for 18 to 24 hours, turning occasionally. Remove the shrimp to a serving bowl, discarding the remaining marinade.

Sauté the artichoke hearts in a nonstick skillet sprayed with nonstick cooking spray until tender. Drain the capers, reserving 1 tablespoon of the liquid. Combine the artichoke hearts, capers, reserved liquid, mushrooms, onion, olives and cherry tomatoes with the shrimp in the serving bowl and mix gently. Chill until serving time. Serve on cupped lettuce leaves.

YIELD: 6 TO 8 SERVINGS AS AN ENTRÉE
12 SERVINGS AS A FIRST COURSE

Bernice Johnson Reagon's Smothered Catfish

When Bernice Johnson Reagon was growing up, her father would not eat fried fish of any kind, so her mother often prepared a dish for him that she called "smothered catfish."

2 small or 1 medium catfish
Salt and pepper to taste
Corn meal
Vegetable oil or butter
1 onion, sliced
1 to 2 cups water

Cut the catfish into 3-inch pieces, leaving the bones in. Season with salt and pepper and coat with corn meal. Coat the bottom of a skillet with the oil and heat until very hot. Add the fish and onion. Sauté until 1 side of the fish is seared but not brown. Turn and add enough water to have no more than 2 cups liquid in the skillet. Simmer for 15 minutes or until the fish flakes easily and most of the liquid has evaporated. Adjust the seasonings.

YIELD: 2 SERVINGS

Monkfish in Wine Sauce

1½ pounds monkfish
Salt and freshly ground pepper to taste
2 tablespoons unsalted butter
2 shallots, minced
1 leek, white part only, washed, julienned
1 medium carrot, peeled, cut into
    2-inch slivers
1 cup muscadet
¾ cup heavy cream
2 tablespoons unsalted butter

Remove the heavy membrane from the fish; cut the fish into 1-inch cubes. Sprinkle with salt and pepper. Heat 2 tablespoons butter in a large skillet over medium heat until the butter has melted and the foam has subsided. Add the shallots and sauté for 2 minutes or until tender. Add the leek and carrot and sauté for 4 minutes or until tender. Add the fish, tossing to coat with butter. Add the wine and bring to a simmer. Cover the skillet and remove from the heat. Let stand for 6 minutes. Remove the fish and vegetables with a slotted spoon and keep warm.

Boil the wine mixture over high heat until reduced to ½ cup. Add the cream and cook until the sauce is slightly thickened and reduced by ½. Remove from the heat and whisk in 2 tablespoons butter. Drain the fish and vegetables and return to the skillet. Heat gently without boiling. Serve garnished with seedless green grapes.

YIELD: 4 SERVINGS

David Shifrin's Baked Salmon

David Shifrin thinks this dish is perfect for entertaining.
He serves it cold after concerts.

2 large Vidalia, Walla Walla
    or other sweet onions,
    sliced
3 pounds salmon fillets
Salt and freshly ground
    pepper to taste
2 or 3 lemons, thinly sliced

Sauce *(optional):*
1 cup yogurt or low-fat yogurt
¼ cup mayonnaise
1 tablespoon lemon juice
⅛ teaspoon hot pepper sauce
3 tablespoons chopped fresh dill
⅛ cup white wine

Spread half the onion slices in a foil-lined large baking pan or casserole. Place the salmon over the onions and sprinkle with salt and pepper. Top with the remaining onion and lemon slices.

Bake, covered with foil, at 300 degrees for 30 minutes. Remove the salmon to a platter and surround with the onion and lemon slices.

Alternately, this salmon may be served cold with a dill sauce on the side. To prepare the sauce, mix the yogurt, mayonnaise, lemon juice, hot pepper sauce, dill and wine in a bowl.

YIELD: 6 TO 8 SERVINGS

Sweet Honey in the Rock

"I first went to hear Sweet Honey in the Rock after reading about it in a concert program," says music lover Nancy Elder, "and I haven't missed one of their concerts since." Sweet Honey is a group of six African-American women who have sung together for twenty-five years. The founder and guiding spirit is Bernice Johnson Reagon, who studies American and African-American music. "They sing a cappella, except for some small percussion instruments they hold. I love the mix—some reggae, African, hymns, American, folk songs. . . . They have power, sweetness, compassion, warmth, and beautiful complex harmonies and underlying rhythms. Their dress is colorful and dramatic. If there's reincarnation, I hope I come back as a member of Sweet Honey in the Rock."

Baked Whole Salmon

1 (6-pound) salmon
¼ cup white wine
1 white onion, sliced
1 lemon, sliced
2 tablespoons chopped parsley
Salt and pepper to taste
1 cup grated cucumber
½ cup sour cream
¼ cup mayonnaise
1 tablespoon chopped parsley
2 teaspoons chopped onion
2 teaspoons vinegar

Fold a large piece of heavy-duty foil into a double thickness. Place the salmon in the center of the foil and pour the wine over the fish. Arrange the onion slices, lemon slices and 2 tablespoons parsley evenly over and inside the salmon. Season with salt and pepper. Seal the foil very tightly. Bake at 350 degrees for 45 minutes.

For the sauce, combine the cucumber, sour cream, mayonnaise, 1 tablespoon parsley, chopped onion and vinegar in a bowl and mix well. Season with additional salt and pepper. Chill, covered, for 1 hour or longer.

Remove the salmon carefully from the foil and place on an oblong platter. Remove the skin from the top side of the salmon. Garnish the platter with watercress, cucumber slices and lemon slices. Serve the sauce on the side.

YIELD: 12 SERVINGS

Grilled Salmon and Pears

¾ cup olive oil
¼ cup balsamic vinegar
2 tablespoons lemon juice
2 tablespoons honey
1 teaspoon salt
½ teaspoon freshly ground pepper
4 (6-ounce) salmon fillets
4 cups baby greens
2 cups thinly sliced unpeeled pears
⅓ cup chopped hazelnuts, toasted

For the sauce, whisk the olive oil, vinegar, lemon juice, honey, salt and pepper in a medium bowl. Rinse the salmon and pat dry. Drizzle each fillet with ½ tablespoon of the sauce. Broil on a lightly oiled grill for 8 to 12 minutes or until the fish flakes easily, turning once.

Toss the greens with half the remaining sauce. Arrange on individual plates. Top each with 1 fillet. Arrange pear slices over the salmon and sprinkle with hazelnuts. Serve the remaining sauce on the side.

YIELD: 4 SERVINGS

Steamed Sea Bass in Black Bean Sauce

1½ pounds sea bass or
   walleye fillets, skin
   removed
1 tablespoon peanut oil
2 tablespoons fermented
   dried black beans
1 teaspoon minced fresh
   gingerroot

⅔ cup chicken stock
1 tablespoon oyster sauce
1 teaspoon soy sauce
2 teaspoons cornstarch
2 tablespoons sherry
1 teaspoon minced garlic
¼ cup chopped scallions

Steam the fish for 8 to 12 minutes or until it flakes easily. Remove to a platter and keep warm.

For the sauce, heat a wok to the smoking point. Add the oil and heat until very hot. Add the beans and gingerroot and cook for 15 seconds. Add the chicken stock, oyster sauce and soy sauce. Boil for 2 minutes or until somewhat reduced. Stir in a mixture of the cornstarch and sherry. Cook briefly until thickened. Stir in the garlic and scallions and pour over the fish. Serve with rice.

Note: The sauce in this recipe can be doubled easily.

YIELD: 4 SERVINGS

Fish Fillets à la Provençal

2 cups chopped plum or
   Roma tomatoes
½ cup chopped fresh fennel
1 cup chopped fresh leeks
2 garlic cloves, chopped
2 teaspoons turmeric
½ cup white wine

½ cup bottled clam juice
Fresh thyme to taste
Fresh parsley or basil to taste
2 to 3 tablespoons Pernod
Salt and pepper to taste
4 (6-ounce) snapper, wolf fish
   or sea bass fillets

Combine the tomatoes, fennel, leeks, garlic, turmeric, wine, clam juice, thyme, parsley, liqueur, salt and pepper in a saucepan. Cook until the sauce is heated through, stirring frequently.

Place the fish fillets in an oven baking bag or wrap in parchment paper. Spoon the sauce over the fish. Bake at 375 degrees for 12 to 15 minutes or until the fish flakes easily.

YIELD: 4 SERVINGS

Myra Hess

Eminent pianist Myra Hess toured for decades. Before one of her several Ann Arbor recitals during the 1950s, she came onto the Hill Auditorium stage to warm applause. She sat down, checked the height of the bench, looked down the length of her gown to the pedals, wiped her palms with a fluttery handkerchief, and opened a book on the music rest. Then she turned to the audience.

"I play with the music before me," she said without apology. "I enjoy it more if I look at it while I play."

Asian Fish Steaks

1 cup soy sauce
½ cup fresh lime juice
¼ cup mirin (see Note)
½ cup dark sesame oil
3 tablespoons minced garlic
3 tablespoons minced fresh gingerroot
3 tablespoons crushed red pepper flakes
4 (1-inch-thick) firm-textured fish steaks,
    such as swordfish
Vegetable oil

Combine the soy sauce, lime juice, mirin, sesame oil, garlic, gingerroot and red pepper flakes in a shallow pan. Add the fish to the marinade 1 hour before grilling, turning once to coat both sides.

Remove the fish from the marinade. Dip the fish lightly into the vegetable oil to prevent the fish from sticking to the grill (omit this step if baking or broiling the fish). Grill for 5 to 7 minutes per side or until the fish flakes easily, brushing once with the marinade. Garnish with lime slices.

Alternately, this fish may be baked or broiled. To bake, brush with the marinade and bake at 375 degrees for 15 to 20 minutes. To broil, brush with the marinade and broil 4 inches from the heat source for 5 to 7 minutes per side, turning once and basting with marinade.

Note: Mirin is a sweet Japanese cooking wine. It is available in Japanese markets and in some supermarkets.

YIELD: 4 SERVINGS

Skewered Trout

¾ to 1 pound boneless trout fillets, skin on,
    split into halves lengthwise
2 stalks lemon grass, cut into quarters
    (see Note)
2 tablespoons Champagne or white wine
2 teaspoons pink peppercorns, crushed
½ teaspoon dried summer savory
¼ teaspoon salt
⅛ teaspoon black pepper

Poke holes in the fish skin with a metal skewer or other sharp object. Thread the fish onto the lemon grass skewers. Spray the skin side with nonstick cooking spray. Place the skewers on a platter and sprinkle the cut sides of the fish with equal amounts of Champagne, peppercorns, summer savory, salt and pepper.

Place the skewers skin side down in the center of a cooking grate. Grill for 4 to 5 minutes or until the fish flakes easily. Turn and grill for 30 seconds longer.

Note: Well-soaked bamboo skewers may be used instead of lemon grass.

**YIELD: 3 TO 4 SERVINGS AS AN ENTRÉE
8 SERVINGS AS AN APPETIZER**

Grilled Tuna with Wasabi Butter

2 tablespoons peeled fresh gingerroot
6 (5-ounce) tuna steaks
¼ cup olive oil
Juice of 1 lemon
6 tablespoons (¾ stick) unsalted butter, softened
¼ cup powdered wasabi (see Note)
Salt and freshly ground pepper to taste

Press the gingerroot through a garlic press. Place the tuna steaks in a single layer in a large shallow pan. Mix the olive oil, lemon juice and ginger in a small bowl and pour over the fish. Let stand for 20 to 30 minutes, turning once.

Combine the butter with enough of the wasabi to make a thick paste and set aside.

Remove the steaks from the marinade, reserving the remaining marinade. Season the steaks lightly with salt and pepper. Grill or broil for 7 to 10 minutes or to desired degree of doneness, turning 2 to 3 times and basting frequently with the reserved marinade.

Remove the steaks to a platter and top each with some of the wasabi butter. Serve immediately.

Note: Wasabi is a Japanese horseradish. It is available in Japanese markets and in some supermarkets.

YIELD: 6 SERVINGS

In the winter of 1959, soprano Renata Tebaldi came to Ann Arbor for a recital at Hill Auditorium. Gail Rector, then president of the University Musical Society, remembers that when the diva arrived by train with her pet poodle, it "caused consternation" at the Michigan League on campus, where she had reserved a room. Summoned by the League's manager, Rector had to promise that UMS would pay for any damage the dog might do. When Rector told her that the League had overlooked its strict no-pets rule for her, Tebaldi replied, "No, for you!" Her meaning was clear: no poodle, no performance.

Tuna Niçoise Kabobs

8 thick scallions (1 bunch)
²/₃ cup Italian salad dressing
1½ tablespoons chopped fresh rosemary, or 1½ teaspoons
    dried rosemary
1 pound fresh tuna steaks, cut into 1½-inch chunks
1 pound small red potatoes, scrubbed
Salt to taste
8 fresh rosemary branches (optional)
1 head romaine, separated into leaves
½ cup black olives
2 plum tomatoes, cut into wedges

Trim the scallions to leave intact 2 inches of the green part. Mix the salad dressing and chopped rosemary in a bowl. Place the tuna in a shallow dish. Pour about ½ cup of the dressing over the tuna and stir to coat well. Marinate in the refrigerator for up to 2 hours. Reserve the remaining marinade.

Cook the potatoes in boiling salted water in a saucepan for 8 minutes or just until fork-tender; drain well. Add the potatoes to the marinade in the shallow dish, turning to coat well. Add the scallions to the marinade in the shallow dish and let stand for 15 minutes.

Thread the scallions, tuna and potatoes onto 4 long metal skewers, beginning and ending with scallions and alternating tuna and potatoes in the center. Dampen the rosemary branches with cold water. Toss the rosemary onto medium coals. Grill the kabobs for 10 minutes or until the tuna is the desired degree of doneness, the potatoes are tender and the scallions are brown, turning 1 to 2 times.

To serve, place the kabobs on a bed of lettuce leaves and drizzle with the reserved marinade. Arrange the olives and tomatoes around the kabobs.

YIELD: 4 SERVINGS

Garrick Ohlsson's Grilled Tuna with Herb Sauce

Garrick Ohlsson says this simple but elegant entrée goes well with red wine.

4 to 6 canned plum tomatoes, chopped
½ cup olive oil
3 tablespoons lemon juice
3 garlic cloves, minced
½ teaspoon salt
1 cup firmly packed shredded herbs, such as oregano, thyme,
    lemon balm or marjoram
4 tablespoons olive oil
1 (3-inch-thick) tuna steak (about 1 pound)

For the sauce, combine the tomatoes, ½ cup olive oil, lemon juice, garlic, salt and herbs in a glass or ceramic bowl. Chill, covered, in the refrigerator for 2 to 4 hours. Let stand to bring to room temperature.

Heat 2 tablespoons of the olive oil in a heavy 10- or 12-inch skillet over high heat. Brush the tuna with the remaining 2 tablespoons olive oil. Place the tuna in the skillet and sear for 1 minute per side or to desired degree of doneness.

Remove the tuna to a heated serving platter and cut into thick slices. Top with half the sauce. Serve the remaining sauce on the side. Serve with plain risotto or steamed new potatoes.

YIELD: 2 TO 3 SERVINGS

Garrick Ohlsson

Garrick Ohlsson is "a genuine giant of the keyboard," the New Yorker said, with "a technique that threatens to incinerate a Bosendorfer." He has Ann Arbor audiences in thrall, having performed the entire solo piano repertoire of Frederic Chopin in a series of six concerts over two successive seasons. The final concert of that series took place in a standing-room-only Hill Auditorium with the artist's parents in the audience.

In 1998, the University Musical Society and the Ford Honors Program chose Ohlsson to receive the third annual Distinguished Artist Award. During his visits to town, Ohlsson has browsed the bookstores, walked the campus, and found a favorite restaurant. "Nowhere else do I feel so well cared for," he says.

Poultry and Game Birds

1957

Friday, May 3, 1957, 8:30 p.m.

Hill Auditorium

Sixty-Fourth Annual May Festival

The Philadelphia Orchestra
The University Choral Union
Thor Johnson   *Guest Conductor*

Soloists
Leontyne Price   *Soprano*
Martha Lipton   *Contralto*
Rudolf Petrak   *Tenor*
Robert McFerrin   *Baritone*
Nicola Moscona   *Bass*

Aïda (in concert form)
Verdi
*An opera in four acts,
for soloists, chorus, and orchestra*

Aïda   Leontyne Price
Amneris   Martha Lipton
Radames   Rudolf Petrak
Amonasro   Robert McFerrin
Ramphis/The King   Nicola Moscona
Messenger   Jerry Langenkamp
*Priestesses, Soldiers, Ministers, Captains,
The People, and Slave Prisoners*
University Choral Union

Leontyne Price (seated, center)

FEW concert-goers on this May Festival evening expected an introduction to one of the era's great voices. But by the end of the concert, few doubted that they had enjoyed precisely that kind of historic moment. It was the debut performance of Leontyne Price in a role she would go on to make her own.

The dramatic soprano's first appearance under University Musical Society auspices occurred without fanfare. "Verdi's vigorous and highly dramatic opera, 'Aïda,' will be presented tonight in the second concert of the May Festival," said the front page of the *Ann Arbor News* that day. "It features five soloists, the Philadelphia Orchestra under the baton of Guest Conductor Thor Johnson and the 330-voice University Choral Union." Not until the seventh paragraph were the soloists named, among them Leontyne Price "in the role of Aïda, Ethiopian slave girl."

Price had sung the role of Bess in a version of Gershwin's "Porgy and Bess" that had toured for several years. Hugh Lee Lyon, her biographer, says her "pure animal drive," in contrast with her "very cultured type of singing," combined to create "a definitive Bess." By the time of this concert, she was poised to enter the realm of grand opera with stunning impact. The next day's newspaper described the audience's sense of discovery. "Those rare occasions when an X quantity, not capable of being planned or sought after, infuses the music are as thrilling as they are memorable....Last night's 'Aïda' was such a time. Leontyne Price, soprano, was magnificently dramatic in the title role, as her intense high voice penetrated and threaded even the most opaque orchestral background."

By the fall, Price had electrified the opera world, debuting with the San Francisco Opera Company, first in Poulenc's "Dialogues of the Carmelites" and then in a full-scale production of "Aïda."

She returned to Ann Arbor many times. In a letter written in 1979 for the hundredth anniversary of the University Musical Society, she spoke of her feeling for Ann Arbor and the "warm surge of nostalgia" that "reminds me that here was the scene of many first performances for me. My first 'Aïda' in concert form, my first...Verdi 'Requiem,'..."

Price included the aria "Ritorna vincitor" from "Aïda" in a concert with the Philadelphia Orchestra at Hill Auditorium in 1971. One concert-goer still remembers: "From where we were sitting, in the middle, four or five rows back from the stage, she looked twelve feet tall, like an African goddess. The audience stopped breathing when she began to sing. It was overpowering. 'Aïda' seemed to be who she was."

After her San Francisco debut in the opera, Leontyne Price went on to sing "Aïda" with all of the major opera companies of the world: New York, Milan, London, and Vienna. She twice recorded the opera, and she chose it for her "farewell to opera" performance at the Metropolitan Opera House in January 1985.

What was cooking?

In 1956 James Beard opened his cooking school in New York City, and Craig Claiborne began a long run as food editor of the New York Times. *Both were leaders in a trend toward a more sophisticated and self-conscious American cuisine. They came along just five years after Poppy Cannon's* Can-Opener Cookbook *and three years after the debut of Lipton's dried onion soup mix, the basis of that ubiquitous dip.*

Frederica von Stade's After-Concert Chicken

1 teaspoon cumin seeds
2 tablespoons (or more) olive oil
1 cup chopped onion
1 garlic clove, minced or pressed
2 jalapeño chiles, seeded, finely chopped
4 whole boneless skinless chicken breasts, cut into halves
2 cups cooked white beans
2 cups cooked corn kernels
1 teaspoon salt
Freshly ground pepper to taste

To toast the cumin seeds, heat a small sauté pan. Spread the cumin seeds in the pan. Cook for 5 minutes, turning occasionally. The seeds will darken and the aroma will intensify. Spoon the seeds into a small bowl to cool. Grind the cooled seeds in a nut grinder or blender.

Heat 2 tablespoons olive oil in a large Dutch oven. Add the onion, garlic, cumin seeds and jalapeños and sauté until tender but not brown. Remove the vegetables from the Dutch oven and keep warm. Add the chicken to the Dutch oven, adding a small amount of olive oil if needed to prevent sticking. Sauté just until brown on both sides.

Return the vegetables to the Dutch oven. Add the beans and corn kernels. Season with salt and pepper. Bake, covered, at 350 degrees for 30 minutes or until the chicken is cooked through. Serve with rice or polenta.

YIELD: 4 SERVINGS

Basil Grilled Chicken

3/4 teaspoon coarsely ground pepper
4 chicken breasts, skin removed
1/3 cup butter or margarine, melted
1/4 cup chopped fresh basil
1/2 cup (1 stick) butter or margarine, softened
2 tablespoons minced fresh basil
1 tablespoon grated Parmesan cheese
1/4 teaspoon garlic powder
1/8 teaspoon salt
1/8 teaspoon pepper

Press 3/4 teaspoon pepper into the meaty side of the chicken. Mix 1/3 cup butter and 1/4 cup basil in a bowl. Brush the chicken lightly with some of the mixture.

For the basil butter, combine 1/2 cup butter, 2 tablespoons basil, cheese, garlic powder, salt and pepper in a small mixer bowl. Beat at low speed until blended and smooth. Remove to a serving bowl and set aside.

Grill the chicken over medium coals for 8 to 10 minutes per side or until cooked through, basting frequently with the remaining melted butter mixture.

Serve with the basil butter. Garnish with fresh basil sprigs.

YIELD: 4 SERVINGS

Broiled Chicken Breasts on a Bed of Greens

4 boneless skinless chicken
   breasts
2 teaspoons olive oil
2 tablespoons fresh lemon
   juice
2 tablespoons chopped fresh
   rosemary, or 1 teaspoon
   dried rosemary
2 teaspoons finely chopped
   garlic

Salt and pepper to taste
1 head radicchio, separated into
   leaves
2 heads Bibb lettuce, separated
   into leaves
4 ounces arugula, cut into bite-
   size pieces
Warm Curry Dressing (below)
¼ cup coarsely chopped fresh
   basil or chervil

Trim away any membrane or fat from the chicken. Combine the olive oil, lemon juice, rosemary, garlic, salt and pepper in a bowl and mix well. Add the chicken, turning to coat well. Marinate, covered, in the refrigerator for 30 minutes to 4 hours.

Remove the chicken from the marinade, discarding the remaining marinade. Place the chicken on a rack in a broiler pan. Broil for 2 to 3 minutes per side or until cooked through. Remove the chicken from the oven and cut diagonally into ¼-inch slices.

Toss the radicchio, Bibb lettuce and arugula in a large bowl. Add half the Warm Curry Dressing and toss again. Top with the chicken slices. Sprinkle with the remaining dressing and basil.

YIELD: 4 SERVINGS

Warm Curry Dressing

2 teaspoons Dijon mustard
1 teaspoon curry powder
2 tablespoons balsamic
   vinegar
¼ cup chopped scallions

⅓ cup olive or vegetable oil
Salt and freshly ground pepper
   to taste
¼ cup coarsely chopped fresh
   basil or chervil

Combine the Dijon mustard, curry powder, vinegar and scallions in a saucepan and whisk to mix. Cook over low heat until heated through, whisking occasionally. Add the olive oil and mix well. Remove from the heat and stir in salt, pepper and basil.

YIELD: 1 CUP

103

Chinese Chicken with Peanuts

1/4 cup soy sauce
2 tablespoons dry sherry
2 tablespoons cornstarch
2 whole chicken breasts, skinned, boned,
    cut into thin strips
1/4 cup vegetable oil
3 green onions, cut into 1/2-inch slices
1 teaspoon chopped fresh gingerroot
1 large green bell pepper, seeded,
    cut into strips
1 to 2 cups fresh bean sprouts
1 tablespoon hoisin sauce
Hot cooked rice
1/2 cup dry roasted peanuts

Combine the soy sauce, sherry and cornstarch in a bowl and mix well. Add the chicken, turning to coat. Marinate, covered, in the refrigerator for 30 minutes. Remove the chicken from the marinade, discarding the remaining marinade.

Heat 2 tablespoons of the oil in a wok or heavy skillet until very hot but not smoking. Add the chicken and stir-fry just until brown and cooked through. Remove the chicken and keep warm.

Add the remaining 2 tablespoons oil to the wok and heat until very hot. Add the green onions, gingerroot and green pepper and sauté for 2 to 3 minutes. Add the bean sprouts and hoisin sauce and stir-fry for 1 minute. Add the chicken and stir to mix well.

Serve over hot cooked rice. Sprinkle each serving with peanuts. Serve additional peanuts on the side if desired.

YIELD: 4 SERVINGS

Low-Fat Grilled Chicken Kabobs

1 cup fat-free plain yogurt
5 tablespoons crumbled low-fat feta cheese
2 tablespoons chopped fresh rosemary
2 tablespoons chopped fresh thyme
3 tablespoons minced garlic
1 1/2 pounds boneless chicken breasts, cut into
    1/2-inch pieces
2 large red bell peppers, cut into 1 1/2-inch
    pieces
Salt and pepper to taste
2 tablespoons crumbled low-fat feta cheese

Mix the yogurt, 5 tablespoons feta cheese, rosemary, thyme and garlic in a shallow pan. Add the chicken, turning to coat well. Marinate, covered, at room temperature for 30 minutes or in the refrigerator for up to 4 hours. Remove the chicken from the marinade, discarding the remaining marinade.

Thread the chicken and red peppers alternately onto 4 to 6 skewers. Season with salt and pepper. Grill for 8 minutes or until the chicken is brown and cooked through. Place the kabobs on plates and sprinkle with 2 tablespoons feta cheese.

Variation: Substitute fresh basil for the rosemary and tomato basil feta cheese for the plain feta cheese.

YIELD: 4 SERVINGS

Dale Warland's Greek Lemon Chicken

1 cup fruity white wine
¼ cup olive oil
¼ cup fresh lemon juice
1 teaspoon freshly grated
    lemon zest
1 teaspoon salt
1 teaspoon freshly ground
    pepper
3 garlic cloves, crushed
6 large whole chicken
    breasts, skinned, boned
3 tablespoons olive oil
1 pound angel hair pasta
2 tablespoons (¼ stick)
    butter

2 tablespoons flour
½ teaspoon salt
2 teaspoons prepared mustard
1 cup milk
2 egg yolks
Freshly grated zest of 1 lemon
1 teaspoon fresh lemon juice
1 teaspoon dillweed
¼ cup minced fresh parsley
1 cup sour cream
¼ cup (½ stick) butter, melted
⅓ cup crumbled feta cheese
½ cup shredded Muenster or
    Monterey Jack cheese

For the marinade, combine the wine, ¼ cup olive oil, ¼ cup lemon juice, 1 teaspoon lemon zest, 1 teaspoon salt, pepper and garlic in a bowl and mix well. Slightly pound the chicken. Place the chicken in a shallow dish or sealable plastic bag. Marinate, covered, in the refrigerator for up to 12 hours. Remove the chicken from the marinade; discard the remaining marinade. Heat 3 tablespoons olive oil in a skillet. Add the chicken; sauté until tender and cooked through. Cut the chicken into strips and set aside.

Cook the pasta to al dente using the package directions; drain well and keep warm.

For the sauce, melt 2 tablespoons butter in a saucepan. Blend in the flour and ½ teaspoon salt gradually, stirring constantly until smooth. Add the mustard. Add the milk gradually, stirring constantly until thickened. Mix the egg yolks, zest of 1 lemon and 1 teaspoon lemon juice in a small bowl. Whisk a small amount of the hot flour mixture into the egg mixture; whisk the egg mixture into the hot flour mixture. Bring to a gentle boil. Remove from the heat; add dillweed and parsley. Stir in the sour cream when parsley has wilted.

Combine the pasta, ¼ cup butter, ¾ cup of the sauce and feta cheese in a bowl and mix well. Spoon into a greased 9x13-inch baking dish. Top with the chicken slices, remaining sauce and Muenster cheese. Broil until the cheese is golden brown.

YIELD: 6 TO 8 SERVINGS

Skillet Chicken with Asparagus

4 boneless skinless chicken breasts
    (about 1 pound)
Paprika to taste
1 teaspoon vegetable oil
½ teaspoon sesame oil
1 cup chicken broth
1 medium onion, sliced
1 medium garlic clove, minced
1 tablespoon chopped fresh dillweed, or
    1 teaspoon dried dillweed
1 pound fresh asparagus, trimmed
1 tablespoon cornstarch
2 tablespoons chicken broth
1 (2-ounce) jar sliced pimiento, drained
1 cup orzo, cooked (about 3 cups)

Trim any fat away from the chicken. Sprinkle lightly with paprika. Heat the vegetable oil and sesame oil in a large nonstick skillet sprayed with nonstick cooking spray. Add the chicken. Cook over medium-high heat for 5 minutes or just until brown on both sides. Reduce the heat. Add 1 cup chicken broth, onion, garlic and dillweed. Simmer, covered, until the chicken is tender and cooked through. Keep warm.

Cook the asparagus in boiling water to cover in a large skillet for 3 to 5 minutes or just until tender-crisp; do not overcook. Drain and rinse under cold water.

Mix the cornstarch and 2 tablespoons chicken broth in a small bowl. Add to the chicken mixture. Add the pimiento and cook until the sauce thickens, stirring constantly. Add 4 of the asparagus spears and heat briefly.

Arrange the remaining asparagus, the chicken mixture and the orzo on plates. Spoon the sauce over the top. Garnish with fresh dillweed.

YIELD: 4 SERVINGS

Thai Chicken Stir-Fry

1 tablespoon cornstarch
1 tablespoon each soy sauce and dry sherry
½ teaspoon minced garlic
8 ounces boneless skinless chicken breasts,
    cut into thin strips
1 tablespoon cornstarch
2 tablespoons soy sauce
½ cup creamy peanut butter
2 teaspoons vinegar
½ teaspoon sugar
⅔ cup water
2 tablespoons vegetable oil
1 bunch green onions, cut into 1-inch pieces
1 red bell pepper, cut into thin strips
½ teaspoon minced garlic
12 ounces fresh bean sprouts
Hot cooked fine egg noodles
2 tablespoons chopped roasted unsalted
    peanuts

Mix 1 tablespoon cornstarch, 1 tablespoon soy sauce, sherry and ½ teaspoon garlic in a shallow dish. Add the chicken, stirring to coat. Marinate for 10 minutes. Remove the chicken, discarding the remaining marinade.

Mix 1 tablespoon cornstarch, 2 tablespoons soy sauce, peanut butter, vinegar and sugar in a bowl. Blend in the water gradually and set aside.

Heat half the oil in a hot wok or large skillet. Add the chicken; stir-fry for 2 minutes. Remove the chicken from the wok. Heat the remaining oil in the wok. Add the green onions, red pepper and ½ teaspoon garlic; stir-fry for 2 minutes. Add the bean sprouts; stir-fry for 1 minute. Stir in the chicken and peanut butter mixture. Cook for 1 minute or until the sauce boils and thickens, stirring frequently. Serve the chicken mixture over the noodles. Sprinkle with peanuts.

YIELD: 4 SERVINGS

Chicken Lori

3 tablespoons capers
9 (6- to 8-ounce) boneless skinless chicken breasts
6 garlic cloves, minced or pressed
Salt and freshly ground pepper to taste
3 tablespoons (or more) olive oil
1 large sweet onion, coarsely chopped
1 tablespoon dried rubbed sage
2 to 3 cups dry bread crumbs
1 cup grated Parmesan cheese
1 cup low-fat milk
¼ cup (½ stick) butter, melted, or butter-flavor nonstick
    cooking spray

Line a baking sheet with sides with oiled parchment paper. Drain the capers, reserving 1 tablespoon of the liquid. Trim any fat or membrane from the chicken. Cut 3 of the chicken breasts into small chunks and set aside. Pound the remaining chicken between 2 sheets of plastic wrap until almost translucent. Rub some of the garlic over the chicken and season lightly with salt and pepper.

For the filling, heat 3 tablespoons olive oil in a large sauté pan. Add the onion and sauté until tender. Add the chicken chunks and sauté until cooked through. Add the remaining garlic, sage and about 1 cup of the bread crumbs. Cook until the chicken is coated with crumbs, stirring frequently with a wooden spatula and adding more olive oil if needed to prevent sticking. Adjust the seasonings. Remove the mixture from the pan and let cool. Coarsely chop the cooked chicken in a food processor; do not purée. Add the capers and reserved liquid.

Spoon the filling evenly down the center of each flattened chicken breast. Fold in the sides of the chicken and roll up tightly. Mix the cheese with the remaining 1 to 2 cups bread crumbs. Dip each chicken roll into the milk, then into the cheese mixture. Place the rolls on the prepared baking sheet. Chill in the refrigerator for 30 minutes.

Brush melted butter on each chicken roll. Bake at 350 degrees for 20 minutes. Turn the chicken rolls over and bake for 5 to 10 minutes or until golden brown. Remove from the oven and let stand for 5 minutes. Slice the rolls diagonally so that the filling is visible.

YIELD: 6 TO 7 SERVINGS

Rudolf Serkin

Even decades later, seasoned concert-goers who were there say that Rudolf Serkin's 1961 recital at Hill Auditorium remains the most memorable of their experience. Serkin's program comprised Beethoven sonatas: Opus 31, No. 1; Opus 27, the "Moonlight"; and, after intermission, Opus 106, the "Hammerklavier."

The last sonata, physically and emotionally daunting, brought people to their feet, clapping and shouting. There was no worthy encore, and they knew it, but they kept it up. Serkin took many bows.

A woman who was there remembers: "At last, Serkin returned to the piano. Four thousand astounded people swooshed as one back into their seats. What would he do?

"The encore was another Beethoven sonata, Opus 57 in F minor, the 'Appassionata.' All of it!"

Baked Chicken with Caperberry Gremolata

Caperberry Gremolata (below)
3½ to 4 pounds assorted chicken pieces, or 4 quarters
Salt and freshly ground pepper to taste
Chicken stock or water

Stuff about 1 tablespoon of the Caperberry Gremolata under the skin of each chicken piece. Flatten the skin to distribute the gremolata evenly. If using chicken quarters, divide the gremolata evenly among them.

Place the chicken in a casserole and add a small amount of chicken stock. Bake, covered, at 325 degrees for 1 hour or until the chicken is cooked through. Remove from the oven and increase the oven temperature to 400 degrees. Bake, uncovered, for 5 minutes or until brown. Garnish with additional caperberries and parsley.

YIELD: 4 TO 6 SERVINGS

Caperberry Gremolata

3 garlic cloves, minced
¼ cup coarsely chopped parsley
3 tablespoons caperberries, chopped, or
*   3 tablespoons drained capers*
1½ tablespoons finely grated lemon zest
1 teaspoon finely grated orange zest
1 tablespoon lemon juice
1 tablespoon orange juice

Combine the garlic, parsley, caperberries, lemon zest, orange zest, lemon juice and orange juice in a small bowl and mix well. Let stand for 15 minutes or longer to allow the flavors to blend.

YIELD: ABOUT ½ TO ¾ CUP

Perfect Grilled Chicken

1 (3½-pound chicken), cut into quarters, or assorted chicken pieces	2 tablespoons soy sauce
	2 large garlic cloves, minced
¼ cup fresh lemon juice	½ teaspoon cumin
¼ cup olive oil	½ teaspoon sugar
	¼ teaspoon pepper

Arrange the chicken in a single layer in a shallow 9x12-inch baking dish. Combine the lemon juice, olive oil, soy sauce, garlic, cumin, sugar and pepper in a bowl and mix well. Spoon half the mixture over the chicken. Marinate, covered, in the refrigerator for 1 to 12 hours. Cover the reserved marinade and store in the refrigerator until needed.

Drain the chicken, discarding the marinade. Place the chicken skin side down on a grill rack and close the cover. Grill over medium-hot coals for 25 minutes. Baste with the reserved marinade. Turn the chicken. Grill for 20 to 25 minutes or until cooked through.

Serve with Cilantro Salsa (below) or one of the other salsas in the Accompaniments chapter of this cookbook.

YIELD: 4 SERVINGS

Cilantro Salsa

2 cups firmly packed cilantro leaves	2 tablespoons water
	1 to 2 jalapeño chiles, seeded, coarsely chopped
½ small red onion, coarsely chopped	¾ teaspoon sugar
2 tablespoons fresh lemon juice	½ teaspoon salt
	¼ teaspoon pepper

Combine the cilantro, onion, lemon juice, water, jalapeños, sugar, salt and pepper in a food processor container. Process until of the desired consistency. Serve at room temperature. Store any leftover salsa in the refrigerator.

This salsa is especially good with grilled chicken, fish, pork or lamb.

YIELD: 1 CUP

Joan Sutherland

Soprano Joan Sutherland performed arias from her most familiar operatic roles in the May Festival of 1964. The dazzled audience included music archivist Richard LeSueur, then a freshman in the music school. The next day, he spotted Sutherland buying toothpaste at the Kresge store on State Street. He hightailed it over to the Music Center on North University, bought a recording of Sutherland in "I Puritani," and ran back to the store. Record in hand, he approached the six-foot diva, red hair piled high on her head. Would she sign it? "You recognized me?" she asked, astonished.

Caribbean Lime Chicken

3 tablespoons lime juice
2 teaspoons minced garlic
½ teaspoon salt
½ teaspoon thyme
½ teaspoon red pepper flakes
½ teaspoon black pepper
3 pounds assorted chicken pieces
2 tablespoons vegetable oil
2 to 3 sweet onions, cut into narrow wedges
    (about 4 cups)
2 medium tomatoes, seeded, chopped
½ teaspoon curry powder
1 tablespoon lime juice
Lime and orange wedges (optional)

Combine 3 tablespoons lime juice, garlic, salt, thyme, red pepper flakes and black pepper in a shallow dish. Add the chicken, turning to coat well. Remove the chicken from the marinade, discarding the remaining marinade.

Heat the oil in an 11- or 12-inch skillet. Place the chicken in the skillet in a single layer. Cook over medium heat for 5 minutes per side or until brown, turning once. Add the onion wedges. Cook for 8 minutes or until the chicken is cooked through and the onions are tender, stirring frequently. Add the tomatoes and curry powder and cook for 2 minutes. Stir in 1 tablespoon lime juice.

Remove the chicken mixture to a platter. Surround with the lime and orange wedges and garnish with fresh chives. Serve with Gingered Citrus Rice (page 156).

YIELD: 4 TO 6 SERVINGS

Sherried Artichoke Chicken

½ teaspoon salt
½ teaspoon freshly ground pepper
1 teaspoon paprika
1 chicken, cut up
2 tablespoons (¼ stick) butter, melted
2 tablespoons vegetable oil
1 (16-ounce) can artichoke hearts, rinsed,
    drained
8 ounces white mushrooms, sliced
3 tablespoons chopped scallions
2 tablespoons (¼ stick) butter, melted
2 tablespoons flour
⅔ cup chicken broth
¼ cup dry sherry
2 tablespoons catsup
⅛ teaspoon hot sauce, or to taste
1 teaspoon dried rosemary, crumbled
1 pound linguini, cooked, drained

Sprinkle a mixture of the salt, pepper and paprika over the chicken. Cook the chicken in 2 tablespoons butter and oil in a skillet until brown. Remove the chicken to a casserole. Arrange the artichoke hearts around the chicken.

Sauté the mushroooms and scallions in 2 tablespoons butter in a skillet. Sprinkle with the flour. Stir in the chicken broth, sherry, catsup, hot sauce and rosemary. Cook for several minutes to allow the flavors to blend. Spoon over the chicken and artichoke hearts.

Bake at 375 degrees for 40 minutes or until the chicken is cooked through. Serve over the linguini.

Variation: Cook 2 pounds potatoes and purée with 1 teaspoon white truffle oil. Substitute the potatoes for the linguini.

YIELD: 4 SERVINGS

Roasted Cantonese Chicken

2 tablespoons citron brown
   peppercorns
3 tablespoons salt
1 (1-inch) piece of fresh
   gingerroot, thinly sliced
½ teaspoon nutmeg
½ teaspoon garlic
½ teaspoon ground
   tangerine zest

1 (3-pound) chicken
3 to 4 green onions, chopped
2 tablespoons chopped fresh
   gingerroot
2 tablespoons honey
1 tablespoon chopped fresh
   gingerroot
Ground nutmeg to taste

Cook the peppercorns in a skillet over medium heat for
2 minutes, stirring constantly. Add the salt and cook for 2 minutes,
stirring constantly.

Combine 2 tablespoons of the salt and pepper mixture, sliced
gingerroot, nutmeg, garlic and tangerine zest in a bowl and mix
well. Reserve the remaining salt and pepper mixture for another
use. Sprinkle inside the chicken. Place the green onions and
2 tablespoons chopped gingerroot inside the cavity. Spread honey
over the chicken skin and sprinkle with 1 tablespoon chopped
gingerroot and nutmeg.

Bake at 350 degrees for 1½ hours.

YIELD: 4 SERVINGS

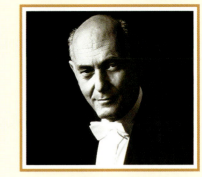

Georg Solti

There have been many cases
of panic, dismay, and last-
minute resourcefulness
throughout the 120 years of
University Musical Society
performances. Tardy artists,
missing instruments or
scores, misplaced items of
clothing, even lost cuff links,
have disrupted backstage
equanimity. Once, conductor
Georg Solti arrived for a
concert without his baton.
The orchestra was onstage,
the audience expectant. Gail
Rector, then UMS president,
enlisted the help of a
backstage custodian, and a
few minutes later presented
the conductor with a
whittled-down stick of wood.
Asked after the concert how
the makeshift baton had
worked, Solti replied, "Well, it
wasn't very well balanced."

Tomato and Basil Turkey Bundles

¼ cup grated Parmesan cheese
¼ teaspoon Italian seasoning
¼ teaspoon salt
¼ teaspoon pepper
1 pound turkey cutlets, pounded thin
½ cup julienned fresh basil
2 Roma tomatoes, seeded, julienned
Olive oil cooking spray
¼ cup seasoned bread crumbs
Mixed greens (optional)
Prepared vinaigrette (optional)

Mix the cheese, Italian seasoning, salt and pepper in a small bowl. Sprinkle evenly over 1 side of the cutlets. Sprinkle with the basil and top with the tomatoes. Roll up as for a jelly roll to enclose the filling. Spray each bundle with olive oil cooking spray and coat with bread crumbs.

Place the bundles seam side down on a 9x14-inch baking sheet sprayed with olive oil cooking spray. Bake at 375 degrees for 20 to 25 minutes or until a meat thermometer inserted into the center of the bundles registers 180 degrees.

Toss the mixed greens with vinaigrette. Arrange the turkey bundles over the mixed greens.

YIELD: 4 SERVINGS

Turkey or Chicken Curry with Honey and Orange

2 tablespoons vegetable oil
1 medium onion, minced
2 garlic cloves, minced
1 tablespoon curry powder
1 tablespoon grated orange zest
1 tablespoon honey
½ cup orange juice
2 cups chopped cooked turkey or chicken
Salt to taste
1 cup plain yogurt
Hot cooked basmati, jasmine or other
    white rice
Chutney (optional)
Toasted coconut (optional)
Toasted almonds or peanuts (optional)
Sliced scallions (optional)

Heat the oil in a medium skillet over medium-high heat. Add the onion and garlic and sauté for 5 minutes. Stir in the curry powder and orange zest and sauté for 1 to 2 minutes. Stir in the honey and orange juice. Add the turkey and salt and simmer for 5 minutes or until heated through. Stir in the yogurt gradually. Simmer over low heat for 5 minutes or until the flavors have blended.

Serve over rice. Garnish with chutney, toasted coconut, toasted almonds or peanuts and/or sliced scallions.

YIELD: 4 SERVINGS

Turkey Breast Braciola

1 to 2 bunches arugula
2 tablespoons olive oil
1 large onion, chopped
½ cup raisins
½ cup chicken broth
⅓ cup freshly grated
   Parmesan cheese
¼ cup pine nuts, toasted

½ cup coarse bread crumbs
1 boneless skinless turkey
   breast (2 to 2½ pounds)
4 ounces thinly sliced prosciutto
1 tablespoon olive oil
½ cup dry white wine
1 cup chicken broth
2 teaspoons lemon juice

For the filling, wash and coarsely chop the arugula. Measure out 3 cups for the filling, reserving the remaining arugula for a garnish. Heat 2 tablespoons olive oil in a 12-inch skillet over medium-high heat until very hot but not smoking. Add the onion; cook until brown, stirring occasionally. Add 3 cups arugula; sauté until wilted. Add the raisins and ½ cup chicken broth. Cook over high heat until most of the liquid has evaporated. Remove from heat; stir in the cheese, pine nuts and bread crumbs.

Butterfly the turkey by making a lengthwise cut in the turkey breast; do not cut all the way through the turkey. Spread out the turkey and place between sheets of plastic wrap. Pound into an 8x12-inch rectangle with a meat mallet, being careful not to make holes in the turkey. Remove the top sheet of plastic wrap. Arrange the prosciutto slices in an overlapping layer over the turkey. Spread a ½-inch-thick layer of the filling over the prosciutto, leaving a ½-inch border. Reserve any remaining filling. Fold 1 long side of the turkey over the filling. Roll up as for a jelly roll. Tie kitchen string around the roll at 1½-inch intervals to maintain the shape. Heat 1 tablespoon olive oil in a skillet over medium-high heat until very hot. Add the turkey; brown on all sides. Add the wine, 1 cup chicken broth and any reserved filling. Cook, covered, over low heat for 35 minutes, turning once. Remove the turkey to a cutting board.

For the sauce, strain the cooking liquid from the skillet into a small saucepan. Boil over high heat until reduced to ½ cup. Skim off the foam. Stir in the lemon juice.

Remove the string from the turkey; cut into ½-inch slices. Toss the reserved arugula with a small amount of sauce. Place the arugula on the platter; arrange the turkey attractively over the top. Drizzle with the remaining sauce. Serve warm or at room temperature.

YIELD: 6 TO 8 SERVINGS

Spinach-Stuffed Game Hens

8 ounces frozen spinach, drained, patted dry
1 cup cottage cheese
¼ cup grated Parmesan cheese
1 egg, beaten
1 teaspoon salt
1 teaspoon pepper
½ teaspoon garlic powder
2 game hens
2 tablespoons vegetable oil
¼ teaspoon oregano
¼ teaspoon thyme
¼ teaspoon rosemary
½ teaspoon paprika

Combine the spinach, cottage cheese, Parmesan cheese, egg, salt, pepper and garlic powder in a bowl and mix well. Loosen the skin of the game hens. Stuff the spinach mixture under the skin of the hens.

Combine the oil, oregano, thyme, rosemary and paprika in a bowl and mix well. Brush on the hens.

Place the hens in a shallow baking pan. Bake at 350 degrees for 45 minutes or until cooked through.

To serve, split each hen into halves with poultry shears.

YIELD: 4 SERVINGS

Goat Cheese-Stuffed Game Hens

3 peaches, thinly sliced
8 ounces pitted cherries
1 cup raisins
½ cup brandy
8 ounces goat cheese, crumbled
2 teaspoons sage
2 teaspoons pepper
4 game hens
½ cup orange preserves
Hot cooked wild rice

Soak the peaches, cherries and raisins in the brandy in a bowl. Combine the goat cheese, sage and pepper in a bowl and mix well. Loosen the skin of the game hens. Stuff the cheese mixture under the skin of the hens. Spread 2 tablespoons orange preserves over each hen.

Place the hens in a shallow baking pan. Spoon the undrained fruit into the baking pan. Bake at 350 degrees for 30 minutes, basting with the pan juices 3 to 4 times.

Serve the hens on a bed of wild rice, spooning the pan drippings over the hens as a sauce.

YIELD: 4 SERVINGS

Duet of Pheasant and Partridge

1 pheasant (legs, thighs, breasts)
1 partridge (legs, thighs, breasts)
3 tablespoons olive oil
3 garlic cloves, minced or pressed
2 teaspoons thyme
1 teaspoon salt
½ teaspoon pepper
1 medium onion, chopped
2 carrots, peeled, chopped
1 tablespoon olive oil
1 pound spicy Italian sausage, casing removed
1½ cups oil-cured black olives
2 cups white wine
2 cups puréed tomatoes
2 cups frozen artichoke hearts, thawed (optional)

Disjoint each game bird. Rub the pieces with 3 tablespoons olive oil, garlic, thyme, salt and pepper.

Sauté the onion and carrots in 1 tablespoon olive oil in a heavy 8-quart Dutch oven until tender. Remove the vegetables and set aside. Brown the sausage in the Dutch oven, stirring until crumbly. Remove the sausage and set aside.

Add a small amount of olive oil to the Dutch oven if needed. Add the game birds and cook until brown. Add the sautéed vegetables and sausage. Add the olives, wine and tomatoes and stir to mix well. Cover with parchment paper or waxed paper and a heavy lid.

Bake at 325 degrees for 1 hour. Add the artichoke hearts and mix well. Bake, covered, for 30 minutes.

YIELD: 6 SERVINGS

Rudolf Serkin performed in Hill Auditorium on eighteen occasions during his long career. Gail Rector, president of the University Musical Society during those years, recalls that Serkin toured with his own piano and his own piano tuner.

Personally, "Rudi" Serkin was an energetic and lovable man with a puckish sense of humor. Once, he concealed a Playboy centerfold just inside the scores of the Juilliard String Quartet, testing their decorum as they began their concert.

Meats

1964

Sunday, May 3, 1964, 2:30 p.m.

Hill Auditorium

Seventy-first Annual
May Festival

The Philadelphia Orchestra
The University Choral Union
Igor Stravinsky *Guest Conductor*
Robert Craft *Guest Conductor*
Soloists: Vera Zorina *Narrator*
John McCollum *Tenor*

Symphony in C   Stravinsky
Moderato alla breve
Larghetto concertante
Allegretto
Largo; tempo giusto, alla breve; largo
Robert Craft *Conducting*

Five Pieces for Orchestra   Schönberg
Vorgefühle ("Presentiments")
Vergangenes ("The Past")
Farben ("Colors")
Péripetie ("Peripeteia")
Das Obligate Rezitativ
(The Obligato Recitative)
Robert Craft *Conducting*

"Perséphone"   Stravinsky
(Melodrama to words by André Gide)
Perséphone ravie
Perséphone aux enfers
Perséphone renaissante
(played without pause)
Vera Zorina and John McCollum
University Choral Union
Igor Stravinsky *Conducting*

Igor Stravinsky

"EVERY composer secretly thinks he knows best how his own music should sound," Aaron Copland wrote. No doubt true, but surely not every composer is able to lead an orchestra to achieve that sound. Ann Arbor audiences realized that Copland could, judging from their response when he came in 1976 to conduct his own works. Igor Stravinsky evoked similar enthusiasm when he came to Ann Arbor in 1964.

Stravinsky came to conduct his "Perséphone," a choral work based on a poem by André Gide. He was an old hand at conducting his own compositions: at age eighty-two, he had led most of the world's major orchestras performing them.

He arrived on the Wednesday before his Sunday afternoon appearance so that he could rehearse with the many participants: the Philadelphia Orchestra, the Choral Union, the Youth Choir, and the soloists, narrator Vera Zorina and tenor John McCollum. A rehearsal photo shows him going over the score with Lester McCoy, then director of the

Choral Union. The composer is wearing one pair of eyeglasses to study the score at hand, and a second pair rests on his forehead.

Stravinsky conducted sitting down, a circumstance that did not reduce the brilliance of the performance. The *Ann Arbor News* wrote that he "guided the Philadelphia Orchestra and the vast Choral Union (supplemented by a children's choir) with uncanny musical instincts," in "an unforgettable musical experience. The months of waiting for that precise moment when the world's greatest living composer would enter Hill Auditorium charged the atmosphere with suspense and emotion, with affection and gratitude."

Aaron Copland, too, frequently conducted his own works, and had conducted his "Orchestral Variations" here in 1961. The program for that 1976 May Festival concert with the Philadelphia Orchestra, performed on Friday, April 30, 1976, at 8:30 p.m., included three of his own compositions.

Eugene Ormandy often planned the annual May Festival around a theme. For the 1976 concerts, to honor the country's bicentennial, he chose primarily American works. Copland, born in 1900 and thus truly a child of the century, picked compositions appropriate to the country's celebration: his "Fanfare for the Common Man," written shortly after the U.S. entered the Second World War, his "Concerto for Clarinet and String Orchestra," written for the brilliant American clarinetist Benny Goodman, and a Concert Suite from his opera "The Tender Land."

"Copland the conductor looked as straightforward, honest and unpretentious as much of his music sounds," wrote a local critic after the concert. "His motions were, at turns, angular and sweeping; his swooping wrists and flapping elbows gave the impression of imminent flight. Particularly infectious rhythms appeared to send waves of energy throughout his body."

Other composers who conducted their own works under UMS auspices include Gustav Holst, Howard Hanson, and Virgil Thomson. Both Holst and Hanson conducted choral works, all of them world or U.S. premieres.

What was cooking?

In the early 1960s, Julia Child began her televised cooking lessons as the "French Chef" and published, with Simone Beck and Louisette Bertholle, the landmark Mastering the Art of French Cooking.

❖

At the same time, the health food movement and vegetarianism were gaining ground, exemplified by Adelle Davis's Let's Eat Right To Keep Fit, *and contrary housewives were making a best-seller of Peg Bracken's* The I Hate To Cook Book. *Nearly four decades later, all three books are still in print.*

Chateaubriand

Thick end of a beef tenderloin (about 1½ pounds)
2 tablespoons olive oil
2 tablespoons cracked pepper
Coarse salt to taste

Wrap the tenderloin in cheesecloth or a clean towel. Flatten to an even thickness with the bottom of a saucepan or sauté pan. Rub the tenderloin with the olive oil and pepper. Season with coarse salt.

Heat a large ovenproof pan. Add the beef and sear on both sides. Bake at 450 degrees until a meat thermometer inserted in the center registers the desired degree of doneness. (Remember that the beef will continue to cook for several minutes after it is removed from the oven.) Remove from the oven and let stand for several minutes.

Cut the beef diagonally into thin wide slices. Serve on heated plates with Savory Oyster Sauce (below) or Béarnaise Sauce (page 190).

YIELD: 6 SERVINGS

Savory Oyster Sauce

2 shallots, finely chopped
1 tablespoon olive oil
1 tablespoon butter
⅔ to 1 cup pan drippings, beef stock or red wine
1 cup bottled oyster sauce
½ cup mixed chopped fresh tarragon, chives and scallions

Sauté the shallots in the olive oil and butter in a saucepan until tender. Add the pan drippings and boil until reduced by ⅓. Add the oyster sauce and herbs and mix well.

YIELD: 2½ CUPS

Isaac Stern's Hearty Borscht

This one-course meal lifts your spirits and warms your bones. It is one of Isaac Stern's favorites and one that he enjoys preparing himself.

3 pounds beef shinbone
2 pounds beef brisket, cut into pieces
2 quarts water
4 cups shredded cabbage
2 cups chopped beets
2 large onions, chopped
3½ cups canned tomatoes
¾ cup lemon juice
6 garlic cloves, minced
¼ cup chopped parsley
1 small bay leaf, crumbled
1 teaspoon paprika
3 tablespoons sugar
1 teaspoon salt
Freshly ground pepper to taste
Sour cream

Combine the shinbone, brisket and water in a large stockpot and bring to a boil. Reduce the heat and simmer, covered, for 1 hour. Add the cabbage, beets, onions, tomatoes, lemon juice, garlic, parsley, bay leaf, paprika, sugar, salt and pepper and mix well. Simmer for 2 hours.

Remove the shinbone from the stockpot. Trim off the meat and discard the bone. Cut the meat into 1-inch pieces and return to the stockpot.

Simmer for 10 minutes. Ladle into bowls and top each serving with sour cream.

YIELD: 6 SERVINGS

Isaac Stern, asked whether he has dietary preferences or restrictions, always replies, "Yes! I like food with my dinner."

Itzhak Perlman, met at the airport before one of his many Ann Arbor concerts, had one question: Where could he buy a Kit-Kat candy bar?

Brazilian Grilled Lamb and Black Beans

2 large oranges, peeled
1 medium red onion
2 (16-ounce) cans black beans, rinsed, drained
1 (8-ounce) bottle red wine vinegar-and-oil salad dressing
½ butterflied leg of lamb (sirloin half), trimmed
*   (about 3 pounds)*
1 teaspoon garlic salt
½ teaspoon red pepper flakes
3 medium red or green bell peppers, cut lengthwise
*   into quarters*

Cut the oranges lengthwise into halves and then crosswise into thin slices. Set aside. Cut the onion crosswise into halves and cut off a thin slice. Separate the onion slice into rings and reserve for a garnish. Finely chop the remaining onion. Combine the chopped onion, beans and ⅓ cup of the salad dressing in a medium bowl and mix well. Cover and store in the refrigerator until serving time.

Brush ⅓ cup of the salad dressing over the lamb. Sprinkle with the garlic salt and red pepper flakes.

Place the lamb and bell peppers on a grid over medium coals. Grill, covered, for 30 to 35 minutes or until the bell peppers are tender and a meat thermometer inserted in the lamb registers 160 degrees for medium; turn the lamb every 10 minutes during grilling and the bell peppers every 15 to 20 minutes. Remove from the grill. Let the lamb stand for 10 minutes before carving into thin slices.

To serve, place the bean mixture in the center of a serving platter. Arrange the bell peppers and orange slices around the beans. Arrange the lamb slices over the beans. Top with the reserved onion rings and drizzle with the remaining salad dressing. Garnish with strips of red bell peppers.

YIELD: 8 TO 10 SERVINGS

Lamb Riblets, Capellini and Sicilian Pasta Sauce

2 pounds lamb riblets
¼ cup water
2 cups Sicilian Pasta Sauce
(below)

1 (16-ounce) package capellini,
cooked, drained
Freshly grated Parmesan cheese

Arrange the lamb in a single layer in a 9x13-inch baking pan. Bake at 450 degrees for 30 minutes or until very brown. Remove the lamb to a 4- or 5-quart saucepan. Drain the pan drippings; return 1 tablespoon drippings to the pan. Pour in water, stirring to scrape up any brown bits. Pour the liquid over the lamb in the saucepan. Add 2 cups Sicilian Pasta Sauce. Bring to a boil and simmer, covered, for 1 hour or until the meat falls from the bone.

Place the pasta on individual plates and top with the lamb and sauce. Sprinkle with Parmesan cheese.

YIELD: 4 TO 6 SERVINGS

Sicilian Pasta Sauce

1 whole head garlic
1 large eggplant
(about 1¾ pounds),
cut into ½-inch cubes
⅓ cup olive oil
4 (15-ounce) cans tomato
sauce
1 (28-ounce) can pear
tomatoes

1½ cups port
1½ cups chopped fresh parsley
3 tablespoons brown sugar
2 tablespoons oregano
2 bay leaves
1 cinnamon stick
Salt and pepper to taste

Peel and mince the garlic cloves. Combine the eggplant, garlic and olive oil in a 5-quart saucepan. Cook over medium-high heat for 50 minutes or until the eggplant is falling apart, stirring frequently. Add the undrained tomatoes; stir to break the tomatoes into chunks. Stir in the tomato sauce, port, parsley, brown sugar, oregano, bay leaves and cinnamon stick. Bring to a boil; reduce heat. Simmer, covered, for 1 hour or until reduced to 3 quarts. Season with salt and pepper. Discard bay leaves and cinnamon stick.

YIELD: 3 QUARTS

Baritone Jerome Hines was the guest of honor at a buffet supper following his performance during a May Festival. His hostess, Lois Stegeman, after setting out an elaborate spread that included beef tenderloin, salads, and desserts, could find no sign of Hines. She finally found him in her kitchen, chatting with one of her young sons and contentedly eating what he preferred: a bowl of puffed wheat cereal with honey and milk.

Finger-Licking-Good Lamb Chops

8 (1- to 1½-inch-thick) baby lamb chops,
    with 3- to 4-inch-long bones
½ cup fresh lemon juice
⅓ cup olive oil
6 garlic cloves, minced
2 tablespoons minced fresh rosemary
Sea salt and freshly ground pepper to taste

Arrange the lamb chops in a single layer in a shallow glass dish. Pour the lemon juice and olive oil over the chops. Sprinkle with the garlic and rosemary. Marinate, covered, in the refrigerator for 3 to 4 hours, turning once.

Season the lamb chops with sea salt and pepper. Place the chops directly over the fire on a grill. Grill for 3 to 4 minutes per side for medium-rare. Serve hot. Garnish with lemon wedges.

Alternately, these chops may be broiled 4 inches from the heat source for about 4 minutes per side.

YIELD: 4 TO 6 SERVINGS

Rack of Lamb Genghis Khan

1 cup finely chopped onion
2 tablespoons minced garlic
3 tablespoons lemon juice
½ cup honey
3 tablespoons curry powder
1½ teaspoons cayenne pepper
1 teaspoon dry mustard
2 teaspoons freshly ground black pepper
2 tablespoons salt
1 cup water
3 racks of lamb or pork, 8 ribs each
1 cup hoisin sauce

Combine the onion, garlic, lemon juice, honey, curry powder, cayenne pepper, dry mustard, black pepper, salt and water in a bowl and mix well. Place the lamb racks in a large sealable plastic bag and add the marinade. Seal the bag and marinate in the refrigerator for 48 hours, turning occasionally.

Remove the lamb from the marinade, discarding the remaining marinade. Let stand at room temperature for 1 hour. Brush with the hoisin sauce.

Place the lamb on a rack in a shallow roasting pan. Bake at 450 degrees for 15 to 25 minutes for rare. Let stand for 6 to 7 minutes before carving.

YIELD: 6 SERVINGS

Lamb Shanks in Red Wine

Flour
Salt and pepper to taste
4 lamb shanks
3 tablespoons olive oil
5 red onions, peeled, thinly
    sliced
¼ cup chopped fresh rosemary
4 garlic cloves, chopped
¾ cup balsamic vinegar
1¼ cups red wine

Mix flour, salt and pepper in a shallow dish. Coat the lamb shanks with the flour. Heat the olive oil in a large Dutch oven. Add the lamb; cook until brown on both sides. Remove the lamb and keep warm. Add the onions to the Dutch oven. Cook over low heat for 10 minutes or until light brown. Add the rosemary and garlic; cook for 2 minutes. Add the vinegar and wine. Increase the heat; cook for 2 to 3 minutes. Return the lamb to the Dutch oven. Place a piece of parchment paper over the top of the pan and then the lid. Bake at 350 degrees for 2 to 2½ hours or to desired degree of doneness, basting every 30 minutes and adding additional wine if needed.

YIELD: 4 SERVINGS

Bill Bolcom's Pork Scallopini with Green Peppercorns

1 pound boneless pork loin
    or tenderloin
Salt and freshly ground
    pepper to taste
1 garlic clove, partially
    crushed
2 tablespoons olive oil
2 tablespoons (¼ stick) butter
2 tablespoons pickled green
    peppercorns
1 teaspoon fresh lemon juice

Cut the pork loin into 8 slices; pound until thin. Sprinkle with salt and pepper; rub with garlic. Heat the olive oil and butter in a skillet over high heat until very hot. Add the pork slices; sauté until cooked through, turning once. Remove the pork slices to a platter; keep warm. Add the peppercorns and lemon juice to the skillet; cook for 30 seconds. Pour over the pork slices. Serve immediately.

YIELD: 4 SERVINGS

David Daniels, William Bolcom, and Itzhak Perlman

In the mostly serious repertoire of William Bolcom, pianist and Pulitzer Prize-winning composer, is a song called "Lime Jello, Marshmallow, Cottage Cheese Surprise." A favorite encore when he and his wife, soprano Joan Morris, present their recitals of American popular songs, it wittily describes the kinds of food that torment touring musicians. But Bolcom isn't fussy. He likes "pretty much anything humans eat. I stop, however, at things that crawl across one's plate. Once we were on Chesapeake Bay enjoying oysters accompanied by little pink oyster crabs, which one is supposed to pop, live, into one's mouth. I couldn't manage to do it. I expect my food to sit still."

Pork Scallopini with Roasted Fennel Seeds

2 tablespoons fennel seeds
1 pound pork scallops or tenderloin
Salt and freshly ground pepper to taste
2 garlic cloves, minced
1 cup milk
1 cup ground Parmesan cheese
1 cup dry bread crumbs
¼ cup olive oil

Brown the fennel seeds in a small sauté pan sprayed with nonstick cooking spray. Let stand until cool. Grind the seeds in a nut grinder or blender.

Season the pork scallops with salt, pepper and garlic. (If using tenderloin, cut into 8 slices and pound thin before seasoning.) Dip the pork into the milk, then into a mixture of the cheese and bread crumbs.

Heat the olive oil in a sauté pan. Add the pork and sauté until light brown and cooked through. Drain on paper towels. Serve hot.

YIELD: 4 SERVINGS

Skitch Henderson's Spit-Roasted Pork Loin

1 (10-pound) pork loin with the bone,
   trimmed
4 garlic cloves, partially crushed
Salt to taste
½ cup prepared mustard
¼ cup peach jam or orange marmalade
2 teaspoons chopped fresh marjoram, or
   ½ teaspoon dried marjoram
¼ cup apple brandy or apple cider
1 tablespoon cider vinegar
½ teaspoon freshly ground pepper
Juice of ½ lemon

Place the pork loin on a rotisserie spit-rod. Rub the pork with the garlic and sprinkle with salt. Combine the mustard, jam, marjoram, brandy, vinegar, pepper and lemon juice in a medium bowl and mix well. Coat the pork with half the mixture.

Roast over medium-hot coals for 3 hours or until a meat thermometer inserted in the pork registers 170 degrees, basting frequently with the remaining mustard mixture. Remove from the heat and let stand for 15 minutes before carving.

YIELD: 16 SERVINGS

Pork Tenderloin with Couscous

1½ pounds pork tenderloin
2 teaspoons sugar
1 tablespoon vegetable oil
⅔ cup beef or chicken broth
1 tablespoon mustard seeds
1 tablespoon balsamic vinegar
2 teaspoons minced fresh oregano, or 1 teaspoon dried oregano
1⅓ cups beef or chicken broth
1 tablespoon butter or margarine
1 cup couscous
½ cup sliced green onions
⅓ cup beef or chicken broth
½ cup dry red wine
2 teaspoons cornstarch
2 teaspoons water
Salt and pepper to taste

Trim away any fat and membrane from the tenderloin. Sprinkle with the sugar.

Heat the oil in a 10- or 12-inch skillet over medium-high heat. Add the pork and cook for 4 minutes or until brown on all sides. Add ⅔ cup beef broth, mustard seeds, vinegar and oregano. Simmer, covered, over medium-low heat for 12 minutes or until a meat thermometer inserted into the thickest part of the tenderloin registers 160 degrees. Set aside and keep warm.

Bring 1⅓ cups beef broth and the butter to a boil in a 2- or 3-quart saucepan over high heat. Stir in the couscous. Cover and remove from the heat. Let stand for 5 minutes or until all the liquid is absorbed. Stir in the green onions with a fork.

Add ⅓ cup beef broth and wine to the skillet. Boil over high heat for 2 minutes or until reduced to ¾ cup. Stir in a mixture of the cornstarch and water. Bring to a boil, stirring constantly.

Cut the tenderloin into slices and arrange on a platter. Mound the couscous beside the slices. Spoon the sauce over the pork slices. Season with salt and pepper.

YIELD: 4 SERVINGS

A University Musical Society staffer, backstage during a concert by Rudolf Serkin, listened to his spectacular performance, which included one-handed double trills and octave glissandos. As Serkin left the stage, she said to him, "I was stunned by that."

His reply: "So was I!"

127

Mediterranean Torte

2 cups flour
½ cup (1 stick) unsalted
    butter
¼ cup sour cream or cottage
    cheese
Cornmeal
2 tablespoons olive oil
3 garlic cloves, pressed
2 bunches scallions,
    chopped
1 pound spinach, cooked,
    chopped
½ cup bread crumbs

2 tablespoons Dijon mustard
12 canned artichoke hearts,
    drained
1 pound ricotta cheese
1 tablespoon oregano
1 tablespoon rosemary
8 ounces sliced Genoa salami
8 ounces provolone cheese
12 sun-dried tomatoes,
    reconstituted in olive oil
4 ounces thinly sliced prosciutto
Sour cream, yogurt or crème
    frâiche

For the crust, process the flour and butter in a food processor until crumbly. Add ¼ cup sour cream; process until a smooth dough forms. Chill for 30 minutes. Sprinkle a 9-inch springform pan with cornmeal. Divide the dough into halves; return 1 half to refrigerator. Roll the remaining dough between 2 sheets of plastic wrap large enough to cover the bottom and side of the pan with 1-inch overhang. Remove the top plastic wrap. Place the dough in prepared pan with the remaining plastic on top. Fit the dough into the pan; remove the plastic wrap. Trim the edge of the dough to an even 1-inch overhang.

For the filling, heat the olive oil in a 12- or 14-inch skillet. Add the garlic and scallions and sauté for 5 minutes or until tender. Add the spinach and cook for several minutes. Remove from the heat and stir in the bread crumbs. Set aside to cool.

Brush the Dijon mustard over the bottom and side of the pastry. Add the spinach mixture, spreading to the edge of the pan. Arrange the artichoke hearts so that each slice will contain 1 artichoke heart. Spread the ricotta cheese over the top. Sprinkle with the oregano and rosemary. Layer the salami, provolone cheese, sun-dried tomatoes and prosciutto over the ricotta cheese.

Roll the remaining dough into a circle large enough to cover the top of torte. Pull up the overhanging dough to enclose the top. Pinch the edge to seal or press with a fork. Brush with sour cream. Bake at 425 degrees for 10 minutes. Decrease the oven temperature to 375 degrees. Bake for 30 to 40 minutes or until the crust is light brown.

YIELD: 12 SERVINGS

Veal Stew Mediterranean

1 tablespoon olive oil
1½ pounds veal, cut into 1-inch cubes
½ teaspoon salt
½ teaspoon pepper
1 tablespoon olive oil
1 medium onion, cut into halves, then into ¼-inch wedges
3 garlic cloves, chopped
1 (14-ounce) can vegetable or chicken broth
½ cup orange juice
1 tablespoon chopped fresh thyme leaves
1 tablespoon balsamic vinegar
2 plum tomatoes, chopped (about 1 cup)
2 tablespoons cornstarch
¼ cup orange juice

Heat 1 tablespoon olive oil in a large nonstick skillet over medium heat. Add half the veal and cook until brown. Season with half the salt and pepper and set aside. Repeat with the remaining veal.

Heat 1 tablespoon olive oil in the skillet. Add the onion. Cook, covered, for 6 to 8 minutes or until golden brown, stirring constantly. Add the garlic and cook for 1 minute, stirring constantly. Add the veal, vegetable broth, ½ cup orange juice, thyme and vinegar and mix well. Bring to a boil and reduce the heat to low. Simmer, tightly covered, for 1 to 1¼ hours or until the veal is tender and cooked through.

Add the tomatoes and cook for 2 minutes. Stir in a mixture of the cornstarch and ¼ cup orange juice. Cook over medium-high heat for 1 to 2 minutes or until thickened and bubbly.

Ladle into bowls and garnish with freshly grated orange zest and chopped fresh thyme. Serve with couscous, rice or orzo.

YIELD: 4 SERVINGS

Osso Buco

4 (3-inch) pieces of veal
    shank
1 large onion, chopped
1 leek, white part only,
    chopped
2 ribs celery, chopped
2 small carrots or 1 large
    carrot, chopped
3 tablespoons tomato paste
2 tablespoons olive oil
3 cups chopped fresh or
    canned Roma tomatoes

1 teaspoon coarse salt
Freshly ground pepper to taste
1 tablespoon oregano
1 tablespoon marjoram
2 tablespoons grated lemon zest
2 tablespoons olive oil
3 garlic cloves, minced
1 cup flour
2 cups dry white wine
Equal parts chopped garlic,
    grated lemon zest and
    chopped parsley (optional)

Secure each piece of veal with kitchen string (this will help keep the meat on the bone as it cooks).

For the sauce, process the onion, leek, celery and carrots in a food processor until finely chopped. Add the tomato paste and mix well. Heat 2 tablespoons olive oil in a sauté pan. Add the vegetable mixture and sauté briefly. Add the tomatoes and simmer for 5 minutes. Add the salt, pepper, oregano, marjoram and lemon zest and simmer for 5 minutes. Remove from the heat and set aside.

Heat 2 tablespoons olive oil in a large heavy ovenproof sauté pan. Rub the veal with the garlic and additional salt and pepper. Coat with the flour. Place the veal in the sauté pan and cook until seared. Stir the wine into the tomato sauce. Spoon the sauce over the veal. Reduce the heat and cover the pan. Cook for 10 minutes.

Place the sauté pan on a baking sheet to catch pan drippings. Bake at 350 degrees for 1½ hours or until the veal is very tender and falls away from the bone, turning once.

Remove the string and place the veal on a platter. Sprinkle with equal parts chopped garlic, grated lemon zest and chopped parsley.

YIELD: 4 SERVINGS

Mushroom-Stuffed Veal Roast

1 tablespoon butter
3 ounces mixed mushrooms, such as shiitake, oyster and
    cremini, coarsely chopped
1/4 cup minced shallots
2 garlic cloves, minced
2 tablespoons chopped fresh herbs, such as rosemary,
    sage and thyme
1 teaspoon coarsely ground pepper
1 (2 1/4- to 2 1/2-pound) boneless veal shoulder roast
1/2 teaspoon salt
3/4 cup dry white wine
2 teaspoons cornstarch
1 tablespoon water
1/3 cup heavy cream
1/4 teaspoon salt (optional)

For the filling, melt the butter in a medium nonstick skillet over medium heat. Add the mushrooms, shallots and garlic. Cook for 2 to 3 minutes or just until tender, stirring occasionally. Mix the chopped fresh herbs and pepper in a small bowl. Stir half the herb mixture into the mushroom mixture and set aside.

Unroll the veal roast and season with 1/2 teaspoon salt. Spread evenly with the mushroom mixture. Roll up as for a jelly roll and tie with kitchen string. Press the remaining herb mixture into the surface of the veal. Place fat side up on a rack in a shallow roasting pan.

Bake at 325 degrees for 30 to 35 minutes per pound or until a meat thermometer inserted in the thickest part of the veal registers 155 degrees for medium. Remove the roast to a cutting board. Tent loosely with foil and let stand for 15 minutes.

For the sauce, add enough water to the pan drippings to measure 1/4 cup. Return the mixture to the roasting pan and stir in the wine. Cook over medium-high heat until the browned bits have dissolved, stirring constantly. Cook for 3 minutes longer, stirring occasionally. Stir in a mixture of the cornstarch and water. Add the cream and cook for 1 to 2 minutes longer or until thickened and bubbly. Add 1/4 teaspoon salt.

Carve the roast into thin slices and serve with the sauce.

YIELD: 6 TO 8 SERVINGS

Arthur Rubinstein

Pianist Arthur Rubinstein, a favorite of local audiences for his graciousness as well as his artistry, played in Ann Arbor fifteen times during his long career. After a benefit concert in 1971, he attended a gala dinner and reception in the second-floor ballroom of the Michigan League.

Waiting on the landing of the stairway between floors was a nervous young woman from the student newspaper, camera poised. As Rubinstein climbed the stairs toward her, she dropped the camera, which clattered to a rest at his feet. He quickly picked it up, handed it to the embarrassed young woman with a smile, posed as she took his picture, and continued on his way to the celebration in his honor.

Venison or Beef Bourguignon with Savory Dumplings

4 garlic cloves, chopped

1 large onion, cut into
    chunks

2 carrots, sliced

1/2 cup chopped parsley

2 teaspoons coarsely ground
    pepper

1 teaspoon salt

1/4 cup Cognac

1 bottle Burgundy or other
    dry red wine

1 tablespoon coarsely
    ground juniper berries

4 pounds venison or beef,
    cut into 1 1/2-inch cubes

12 ounces bacon, cut into
    1/2-inch cubes

1 teaspoon salt

1/2 teaspoon pepper

1/3 cup (about) vegetable oil

1/4 cup flour

2 tablespoons tomato paste

Beef, chicken or vegetable stock

1 pound mushrooms, cleaned,
    cut into quarters

1 pound pearl onions, blanched,
    peeled

1 tablespoon sugar

Salt and pepper to taste

2 tablespoons potato starch

1/4 cup red wine or beef, chicken
    or vegetable stock

1/2 cup chopped parsley

For the marinade, combine the garlic, onion, carrots, 1/2 cup parsley, 2 teaspoons pepper, 1 teaspoon salt, Cognac, Burgundy and ground juniper berries in a shallow pan and mix well. Add the meat. Marinate, covered, in the refrigerator for 12 hours. Remove the meat and vegetables from the marinade, reserving the remaining marinade. Pat the meat dry and set aside.

For the stew, fry the bacon in a Dutch oven over medium heat until crisp. Remove with a slotted spoon and set aside. Strain the pan drippings and return half the drippings to the Dutch oven. Season the meat with 1 teaspoon salt and 1/2 teaspoon pepper. Sauté a few pieces at a time in the bacon drippings, adding a small amount of the oil if needed.

Return all the meat to the Dutch oven and sprinkle with the flour. Cook for 1 minute. Stir in the tomato paste and cook for several minutes. Add the bacon, reserved marinade and vegetables. If needed, add enough beef stock so that the vegetables and veal are completely covered with liquid. Place a piece of parchment paper or waxed paper over the top of the Dutch oven and then a tight-fitting lid. Bake at 350 degrees for 2 1/2 hours or until the meat is tender and cooked through.

Sauté the mushrooms in the remaining bacon drippings or 1 tablespoon of the oil in a sauté pan. Remove from the pan and set aside. Add additional bacon drippings or oil to the pan as needed. Sauté the onions in the drippings until light brown. Sprinkle the sugar over the onions to lightly caramelize them. Mix the onions and mushrooms in a bowl and season with salt and pepper. Return the mixture to the sauté pan and mix well. Cook for 5 minutes. Stir in a mixture of the potato starch and wine if the stew is too thin. Cook for 5 minutes longer.

Garnish with ½ cup parsley and serve with Savory Dumplings (below) and Red Cabbage and Beet Relish (page 184).

YIELD: 8 TO 10 SERVINGS

Savory Dumplings

2 cups flour
2 teaspoons baking powder
1 teaspoon kosher salt
½ teaspoon freshly ground pepper
¼ teaspoon nutmeg (optional)
3 tablespoons vegetable oil
1 cup milk, water or beef stock
¼ cup chopped fresh thyme or oregano, or sage and parsley

Combine the flour, baking powder, kosher salt, pepper and nutmeg in a bowl. Add the oil and milk and mix lightly until a smooth dough forms, adding chopped fresh herbs you prefer.

Drop the dough by tablespoonfuls into a large stockpot of boiling water. Simmer, uncovered, for 10 minutes. Cook, covered, for 5 to 10 minutes or until the dumplings are cooked through.

Serve with Venison or Beef Bourguignon (page 132) or other hearty stews.

Alternately, these dumplings can be dropped by tablespoonfuls directly onto a simmering stew.

YIELD: 16 DUMPLINGS

On St. Patrick's Day 1973, a late winter storm hit, and by 3 p.m. a foot of snow had fallen. The Mozarteum Orchestra of Salzburg was to perform the "Coronation Mass" that evening with the local Festival Chorus. Orchestra members arrived safely; so did their instruments, after the truck transporting them was pulled from a snow bank along the highway.

The four soloists made it to Hill Auditorium, and of 125 chorus members, seventy-five managed to get there, too. Conductor Donald Bryant recalls his relief at finding that the diminished group remained "well-balanced." Mozart's mass was performed in memory of Charles Sink, who had died a few months earlier at ninety-two. Sink would have delighted in knowing that, to enjoy the glorious music in his honor, 2,500 hardy souls made it through the snow—some on snowshoes or cross-country skis.

Pasta

1978

Sunday, October 8, 1978, 4 p.m.

Hill Auditorium

Opening Concert of the 100th Choral Union Series

Vladimir Horowitz *Pianist*

Polonaise-Fantaisie,
Op. 61   Chopin

Nocturne in F minor,
Op. 55   Chopin

Mazurka in B minor,
Op. 33, No. 4   Chopin

Sonata in B-flat minor,
Op. 35   Chopin

Moment Musical in B minor,
Op. 16, No. 3   Rachmaninoff

Moment Musical in E-flat minor,
Op. 16, No. 2   Rachmaninoff

Consolation   Liszt

Mephisto Waltz   Liszt

Vladimir Horowitz

FOR the inaugural concert of the hundredth season of University Musical Society concerts, no artist could have been more fitting than Vladimir Horowitz. Adding to the centennial pride of the local audience, the great pianist was celebrating the fiftieth anniversary of his own American debut.

After that debut year, Horowitz appeared in Ann Arbor on another eight occasions before 1953, when he began a long "intermission" from the concert stage. His late wife, Wanda Horowitz, recalled "very difficult times. For twelve years he was not playing, and for twelve years I heard, 'I will never play again.'" For music lovers, those years only enhanced his legend, and his return in the 1970s caused a sensation.

His first local concert, at the 1975 May Festival, was arranged at the last minute and announced only three weeks in advance. Concert-goers were in a frenzy to get tickets. Hill

Auditorium sold out in twenty-four hours. UMS box office manager Michael Gowing recalls that "we had so many orders, we ended up dumping them all in this huge box and pulling them out until all the seats were gone. There was just no other way to do it."

Between that concert and this one in 1978, Horowitz gave three other Ann Arbor performances, and he would return once more in 1980. "That was Mr. Rector's doing," comments UMS staffer Sally Cushing. Gail Rector, president of UMS, and Harold Shaw, Horowitz's manager, were good friends. Furthermore, Cushing remembers, "we took really good care of him."

In 1978, Horowitz played in Ann Arbor twice, in April and again in October. The first time was at the May Festival with Eugene Ormandy and the Philadelphia Orchestra, when he performed a signature piece, Rachmaninoff's Third Piano Concerto. Just one month earlier, with Ormandy and the Philadelphia, Horowitz had recorded it in a masterly performance that is still considered a touchstone. Those who heard the work on that May Festival night have never forgotten it. Michael Gowing remembers that "afterwards, Wanda said, 'This is the performance we should have recorded!' "

The happy coincidence of Horowitz's golden jubilee year and the hundredth season of UMS occasioned many festivities around this concert. Wanda Horowitz made what she playfully referred to as her Ann Arbor "debut," giving a brief talk about her father, maestro Arturo Toscanini, the other musical genius in her life. (When Wanda Toscanini Horowitz died in 1998, the obituary in the *New York Times* quoted her on her famous father and husband: "Don't talk to me about them. My father made me neurotic and my husband made me crazy.")

The concert, before an overflow crowd, featured works of Chopin, Rachmaninoff, and Liszt, and an enraptured audience found it hard to let Horowitz go, calling him back for four encores.

What was cooking?

"Nouvelle cuisine," a departure from the calories and rigidities of haute cuisine, developed by renegade young chefs from France, grew under the influence of innovative restaurateurs like Alice Waters of Chez Panisse in Berkeley, California. At about the same time, Calvin Trillin's mirthful Alice, Let's Eat *glorified voluptuous Kansas City barbecue.*

Black Olive Pasta
with Roasted Pepper Sauce

½ pound bread flour (about 2 cups)
¼ pound semolina flour (about 1 cup)
¼ teaspoon salt
3 eggs
4 ounces black olives, pitted, puréed
1 medium onion, finely chopped
1 tablespoon olive oil
2 garlic cloves, finely chopped
Salt and freshly ground pepper to taste
2 red bell peppers, roasted, peeled (see page 39)
¼ cup chicken stock
1 tablespoon minced parsley
2 tablespoons heavy cream

For the pasta, combine the bread flour, semolina flour and salt in a bowl and mix well. Make a well in the center and add the eggs, mixing well with a fork. Add the puréed olives and mix until a smooth dough forms. Cut the dough into 3 equal portions and let stand for 10 minutes.

Place 1 portion of the dough in a pasta machine. Knead, roll thin and cut into narrow flat noodles. Repeat the process with the remaining dough.

For the sauce, sauté the onion in the olive oil in a large saucepan over medium heat until translucent. Add the garlic, salt and pepper and cook for 30 seconds. Remove from the heat. Purée the onion mixture, roasted peppers, chicken stock and parsley in a blender or food processor. Pour into the saucepan. Cook over medium heat until slightly reduced. Stir in the cream and reduce the heat. Simmer until the sauce is slightly thickened.

Cook the noodles in boiling salted water in a stockpot for 2 to 3 minutes or until al dente; drain well. Stir the pasta into the sauce in the saucepan and mix well. Cook until heated through.

YIELD: 4 SERVINGS

Fettuccini al Carciofi

2 tablespoons (¼ stick) butter
14 ounces canned or jarred artichokes, drained,
    rinsed, patted dry
2 tablespoons water
1 tablespoon butter
2 to 3 ounces prosciutto, chopped
3 shallots, minced
1 red bell pepper, chopped
2 large garlic cloves, minced
½ cup dry white wine
1 cup heavy cream
½ cup Pesto Italiano (page 186) or other pesto
Salt and freshly ground pepper to taste
16 ounces fresh fettuccini
½ cup freshly grated Parmesan cheese
¼ cup pine nuts, toasted

Melt 2 tablespoons butter in a large skillet. Add the artichokes and sauté briefly. Add the water and simmer, covered, until the artichokes are tender and lightly browned.

Melt 1 tablespoon butter in a large heavy saucepan. Add the prosciutto, shallots, red pepper and garlic. Sauté for 5 minutes or until the red pepper is tender. Add the wine. Boil for 3 minutes or until the liquid is reduced by ½. Stir in the cream and Pesto Italiano. Cook for 5 minutes or until the sauce thickens, stirring frequently. Season with salt and pepper. Set aside and keep warm.

Cook the fettuccini in boiling salted water in a stockpot until al dente; drain well.

Place the pasta in a large serving bowl and top with the artichokes. Spoon the sauce over the top. Add the cheese and pine nuts and toss to mix well. Serve immediately.

YIELD: 4 SERVINGS

Thai'd Up Fettuccini

12 ounces fettuccini
1 tablespoon vegetable oil
1 small onion, sliced (about ¼ cup)
1 tablespoon chopped seeded jalapeño chile
2 cups shredded chicken, turkey, pork or beef
    (optional)
2 cups chopped broccoli florets
3 garlic cloves, chopped
3 plum tomatoes, cored, cut into quarters
⅛ teaspoon red pepper flakes
1 cup low-sodium chicken broth
¼ cup loosely packed cilantro leaves
2 tablespoons lime juice
Zest of 1 lime (optional)
2 tablespoons chopped cilantro (optional)
2 tablespoons chopped onion (optional)
2 tablespoons peanuts, crushed (optional)

Cook the fettuccini in a stockpot using the package directions; drain well. Return the pasta to the stockpot and set aside.

Heat the oil in a large heavy skillet over high heat. Add the sliced onion and jalapeño. Sauté for 3 minutes or until wilted. Add the chicken and reduce the heat to medium. Cook for 4 minutes or until heated through. Add the broccoli, garlic, tomatoes and red pepper flakes and sauté for 2 minutes. Add the chicken broth, ¼ cup cilantro leaves, lime juice and lime zest. Boil for 4 minutes or until the liquid is reduced by ½. Remove and discard the lime zest.

Add the sauce to the pasta in the stockpot. Cook over low heat until heated through, stirring until the pasta is evenly coated. Remove the pasta to a serving platter or plates. Top with chopped cilantro, onion and peanuts and serve immediately.

YIELD: 4 SERVINGS

Fusilli Portofino

16 ounces fusilli or other medium pasta shape
Salt to taste
1 pound medium shrimp, peeled, deveined
12 sun-dried tomatoes, drained,
    cut into strips
8 fresh plum tomatoes, cut into small pieces
2 bunches arugula, torn into bite-size pieces
6 sprigs of fresh flat-leaf parsley, coarsely
    chopped
Leaves of ½ small bunch fresh basil, coarsely
    chopped
¼ cup olive oil
Juice of 1 lemon
Freshly ground pepper to taste

Cook the fusilli in boiling salted water in a saucepan until al dente. Drain well and keep warm.

Steam the shrimp until they turn pink and are no longer translucent.

Combine the shrimp, sun-dried tomatoes, plum tomatoes, arugula, parsley and basil in a large bowl and mix well. Add the pasta, olive oil, lemon juice, salt and pepper and toss to mix well. Serve immediately.

YIELD: 6 SERVINGS

Bill T. Jones' Sage Fusilli

16 ounces fusilli
Salt to taste
10 ounces cherry tomatoes,
    cut into halves
2 small garlic cloves, thinly
    sliced
3 tablespoons extra-virgin
    olive oil

½ cup fresh sage leaves,
    chopped
1 tablespoon minced parsley
Freshly grated pepper to taste
Freshly grated Parmesan cheese
Sea salt to taste

Cook the fusilli in boiling salted water until al dente. Drain well and keep warm. Sauté the cherry tomatoes and garlic briefly in the olive oil in a skillet. (The tomatoes should be warm but still firm.) Remove from the heat and stir in the sage, parsley and a lot of pepper.

Combine the pasta and sauce in a bowl and mix well. Add the cheese and toss to mix well. Remove to a warm serving bowl and sprinkle with sea salt.

YIELD: 3 TO 4 SERVINGS

Linguini with Roquefort Sauce

8 ounces prosciutto, thinly
    sliced, julienned
6 ounces Roquefort cheese,
    coarsely crumbled
2 cups large walnut pieces
1 cup chopped flat-leaf
    parsley
¼ cup finely chopped
    fresh rosemary

3 garlic cloves, minced
1½ teaspoons freshly ground
    pepper
¾ cup olive oil
½ cup heavy cream or
    half-and-half
16 ounces linguini, cooked
1½ cups freshly grated
    Parmesan cheese

Mix the prosciutto, Roquefort cheese, walnuts, parsley, rosemary, garlic, pepper and olive oil in a large bowl. Let stand at room temperature for 3 hours. Stir in the cream and let stand for 1 hour. Add the linguini. Add ½ cup of the Parmesan cheese; mix well. Serve the remaining 1 cup Parmesan cheese on the side.

YIELD: 4 TO 6 SERVINGS

Dancer and choreographer Bill T. Jones says his favorite food "is the food I eat at home, prepared by my companion, Bjorn, while I improvise about our living room or read to him food writers' letters, memoirs, and essays, such as M. F. K. Fisher's or James Beard's. We sit at the table, candlelight, soft music in a glowing room, enjoying the ebb and flow of conversation."

Linguini with Sautéed Asparagus

16 ounces linguini or fettuccini
Salt to taste
12 jumbo asparagus spears
2 tablespoons olive or vegetable oil
¾ cup chopped red onion
¼ cup capers, drained
½ cup black olives, pitted, chopped
1 tablespoon chopped fresh basil
4 medium fresh tomatoes, peeled,
    seeded, puréed
Freshly ground pepper to taste

Cook the linguini in boiling salted water in a stockpot until al dente. Drain well and keep warm.

Cut the asparagus diagonally into 1-inch pieces. Cook briefly in boiling water in a saucepan. Plunge immediately into cold water. Drain and set aside.

Heat the olive oil in a large skillet over medium heat. Add the onion and sauté for 2 minutes. Add the capers, olives, basil and puréed tomatoes and cook for 4 minutes. Add the pasta and simmer for 2 minutes. Stir in the asparagus at serving time. Season with additional salt and pepper.

Note: Peeling and seeding the tomatoes is optional.

YIELD: 6 SERVINGS

Orzo Oliva

16 ounces orzo
Salt to taste
2 tablespoons olive oil
2 tablespoons (¼ stick) butter
1½ cups chopped onions
3 shallots, chopped
2 cups chopped celery
2 garlic cloves, chopped
2 tablespoons flour
1 cup chicken broth
¼ cup chopped fresh basil, or 1 teaspoon
    dried basil
1 teaspoon dried oregano
¼ teaspoon cayenne pepper
1 (35-ounce) can plum tomatoes, drained
8 ounces kalamata olives, pitted, coarsely
    chopped
8 ounces mozzarella cheese, shredded
Salt and freshly ground black pepper to taste
4 ounces mozzarella cheese, shredded

Cook the orzo in boiling salted water in a saucepan until al dente; drain well and keep warm.

Heat the olive oil and butter in a large heavy skillet over medium-low heat. Add the onions, shallots and celery and sauté for 5 minutes or until tender. Add the garlic and sauté for 30 seconds. Add the flour and sauté for 2 minutes. Add the chicken broth, basil, oregano, cayenne pepper and tomatoes. Break up the tomatoes with a spoon. Simmer for 5 minutes, stirring occasionally.

Remove the orzo to a large casserole. Stir in the tomato mixture, olives and 8 ounces mozzarella cheese. Season with salt and black pepper. Sprinkle 4 ounces mozzarella cheese over the top.

Bake at 400 degrees for 30 minutes or until heated through.

YIELD: 6 SERVINGS

Penne with Stilton Sauce

2 quarts water
½ teaspoon salt
1½ pounds penne
½ tablespoon olive oil
Stilton Sauce (below)

¾ cup fresh or frozen tiny peas
2½ tablespoons scallions or
    chives
1 cup freshly grated Parmesan
    cheese

Bring the water and salt to a boil in a stockpot and add the penne. Cook for 12 minutes or until the pasta is al dente. Drain the pasta and submerge in cold water; drain again. Toss the pasta with the olive oil to prevent sticking. Toss the pasta, Stilton Sauce and peas in a large warm bowl or casserole until well mixed. Sprinkle the scallions over the top. Serve immediately with the Parmesan cheese.

YIELD: 6 SERVINGS AS AN ENTRÉE
8 TO 12 SERVINGS AS A SIDE DISH

Stilton Sauce

4 ounces shallots, peeled
½ tablespoon olive oil
1 cup milk or half-and-half
½ cup chicken, beef or
    vegetable stock
½ medium onion, peeled,
    cut into quarters
1 medium carrot, chopped

½ stalk celery with leaves, cut
    into halves
1 bay leaf
3 peppercorns
½ teaspoon salt
6 to 8 ounces Stilton cheese,
    crumbled
3 garlic cloves, minced

Toss the shallots with the olive oil in a small bowl. Spread on a baking sheet. Bake at 375 degrees for 15 to 20 minutes or until tender. Let stand until cool. Coarsely chop the shallots. Combine the milk, chicken stock, onion, carrot, celery, chopped shallots, bay leaf, peppercorns and salt in a 1-quart saucepan. Simmer for 20 minutes or until the liquid is reduced by ⅓. Strain through a sieve; return the liquid to the saucepan. Add the cheese. Cook until the cheese is melted and the sauce coats a spoon, stirring constantly. Add the garlic. Sauce can be stored, covered, in the refrigerator for several days. Reheat gently before tossing with pasta.

YIELD: 2 TO 2½ CUPS

Luciano Pavarotti

Luciano Pavarotti's 1974 recital in Ann Arbor was only the second of his career. At lunch with Carol Wargelin, former University Musical Society artistic administrator, he ordered two steak dinners and devoured both as she made notes on changes in his program for the evening.

Looking up from her notes, she caught him stealing ice cream from her dessert plate. Playing to his undeniable charm, she exacted repayment by asking him to sing a favorite aria. He sang it to her, right there, sotto voce.

Penne Wild and Earthy

1 ounce dried porcini mushrooms or other dried wild
    mushrooms
1 cup warm water
3 tablespoons prosciutto or pancetta
2 tablespoons finely chopped onion
1 tablespoon olive oil
3 tablespoons butter
2 garlic cloves, finely chopped
1 (16-ounce) can chopped plum tomatoes
1 teaspoon finely chopped fresh chile pepper, or to taste
¼ cup sliced pitted kalamata olives
½ teaspoon salt
Freshly ground pepper to taste
16 ounces ribbed penne
A few drops of truffle oil (optional)
Freshly grated Parmesan cheese

Soak the mushrooms in the warm water for 30 minutes.
Remove the mushrooms, reserving the liquid. Rinse the mushrooms
in several changes of fresh water. Chop the mushrooms and set
aside. Strain the soaking liquid through a paper towel-lined sieve
and set aside. Cut the prosciutto into ⅛-inch-thick slices, then into
¼-inch strips.

Sauté the onion in the olive oil and butter in a skillet over
medium heat until golden brown. Add the garlic and prosciutto and
sauté for 1 to 2 minutes. Add the undrained tomatoes, mushrooms,
reserved liquid, chile pepper, olives, salt and pepper and mix well.
Simmer for 40 minutes, stirring occasionally.

Cook the penne in boiling salted water in a stockpot until al
dente; drain well. Combine the pasta and sauce in a bowl and mix
well. Stir in the truffle oil. Serve the Parmesan cheese on the side.

YIELD: 4 SERVINGS

Moroccan Chicken Pasta

4 garlic cloves, minced
2 tablespoons minced fresh
    gingerroot
1 scallion, thinly sliced
1/3 cup chopped cilantro
1/2 cup chopped mint leaves
1/4 cup currants
1/3 cup chicken stock
1/3 cup fresh lemon juice
2 tablespoons honey
1 teaspoon cumin
1 teaspoon curry powder
2 teaspoons paprika
2 teaspoons cornstarch

1 to 2 teaspoons finely chopped
    fresh chile pepper
1/2 cup pine nuts
1 pound boneless skinless
    chicken breasts
8 ounces pasta
Salt to taste
1/4 cup finely chopped onion
2 tablespoons olive oil
1 cup black olives, pitted, cut
    into halves
Freshly ground pepper to taste
1/4 cup chopped fresh parsley
Freshly grated nutmeg to taste

For the sauce, combine the garlic, gingerroot, scallion, cilantro, mint, currants, chicken stock, lemon juice, honey, cumin, curry powder, paprika, cornstarch and chile pepper in a bowl and mix well.

Spread the pine nuts on a baking sheet. Bake at 325 degrees for 10 minutes or until golden brown. Cut the chicken into 1-inch cubes. Combine the chicken and 1/4 cup of the sauce in a bowl and mix well.

Cook the pasta in boiling salted water in a stockpot until al dente. Drain well and keep warm.

Sauté the onion in the olive oil in a skillet over medium heat until golden brown. Increase the heat to medium-high. Add the chicken and sauté until cooked. Add the pine nuts, pasta, olives and remaining sauce and mix well. Cook until heated through. Season with salt and pepper. Remove to a serving dish and sprinkle with parsley and nutmeg. Serve immediately.

YIELD: 4 SERVINGS

Pumpkin Gnocchi with Butter Thyme Sauce

1 (15-ounce) can pumpkin,
    or 1½ pounds pumpkin
    (see Note)
2 tablespoons butter
1¼ cups flour
1 egg
1 egg yolk
Salt and freshly ground
    pepper to taste
1 teaspoon freshly grated
    nutmeg, or to taste
Hot pepper sauce to taste
Boiling water or chicken
    bouillon
Butter Thyme Sauce
Coarsely grated Parmesan
    cheese

Combine the pumpkin and butter in a saucepan. Cook over low heat until the pumpkin has thickened and dried, stirring frequently. Remove from the heat. Add the flour, egg, egg yolk, salt, pepper, nutmeg and hot pepper sauce gradually, mixing until a soft dough forms.

Shape 1 to 1½ teaspoons of the dough into a flat disk with floured hands. Place on a baking sheet and press with a fork to indent. Repeat until there are 10 gnocchi. Drop the gnocchi into boiling water in a large stockpot. Cook until the gnocchi rise to the surface. Remove to a casserole with a slotted spoon. Repeat the process until all the dough is used.

To serve, spoon Butter Thyme Sauce over the gnocchi. Sprinkle with Parmesan cheese and additional pepper.

Note: Fresh pumpkin should be peeled and chopped and cooked in boiling water to cover until tender. Purée the drained pumpkin in a food processor or blender.

YIELD: 4 TO 6 SERVINGS

Butter Thyme Sauce

¼ cup (½ stick) butter
2 tablespoons chopped thyme leaves

Combine the butter and thyme leaves in a saucepan. Simmer over low heat for 1 to 2 minutes.

YIELD: ¼ CUP

146

Cecilia Bartoli's Family Cicche

1⅓ *pounds potatoes, peeled*
2 *quarts water*
3 *teaspoons salt*
3 *quarts water*
⅔ *pound spinach, cooked, drained, squeezed dry*
⅔ *pound ricotta cheese*
1 *egg*
1 *cup (about) flour*
2 *tablespoons extra-virgin olive oil*
Grated Parmesan cheese or tomato sauce

Combine the potatoes, 2 quarts water and 1 teaspoon of the salt in a saucepan. Boil until the potatoes are tender; drain well. Press the potatoes through a ricer and then mash them.

Bring 2 quarts water and 1 teaspoon of the salt to a boil in a stockpot. Mix the potatoes, spinach, ricotta cheese, egg and ½ teaspoon of the salt in a large bowl. Add the flour and mix until a very soft dough forms. Shape some of the dough into small balls and drop into the boiling water. Add the remaining ½ teaspoon salt to the water. Remove and drain the cicche as soon as they rise to the surface. Place the cicche in a very lightly greased shallow baking dish. Repeat the process until all the dough is used.

Drizzle the olive oil over the cicche. Sprinkle with Parmesan cheese or top with tomato sauce. Bake at 350 degrees for 30 minutes.

YIELD: 4 SERVINGS

Cecilia Bartoli, the sensational young Italian mezzo-soprano, visited Dascola's barbershop after her second Ann Arbor recital. Barbers Ernie, Dominic, and Bob Dascola are outspoken Bartoli fans, so Ken Fischer, University Musical Society president and a regular customer, brought her there. Bartoli, delighted to converse in her native tongue, had a warm exchange with the Dascolas, charming them and the fifty or so people who crowded into the downtown shop as word spread. The "Cecilia shrine," complete with autographed pictures, ticket stubs, and even a lock of the singer's thick, dark hair, has amused the barbers' customers—and sold a lot of tickets.

Rice and Grains

1986

Saturday, March 22, 1986, 8 p.m.

Hill Auditorium

A Special Benefit Performance Benny Goodman and His Big Band

Benny Goodman and His Big Band
Blue Room
I Would Do Most Anything for You
Stealin' Apples
Goodbye
Blue Skies
Big John Special
You've Turned the Tables on Me
Let's Dance
Rappin' It Up
Sunrise Serenade
New Kind of Love
My Honey's Lovin' Arms
Sometimes I'm Happy
King Porter Stomp
Devil and the Deep Blue Sea
Don't Be That Way
Stompin' at the Savoy
You've Changed
Ja Da

Opening Act:
James Dapogny's Chicago Jazz Band
Chicago
Benny's Bugle
After Awhile
California, Here I Come
Delta Bound
Sweet Georgia Brown
Love's In My Heart
Mood Indigo
Breezin' Along With the Breeze
Lawd, Lawd
Squareface
Swing, Mr. Charlie

Benny Goodman

WHEN Benny Goodman, the "King of Swing," first played Carnegie Hall in 1938, his band's great trumpet soloist, Harry James, joked that he felt "like a whore in church." Jazz was still not quite legitimate, still shunned by purists and feared by self-appointed protectors of public virtue.

Nearly fifty years later, by the time of this 1986 concert—Benny Goodman's second at Hill Auditorium—jazz had long since been recognized as America's single most important contribution to the world's music. Goodman had brought his clarinet and a sextet in 1976, and the University Musical Society had presented many other jazz greats— among them Duke Ellington, Dave Brubeck, and the Modern Jazz Quartet. Jazz was part of the curriculum of the University of Michigan music school; in fact, the opening act for this concert was Professor James Dapogny's Chicago Jazz Band.

"Goodman set the standard for clarinet playing," Dapogny says. "There hasn't been anyone better."

Goodman was playing professionally at thirteen, and he was only fifteen when he left home to join a dance band. By the time he was twenty, his clarinet playing was already recognized for its trail-blazing, boundary-bashing musicianship. His "hot" notes glided between grief and joy before being released in the dazzling uplift of a swing—a note just barely off the beat.

In 1934, just four years before the historic Carnegie Hall concert, Goodman put together a group that evolved into the classic swing band of the era and brought him fame as a band leader to match his fame as a clarinetist. It consisted of five brass instruments, four saxophones, and four rhythm instruments. As Goodman's band and others grew in popularity during the 1930s and 1940s, they expanded to about eighteen instruments. "There's not a great difference between a thirteen- or fourteen-piece and a seventeen- or eighteen-piece band, but musicians can hear it," Dapogny says. He thinks it significant that for this 1986 UMS concert, Goodman appeared with a smaller band. It was like a recognition of his roots, Dapogny says, "a return to the sort of group with which he made his first big splash."

Goodman's influence endures, evidenced most recently by the revival of swing dancing, often to songs identified with Goodman himself. In the years since his concert, UMS has begun an annual Jazz Directions Series, and the list of artists presented continues to grow. In 1996, Wynton Marsalis and the Lincoln Center Jazz Orchestra came for the first time, returning the following year in the premiere tour of Marsalis's Pulitzer Prize-winning composition, "Blood on the Fields."

What was cooking?

Regional foods were going mainstream, reflected by Jane and Michael Stern's Coast-to-Coast Cookbook: Real American Food, from Yankee Red Flannel Hash and the Ultimate Navajo Taco to Beautiful Swimmer Crab Cakes and the General Store Fudge Pie. Pasta was the food of the decade, and "fusion" cooking, the combination of Japanese and French (and eventually many other) ingredients and methods, was catching on in Los Angeles.

151

Baked Red Wine Risotto

3 cups red wine
4 cups chicken or vegetable stock
1 cup chopped radicchio
1 garlic clove, minced
1/2 cup golden raisins
2 tablespoons olive oil
1/4 teaspoon salt
1/8 teaspoon pepper
1 onion, finely chopped
3 tablespoons butter
2 tablespoons tomato paste
2 cups arborio rice
Salt to taste
1 1/2 cups grated Parmesan cheese
2 tablespoons chopped fresh chives (optional)

Bring the wine to a simmer in a saucepan. Cook until reduced to 2 cups. Combine 1 1/2 cups of the reduced wine with the chicken stock and keep warm. Keep the remaining 1/2 cup wine warm.

Sauté the radicchio, garlic and raisins in the olive oil in a skillet until the radicchio is wilted. Season with 1/4 teaspoon salt and the pepper. Set aside and keep warm.

Sauté the onion in the butter in a skillet until tender. Add the tomato paste and mix well. Add the rice, stirring until each grain is coated. Spoon into a 3-quart casserole. Pour the chicken stock mixture over the rice mixture. Add salt to taste and 3/4 cup of the cheese. Bake, covered, at 375 degrees for 10 minutes. Remove from the oven. Add the radicchio mixture and the reserved 1/2 cup wine and mix well. Bake, covered, for 20 minutes or until the rice is completely cooked and all liquid has been absorbed. Remove from the oven and sprinkle with 3/4 cup cheese and chopped chives.

This risotto is a good accompaniment to veal or chicken, or it can be served as a first course in warm shallow bowls.

YIELD: 8 SERVINGS

Martin Katz's Risotto all'erbe

Martin Katz recalls eating this simple and very tasty dish in Taormina, Sicily. A self-described "risotto freak," he says this is about the best risotto he has ever eaten.

½ cup (1 stick) butter, softened
3½ ounces herbed cream cheese such as boursin, softened
5 cups water
7 ounces fresh spinach
4 cups arugula
7 tablespoons heavy cream
1 cup finely chopped fresh basil
Salt and freshly ground pepper to taste
3 tablespoons vegetable oil
2 tablespoons (¼ stick) butter
2 tablespoons finely chopped shallots or yellow onion
1½ cups arborio rice

Combine ½ cup butter with the cream cheese in a large bowl. Mix well and set aside.

Bring the water to a boil in a large saucepan. Add the spinach and arugula and cook until almost tender. Drain well, reserving the cooking liquid. Coarsely chop the spinach and arugula. Add to the cream cheese mixture and mix well. Place the mixture in the saucepan and add the cream, reserved cooking liquid, basil, salt and pepper. Simmer over very low heat while preparing the rice.

To prepare the rice, heat the oil and 2 tablespoons butter in a saucepan over medium-high heat until the butter is melted. Add the shallots and sauté until translucent. Add the rice, stirring until each grain is coated. Add ½ cup of the simmering vegetable mixture and reduce the heat to medium. Cook until the rice has absorbed all the liquid, stirring constantly. Add another ½ cup of the simmering vegetable mixture. Cook until the rice has absorbed the liquid, stirring constantly. Add ¼ cup of the simmering vegetable mixture. Cook until the rice has absorbed the liquid, stirring constantly. Repeat the process with ¼ cup of the vegetable mixture at a time until the rice cannot absorb any more liquid. The rice should be creamy but not runny. Adjust the seasonings.

YIELD: 4 SERVINGS

Pianist Martin Katz, a member of the University of Michigan music school faculty, has accompanied some of the world's greatest singers in recital all over the world. Because their bodies are their instruments, Katz believes that singers feel particularly vulnerable.

When they first walk onto the Hill Auditorium stage, he says, singers are overwhelmed by the immensity of the 4,200-seat space. When they begin to rehearse their songs, he watches with pleasure as nervousness turns to relief, then amazement. Once they experience Hill's brilliant acoustics, they realize that even their softest notes will reach to the topmost seats of the second balcony.

Michigan Risotto

2 tablespoons (¼ stick) unsalted butter
2 tablespoons olive oil
1 cup coarsely chopped morels or sliced
    wild mushrooms
1 cup asparagus tips
Salt and freshly ground pepper to taste
2 tablespoons (¼ stick) unsalted butter
2 tablespoons olive oil
⅔ cup minced shallots
1 medium onion, minced
1½ cups arborio rice
½ cup dry sherry
2 garlic cloves, minced
5 to 6 cups chicken or vegetable stock, heated
1 cup chopped spinach
½ cup shredded asiago cheese

Heat 2 tablespoons butter and 2 tablespoons olive oil in a small skillet. Add the mushrooms and asparagus tips and sauté for 3 minutes. Season with salt and pepper. Set aside and keep warm.

Heat 2 tablespoons butter and 2 tablespoons olive oil in a large saucepan. Add the shallots and onion. Sauté over medium heat for 5 minutes or until translucent. Stir in the rice and cook until translucent. Stir in the sherry and garlic. Cook until the rice has absorbed all the liquid. Add 1 cup of the chicken stock and cook until the rice has absorbed all the liquid, stirring occasionally. Repeat the process with 1 cup of the chicken stock at a time until the rice cannot absorb any more liquid. Stir in the spinach with the final addition of chicken stock.

Remove from the heat and stir in the mushroom mixture and cheese. Adjust the seasonings.

YIELD: 4 SERVINGS

Malaysian Brown Basmati Rice

1½ tablespoons butter
½ cup finely chopped onion
¼ cup chopped shallots
1 garlic clove, minced
1¼ cups brown basmati rice
2 teaspoons curry powder
1 teaspoon cumin
¼ teaspoon cayenne pepper
2 bay leaves
½ cup currants
Salt and freshly ground black pepper to taste
1½ cups chicken stock
1¾ cups unsweetened coconut milk
½ tablespoon butter
¼ cup sliced almonds or crushed peanuts
¼ cup shredded unsweetened coconut

Heat 1½ tablespoons butter in a heavy Dutch oven over medium heat. Add the onion and shallots and sauté until translucent. Add the garlic and stir briefly. Add the rice, curry powder, cumin, cayenne pepper, bay leaves, currants, salt and black pepper and mix well. Add the chicken stock and coconut milk. Bring to a boil, stirring frequently. Remove from the heat. Bake, covered, at 350 degrees for 45 minutes or just until the rice is tender and all the liquid has been absorbed. Remove from the oven and let stand for 5 to 10 minutes. Remove and discard the bay leaves.

Heat ½ tablespoon butter in a skillet over medium heat. Add the almonds and coconut and sauté until lightly browned. Remove from the heat and stir into the rice mixture.

YIELD: 4 SERVINGS

Microwave Pilaf

2 cups basmati rice
1 cup fresh cilantro leaves
½ cup shredded coconut
1 small jalapeño chile,
    seeded, minced

1 teaspoon cinnamon
¼ teaspoon ground cloves
1 tablespoon vegetable oil
Salt to taste
2½ cups hot water

Rinse the rice under cold running water using package directions. Set aside to drain. Process the cilantro, coconut, jalapeño, cinnamon, cloves and oil in a blender until a thick paste forms. Season with salt. Combine the rice and herb mixture in a 2-quart microwave-safe casserole. Add the hot water; mix well. Microwave, covered, on High for 14 to 16 minutes or until most of the liquid is absorbed. Let stand, covered, for 5 minutes.

Fluff the rice with a fork and serve immediately.

YIELD: 8 SERVINGS

Dilled Rice

¼ cup red wine vinegar
⅔ cup olive oil
⅓ cup corn oil
1 garlic clove, minced
1 tablespoon honey mustard
Salt and freshly ground
    pepper to taste
1 each large red, green, and
    orange bell pepper, cut
    into bite-size pieces

1 medium or large red onion,
    cut into bite-size pieces
1 cup dried cherries
1 cup dried currants
2 cups long grain rice, cooked
2 cups very fresh dill
1 package frozen baby peas,
    thawed (optional)

Mix the vinegar, olive oil, corn oil, garlic, honey mustard, salt and pepper in a bowl. Mix the bell peppers, onion, cherries and currants in a bowl. Place the rice in a large bowl. Mix in the garlic mixture. Mix in the bell pepper mixture and dill. Adjust the seasonings. Spoon into a serving bowl. Sprinkle the peas over the top. Serve with grilled chicken or pork tenderloin and fresh green beans amandine.

YIELD: 10 TO 12 SERVINGS

Victor Vaughan was dean of the medical school from 1890 to 1921 and a longtime member of the University Musical Society board. In his autobiography, A Doctor's Memories, *he acerbically dismisses jazz, the new music of his time:*

"I wish to say that my training in the appreciation of good music has entered so far into my inward self that when I hear jazz, even Whiteman's improved variety, in a hotel dining room, I am either seized with acute indigestion or my proclivity to forceful expression is restrained with difficulty or not at all."

Gingered Citrus Rice

3 tablespoons butter
1 medium onion, finely chopped
2 tablespoons finely chopped shallots
1 cup long grain rice
1 garlic clove, minced
Grated zest of 1 orange
1 tablespoon grated fresh gingerroot
½ cup fresh orange juice
1½ cups chicken broth
3 tablespoons finely chopped parsley
1 teaspoon minced lemon zest (optional)

Melt the butter in a heavy skillet over medium heat. Add the onion and shallots and sauté until tender and golden brown. Add the rice and garlic and sauté until the rice is coated and golden brown. Add the orange zest and gingerroot and sauté for 1 minute.

Stir in the orange juice and chicken broth. Bring to a boil and reduce the heat. Simmer, covered, for 15 to 20 minutes or until all the liquid has been absorbed. Remove to a serving dish and sprinkle with the parsley and lemon zest.

YIELD: 4 SERVINGS

Incan Brown Rice and Beans

⅔ cup long grain brown rice
2 cups chicken stock
2 cups chopped onions
2 large garlic cloves, minced
2 tablespoons vegetable oil
1 to 2 hot chiles, minced
2 teaspoons cumin
2 cups red kidney beans, cooked
½ cup tomato juice
3 tablespoons minced fresh basil, or
    1 tablespoon dried basil
1 tablespoon minced fresh oregano, or
    1 teaspoon dried oregano
2 tablespoons minced fresh parsley
1 cup yogurt or sour cream

Combine the rice and chicken stock in a medium saucepan. Bring to a boil and stir to mix well. Reduce the heat to low. Cook, covered, for 45 minutes; do not uncover the saucepan during cooking. Remove from the heat and let stand, covered, for 5 minutes.

Sauté the onions and garlic in the oil in a skillet for 3 minutes. Add the chiles and cumin and sauté for 2 minutes.

Combine the rice, onion mixture, beans, tomato juice, basil, oregano and parsley in a 2-quart casserole. Bake, covered, at 350 degrees for 20 minutes. Serve with yogurt or sour cream.

YIELD: 4 SERVINGS

Jasmine Rice with Portobello Mushrooms

3 tablespoons canola oil
1 cup chopped red onion
3 garlic cloves, minced
1 tablespoon minced fresh
   gingerroot
2 teaspoons five-spice
   powder
1 pound portobello
   mushroom caps, cut into
   ¾-inch pieces
1½ cups jasmine rice

2½ cups chicken stock
1 cup finely chopped green
   bell pepper
Salt and freshly ground pepper
   to taste
2 tablespoons finely chopped
   cilantro
¼ cup thinly sliced scallions
2 tomatoes, cut into wedges
   (optional)

Heat the oil in a heavy saucepan over medium heat. Add the onion and sauté until translucent. Add the garlic and gingerroot and sauté for 1 minute. Add the five-spice powder and mushrooms and sauté for 2 to 3 minutes. Stir in the rice.

Add the chicken stock and bring to a boil. Reduce the heat to very low. Cook, covered, for 15 minutes or until the rice is tender. Remove from the heat and add the green pepper, salt and pepper. Let stand, covered, for 5 to 10 minutes. Stir in the cilantro and scallions. Serve with the tomato wedges.

YIELD: 6 SERVINGS

Jazz, the new music that gave its name to the 1920s, was considered lowbrow, dangerous, and even evil by many people. In January 1925, The Etude, a magazine about music published in Philadelphia, carried a long essay entitled, "Is Jazz the Pilot of Disaster?" The answer: Yes. "The whole land," it said, "is still in the throes of this form of musical epilepsy."

Quoted at length in the article, a Dr. M. P. Schlapp "of the New York Post Graduate Hospital," claimed that ". . . our emotional instability is the product of immigration, automobiles, jazz, and the movies."

Polynesian Fried Rice

2¼ cups chicken stock
½ cup unsweetened coconut milk
2 tablespoons light soy sauce
1 tablespoon lime juice
1 tablespoon brown sugar (optional)
2 tablespoons curry powder
1 to 2 teaspoons Chinese chili sauce
½ teaspoon salt
½ teaspoon finely chopped lime zest
1½ cups long grain rice
2 tablespoons peanut or vegetable oil
1 tablespoon minced fresh gingerroot
¼ cup raisins
⅓ cup slivered almonds, toasted
2 cups chopped seeded tomatoes
½ cup thinly sliced scallions
½ cup finely chopped green bell pepper
½ cup chopped fresh pineapple
2 tablespoons lime juice

For the sauce, combine the chicken stock, coconut milk, soy sauce, 1 tablespoon lime juice, brown sugar, curry powder, chili sauce, salt and lime zest in a bowl. Mix well and set aside.

Rinse and drain the rice. Heat the oil in a large saucepan over medium heat. Add the gingerroot and sauté for 1 minute. Add the rice and sauce and mix well. Bring to a boil and reduce the heat to very low. Cook, covered, for 20 minutes or until all the liquid has been absorbed. Stir in the raisins, almonds, tomatoes, scallions, green pepper, pineapple and 2 tablespoons lime juice. Serve immediately.

YIELD: 6 SERVINGS

Vegetarian Paella

2 cups chopped onions
1 tablespoon chopped garlic
1 tablespoon olive oil
4 cups rice
8 cups mushroom or vegetable stock
⅛ teaspoon saffron, or to taste
1 tablespoon pepper
½ to 1 cup chopped fresh herbs
2 cups asparagus, cut into bite-size pieces
2 cups julienned leeks
2 cups sliced exotic fresh mushrooms, such as crimini or shiitake
1 cup julienned bell peppers
1 cup julienned radicchio
1 whole head garlic, roasted, separated into cloves
1 cup julienned sun-dried tomatoes
1 cup garbanzo beans, cooked, drained
1 cup red beans, cooked, drained
1 cup black beans, cooked, drained

Sauté the onions and chopped garlic in the olive oil in a skillet until the onions are translucent. Add the rice, stirring until the rice is coated. Add the mushroom stock, saffron, pepper and chopped herbs. Bring to a boil and reduce the heat to low. Cook, covered, until the rice is tender.

Boil the asparagus in water to cover in a saucepan for 30 seconds. Plunge immediately into cold water. Sauté the leeks briefly in a nonstick skillet sprayed with nonstick cooking spray. Remove and keep warm. Sauté the mushrooms, bell peppers and radicchio separately in the skillet. Remove and keep warm.

Combine the rice, asparagus, leeks, mushrooms, bell peppers, radicchio, roasted garlic, sun-dried tomatoes and all the beans in a bowl and toss to mix well. Serve immediately.

YIELD: 8 TO 10 SERVINGS

Peppered Rice, Pork and Tomatillos

2 ancho chiles
1½ cups short grain rice
1 cup finely chopped tomatoes
¼ cup finely chopped onion
2 garlic cloves
1 teaspoon cumin
1 teaspoon rosemary
3 tablespoons vegetable oil
3½ cups chicken broth
8 tomatillos, cored, cut into 8 wedges each
1 teaspoon salt
Freshly ground pepper to taste
1 pound pork tenderloin
¼ cup minced parsley

Combine the ancho chiles with boiling water to cover in a bowl. Let stand for 10 minutes or until softened. Drain, stem and seed the chiles.

Soak the rice in hot water in a bowl for 10 minutes; drain well. Rinse in cold water and drain again.

Purée the tomatoes, onion, garlic, cumin, rosemary and chiles in a blender or food processor. Set aside.

Heat the oil in a large heavy saucepan over medium-high heat. Add the rice. Cook for 5 minutes or until the rice is light golden brown, stirring constantly. Add the puréed tomato mixture and cook for 5 minutes, stirring constantly. Add the chicken broth, tomatillos, salt and pepper. Bring to a boil and reduce the heat to medium. Cook for 20 minutes or until all the liquid has been absorbed.

Place the pork tenderloin in a baking pan. Bake at 425 degrees for 15 minutes or just until cooked through; do not overcook. Cut the pork into 1-inch cubes.

Place the pork cubes directly on the rice in the saucepan. Reduce the heat to very low. Cook, loosely covered, for 5 minutes. Remove from the heat and let stand for 10 to 15 minutes. Stir in the parsley.

YIELD: 6 SERVINGS

During a "Messiah" performance one year, a bat swooped down from the reaches of Hill Auditorium's soaring ceiling, circled and skimmed some heads in the audience, then continued back up, down, and around. Programs fluttered, and a restless murmur grew. Eventually, "the bat was captured in the coat of a brave patron and taken outside," an audience member recalls. Afterward, the soprano soloist said the bat came so close during one recitative that she was almost afraid to open her mouth.

Wild Rice and Snow Peas

2 cups wild rice
4 scallions
2 tablespoons (¼ stick) butter
4 cups chicken broth or consommé
2 tablespoons (¼ stick) butter
8 ounces mushrooms, thinly sliced
1 cup sliced water chestnuts
8 ounces snow peas, trimmed
¼ cup almonds, toasted
Salt and pepper to taste

Rinse the rice in several changes of water. Cut the green stems of the scallions diagonally into 2-inch pieces. Finely chop the white parts.

Sauté the white parts of the scallions in 2 tablespoons butter in a large skillet. Add the rice and stir to mix well. Add the chicken broth. Bring to a boil and reduce the heat. Cook, covered, for 35 to 40 minutes or until the rice is tender and all the liquid has been absorbed.

Heat 2 tablespoons butter in a heavy skillet. Add the scallion stems, mushrooms and water chestnuts. Sauté until the scallion stems and mushrooms are tender.

Boil the snow peas in water to cover in a saucepan for 1 to 2 minutes or just until tender but still very green. Plunge immediately into ice water; drain well.

Add the mushroom mixture to the rice just before serving time. Stir in the snow peas and almonds. Season with salt and pepper.

YIELD: 4 TO 6 SERVINGS

Barley with Herbed Butter

1 cup barley
4 cups chicken, beef or vegetable broth, or water
1 teaspoon salt
½ cup finely chopped onion
½ cup (1 stick) butter
1 teaspoon rubbed sage
1 teaspoon crushed dried rosemary
1 teaspoon crushed dried thyme
⅓ cup chopped parsley
Freshly ground pepper to taste

Rinse and drain the barley. Combine the barley, chicken broth and 1 teaspoon salt in a saucepan. Bring to a boil and reduce the heat to low. Simmer, covered, for 1 hour or until the barley is tender and the liquid has been absorbed. Remove from the heat. Let stand, covered, until needed.

Sauté the onion in the butter in a skillet over medium heat for 5 minutes or until lightly browned. Stir in the sage, rosemary and thyme.

Combine the barley and onion mixture in a bowl and mix well. Stir in the parsley. Season with additional salt and pepper.

YIELD: 4 TO 6 SERVINGS

Black Bean Cakes

½ cup finely chopped red onion
2 to 4 garlic cloves, minced
¼ cup finely chopped red bell pepper
¼ cup finely chopped green bell pepper
2 tablespoons finely chopped seeded poblano chile
1 tablespoon unsalted butter
2 cups drained cooked black beans
2 egg yolks, lightly beaten
1 tablespoon finely chopped fresh cilantro
1 teaspoon hot pepper sauce
1 teaspoon cumin
1 teaspoon crushed dried oregano
1 tablespoon thinly sliced scallions
½ teaspoon freshly ground pepper
1 cup fine dry bread crumbs
2 tablespoons (or more) vegetable oil

Sauté the onion, garlic, bell peppers and poblano chile in the butter in a skillet until tender.

Combine the onion mixture, beans, egg yolks, cilantro, hot pepper sauce, cumin, oregano, scallions and pepper. Add half the bread crumbs and mix well. Shape ¼ of the mixture at a time into ½-inch-thick patties. Coat with the remaining bread crumbs.

Heat the oil in a skillet over medium-high heat. Add the patties and cook for 4 minutes per side or until golden brown and heated through. Add additional oil during cooking if needed. Drain each batch on paper towels and keep warm in a 300-degree oven.

Serve with sour cream, chives and/or salsa.

YIELD: 4 TO 6 SERVINGS

Vladimir Horowitz took long walks around Ann Arbor with Gail Rector, former president of the University Musical Society. Rector remembers that on one campus walk, they entered the beautiful parlor of the Martha Cook Residence for undergraduate women, where a student was playing the grand piano. Horowitz "went to her side, listened for a moment, then motioned to her to move off the bench," Rector recalls. "He sat down and played a few soft chords, then stood up, without comment. I never knew whether that girl knew that she gave up her seat for Horowitz."

Couscous with Dried Fruit and Pistachios

3 cups water
4½ tablespoons olive oil
2 teaspoons salt
1½ (10-ounce) packages couscous
    (about 2¼ cups)
1 cup thinly sliced dried apricots
2¼ teaspoons cinnamon
½ teaspoon allspice
1¼ cups unsalted pistachios, toasted,
    chopped
¾ cup chopped green onions
6 tablespoons thinly sliced fresh basil, or
    ½ teaspoon cumin, or
    ½ teaspoon cardamom
Salt and pepper to taste

Combine the water, olive oil and salt in a medium saucepan and bring to a boil. Combine the couscous, apricots, cinnamon and allspice in a large bowl. Add the boiling water mixture and cover immediately. Let stand for 5 minutes or until the water has been absorbed. Uncover and fluff with a fork. Let stand until cool. At this point the couscous can be stored in the refrigerator for up to 6 hours. Bring to room temperature before proceeding.

Add the pistachios, green onions and basil to the couscous and mix well. Season with salt and pepper.

YIELD: 8 TO 10 SERVINGS

Gorgonzola Polenta

3 cups milk
3 tablespoons unsalted butter
¾ cup cornmeal
3 tablespoons sour cream
2½ tablespoons freshly shredded Gruyère or
    Emmenthaler cheese
2½ tablespoons freshly grated Parmesan
    cheese
½ cup crumbled Gorgonzola cheese
⅓ cup golden raisins, chopped (optional)
Freshly grated nutmeg to taste
Salt and freshly ground pepper to taste
1½ tablespoons finely chopped parsley
Fine bread crumbs

Bring the milk and butter to a boil in a heavy saucepan. Add the cornmeal very gradually, whisking constantly. Bring to a boil, stirring constantly with a wooden spoon. Boil for 5 minutes or until the mixture is very thick and smooth, stirring constantly. Add the sour cream, all the cheese, raisins and nutmeg and beat until smooth. Remove from the heat and season with salt and pepper.

Spoon the mixture into 6 buttered ½-cup custard cups or ramekins. Smooth the tops with a spoon. Let stand for 15 to 20 minutes.

Loosen the mixture from the custard cups and unmold onto a buttered baking dish or platter. Mix the parsley and bread crumbs in a bowl. Sprinkle a thin layer of the bread crumbs over the top of each serving. Bake at 450 degrees for 10 to 12 minutes or until light golden brown. Serve immediately.

YIELD: 6 SERVINGS

Quinoa with Roasted Vegetables

1 red bell pepper, cut into halves lengthwise
1 yellow squash, sliced lengthwise
1 zucchini, sliced lengthwise
1 small eggplant, sliced lengthwise
2 cups vegetable stock or water
1 cup quinoa (see Note)
Juice of 1 lemon
3 tablespoons olive oil
1 teaspoon minced garlic
1 cup coarsely chopped fresh basil
1 tablespoon finely chopped fresh mint
Kosher salt and freshly ground pepper to taste

Seed the red pepper and remove the membranes. Place the red pepper, squash, zucchini and eggplant cut side down on a large baking sheet sprayed with nonstick cooking spray. Prick the eggplant several times with a fork. Bake at 425 degrees for 12 to 20 minutes or until tender. Remove vegetables from the oven as soon as they are done (the smaller vegetables may be done sooner than the larger ones). Let stand until cool enough to handle. Cut into 1-inch pieces.

Bring the vegetable stock almost to a boil in a saucepan. Spread the quinoa in a heavy-bottomed skillet. Cook over medium heat for 5 minutes or until toasted, stirring occasionally. Add the vegetable stock. Bring to a boil and reduce the heat. Simmer, covered, for 12 to 15 minutes or until the quinoa is translucent. Remove from the heat and let stand, covered, for 5 minutes.

Whisk the lemon juice, olive oil, garlic, basil and mint in a bowl until mixed. Add the quinoa and vegetables. Season with kosher salt and pepper. Garnish with sprigs of fresh basil.

Note: Quinoa (pronounced "keen-wah") is a grain similar to rice. It can be found in most health-food stores and many supermarkets.

YIELD: 6 TO 8 SERVINGS

Michael Gowing, head of the University Musical Society box office since 1971, sometimes chauffeurs visiting performers to and from Detroit Metro Airport. During the May Festival in 1980, he picked up violinist Isaac Stern, whose flight was very late. He tore back to Ann Arbor, delivering Stern to the back door of Hill Auditorium fifteen minutes after the concert had begun. A mere ten minutes later, Stern calmly walked onstage to deliver a grand performance of the Beethoven Violin Concerto with the Philadelphia Orchestra under Eugene Ormandy.

Side
Dishes

1988

Saturday, October 29, 1988, 8 p.m.

Hill Auditorium

A Celebration of Leonard Bernstein's 70th Birthday Year and Hill Auditorium's 75th Anniversary

Vienna Philharmonic Orchestra
Leonard Bernstein   *Conductor*

"Leonore" Overture No. 3 in C major, Op. 72   Beethoven

Halil (1981)   Bernstein
Wolfgang Schulz   *Flutist*

Prelude, Fugue, and Riffs (1949) Bernstein
Peter Schmidl   *Clarinetist*

Symphony No. 4 in E minor, Op. 98   Brahms
Allegro non troppo
Andante moderato
Allegro giocoso
Allegro energico e passionata

Leonard Bernstein

THIS gala benefit concert stands out in the long history of the University Musical Society: Leonard Bernstein was back with the Vienna Philharmonic, with which he had forged a rare and empathetic relationship, for an event that galvanized UMS and its audience. It happened through the mutual affection of Bernstein, members of the Vienna orchestra, and the local community.

Bernstein had made six visits to Ann Arbor beginning in 1963, including two concerts with the Vienna Philharmonic in 1984 and two in 1987 with the same marvelous orchestra. He loved Hill Auditorium's superb performing space, and he loved the town, too. He was an ebullient presence, sweeping into post-concert receptions in a white silk scarf, switching languages easily, radiating vitality.

Newly appointed UMS president Ken Fischer knew that in 1988 Bernstein and the orchestra would set out together on an international tour in celebration of the maestro's seventieth birthday. He also knew that of the thirty American cities bidding for the tour, only three would be chosen. He wanted Ann Arbor to be one. But to make it financially viable required unprecedented community support.

And a commitment from Bernstein.

After the second concert in 1987, Fischer found the maestro sitting backstage, relaxing with a Scotch in one hand and a cigarette in the other. To look him in the eye, "I got down on one knee," Fischer recalls, "and I said, 'We want you back next year.'"

Bernstein considered for what seemed an age. Finally he said, "Ken, I love Ann Arbor. I love the people of Ann Arbor. I love this hall. I'll be back."

Fischer's ambitious plan included sales of blocks of premium tickets to supportive area businesses, and gala dinners before the concert. Ticket prices were high for corporate patrons, but there were also $10 tickets, some of them for prime seats, set aside for university students. A long line of students waited for hours for the box office to open, some even sleeping overnight on the steps of Burton Tower. At the concert, "you had this corporate executive in a tux sitting next to a kid in a sweater and khakis," Fischer recalls.

The evening before the concert, students from a high school orchestra hosted a reception in the lobby of the Power Center for the members of the Philharmonic. After enjoying food and drink provided by local merchants, and music provided by the kids, the orchestra members could be seen around town in ones and twos with the students and their families, having dinner at local restaurants and attending local events, including a football game.

The concert surpassed all expectations. One audience member recalls " . . . a chemistry. There are places where a musician goes beyond himself, and for Bernstein, Hill Auditorium was one of those places." In the last work of the evening, Brahms's Fourth Symphony, "he, the orchestra, and the audience were as one."

What was cooking?

Nouvelle cuisine was melded with "fusion cooking," and restaurants offered flamboyant combinations of ingredients from all over the map. James Trager in his Food Chronology *cites a New York City restaurant menu that included grilled lobster with poblano sauce and pierogi filled with crab meat. The influence of Japanese design could be seen in presentations of food so artful that diners were intimidated. Radicchio, arugula, and mesclun appeared even in supermarkets.*

Roasted Asparagus with Mushrooms

1 pound fresh asparagus, trimmed
8 ounces shiitake or button mushrooms,
    cleaned, trimmed
2 teaspoons olive oil
½ teaspoon chopped fresh rosemary, or
    ¼ teaspoon crushed dried rosemary
Freshly ground pepper to taste
Garlic powder (optional)

Place the asparagus spears and mushrooms in a large sealable plastic bag. Drizzle the olive oil over the vegetables. Add the rosemary. Seal the bag and shake gently to coat the vegetables.

Remove the vegetables from the plastic bag and arrange in a single layer on a large baking sheet. Season with pepper and garlic powder.

Bake at 450 degrees for 10 minutes or until the asparagus is tender-crisp.

YIELD: 4 SERVINGS

Hot and Spicy Green Beans

1 teaspoon dark soy sauce
½ teaspoon sugar
½ teaspoon sesame oil
½ teaspoon white vinegar
½ teaspoon sherry
1 teaspoon cornstarch
3 tablespoons water
3 cups peanut oil
1 pound green beans, rinsed, patted dry
2 teaspoons finely chopped fresh gingerroot
2 teaspoons finely chopped garlic
2 small fresh red hot chiles, finely chopped

Combine the soy sauce, sugar, sesame oil, vinegar, sherry, cornstarch and water in a bowl. Mix well and set aside.

Heat a wok over high heat. Add the peanut oil and heat until very hot. Place the green beans in a shallow heatproof strainer and lower gently into the hot oil. Cook for 2 minutes or until the beans soften. Remove with the strainer and drain over a bowl.

Drain all but 1½ tablespoons oil from the wok. Add the gingerroot, garlic and chiles. Stir-fry over high heat for 1 minute. Add the beans and stir-fry for 1 minute.

Make a well in the center of the beans. Stir the soy sauce mixture and pour into the well. Stir to mix well. Cook until the sauce has thickened. Spoon into a serving dish.

YIELD: 4 TO 6 SERVINGS

Glazed Carrots with Pistachios

1 pound carrots, julienned or cut into chunks, or
    1 pound baby carrots
2 to 3 beef bouillon cubes
2 tablespoons brown sugar
2 tablespoons (¼ stick) butter
1 to 1¼ cups chopped pistachios

Combine the carrots and bouillon cubes in a saucepan. Add enough water to cover the carrots by 1 inch. Simmer until the liquid has evaporated.

Add the brown sugar, butter and pistachios and mix well.

YIELD: 3 TO 4 SERVINGS

Carrots Sebastian

1 tablespoon butter
1 tablespoon extra-virgin olive oil
6 to 8 medium carrots, peeled, cut diagonally into ¼-inch slices
1 cup water
¼ cup bourbon, Scotch or Cognac
½ teaspoon salt
Freshly ground pepper to taste
2 tablespoons chopped flat-leaf parsley

Heat the butter and olive oil in a 1½-quart saucepan. Add the carrots and water. Bring to a boil and reduce the heat. Simmer, covered, for 15 minutes or until the carrots are tender.

Remove the saucepan from the heat and add the bourbon. Have a lid at hand to cover the saucepan in the event adding the liquor causes a flare-up. Simmer for 10 minutes or until all the bourbon has evaporated.

Spoon into a warm serving dish. Season with salt and pepper and sprinkle with the parsley.

YIELD: 4 SERVINGS

Among the pleasures of Donald Bryant's twenty-year tenure as director of the Choral Union was conducting the annual "Messiah" performances. There was annual frustration, too, at having to pause after the Sinfonia, the orchestral introduction, and wait while latecomers were seated.

One year Bryant jokingly wished for a dry martini to sip on while he, a keyed-up chorus and orchestra, and a nervous tenor endured the forced interval. At the second performance, he found a note on the podium. "Look down," it read. At the base of the podium, he saw a brown paper bag; inside it, as he discovered while the inevitable latecomers were seated, was a small glass of clear liquid containing an olive.

Backstage at the first intermission, Bryant had a sip of what was indeed a very dry, very warm martini.

Ida Kavafian's Aromatic Armenian Eggplant

"I learned this recipe from my mother, who was the greatest cook I've ever known, bar none," says violinist Ida Kavafian. "I would like to dedicate everyone's enjoyment of this dish to her."

2 firm medium eggplant
Salt to taste
2 garlic cloves, minced
Olive oil
2 fresh tomatoes, chopped
Pepper to taste
1 (8-ounce) can tomato sauce
2 tablespoons balsamic or wine vinegar, or to taste
1 cup plain yogurt or sour cream

Wash the eggplant and peel 3 strips lengthwise down each, creating a striped effect. Cut into ½-inch slices and sprinkle salt on both sides. Drain on paper towels for 45 minutes, turning the slices several times and changing paper towels as needed.

For the sauce, sauté the garlic in olive oil in a medium skillet until light brown. Add the tomatoes. Season with additional salt and pepper. Cook over medium-low heat for 10 minutes. Add the tomato sauce and bring to a boil. Simmer for 8 minutes. Add the vinegar and simmer for 1 to 2 minutes or until the flavors have blended. Let stand until cool.

Arrange the eggplant slices in a single layer in a large broiling pan or on a baking sheet. Brush both sides with olive oil. Cook under a preheated broiler until evenly light to medium brown, turning once. Let stand to cool slightly.

Place a single layer of eggplant on a serving platter. Spoon the yogurt over the top to almost cover each slice. Spoon the sauce over the top to cover completely. Continue adding layers until all the ingredients are used, ending with the sauce.

Serve at room temperature. This recipe can be prepared earlier in the day and kept at room temperature until serving time, or it can be made 1 day ahead and kept in the refrigerator.

YIELD: 6 SERVINGS

Meredith Monk's Szechuan Eggplant

6 cups peeled eggplant

3 tablespoons soy sauce

1 tablespoon sugar, or
½ teaspoon honey

2 tablespoons red pepper
sauce, or to taste

1 to 2 teaspoons vinegar

½ cup cold water

1 tablespoon minced fresh
gingerroot

1 tablespoon minced fresh garlic

6 tablespoons vegetable oil

1 tablespoon cornstarch
(optional)

1 tablespoon water (optional)

Cut the eggplant into 1½x¼x¼-inch pieces. Soak in cold water until needed. Combine the soy sauce, sugar, red pepper sauce, vinegar and ½ cup cold water in a bowl and mix well.

Heat the gingerroot and garlic in the oil in a large skillet or wok. Drain the eggplant and add to the skillet. Cook for 3 minutes. Stir in the soy sauce mixture and mix well. Cook, covered, over low heat for 5 to 6 minutes or until the eggplant is tender. Add ¼ cup water during cooking time if all the liquid has been absorbed. If the sauce is too thin, add a mixture of the cornstarch and 1 tablespoon water. Serve over rice.

YIELD: 3 TO 4 SERVINGS

Benita Valente's Okra Valente

1 pound okra

2 tablespoons olive oil

1 medium sweet onion, cut
into strips lengthwise

2 small garlic cloves, minced

3 firm plum tomatoes, cut into
wedges lengthwise

Salt and pepper to taste

Peel the stem ends of the okra; cut the okra into halves lengthwise. Heat the olive oil in a heavy skillet over medium to medium-high heat. Add the okra and sauté for 2 minutes or just until it begins to brown.

Add the onion, stirring constantly. Sauté until the onion begins to soften. Add the garlic and tomato wedges. Sauté just until the tomatoes are tender but not mushy. Season with salt and pepper.

YIELD: 4 SERVINGS

Benita Valente

Only light food after concerts for many artists: mezzo-soprano Frederica von Stade eats "fresh fruit with a glass of vin," and soprano Barbara Bonney has grilled vegetables and Parma ham with Bordeaux wine. Benita Valente, with a "glass of good wine," likes a cheese-less pizza and a mixed salad.

Others like much more. "No snacks!" says pianist Menahem Pressler, of the Beaux Arts Trio. For him, it must be a "real dinner!" Violinist Leila Josefowicz, whose favorite food is "just about everything," likes "lots of San Pellegrino water for thirst quenching, followed by lots of food!" Violinist Ida Kavafian, too. After a concert, she likes "anything. I'm always starved!"

Portobello Asparagus Grill

1 cup unpeeled garlic cloves
2 pounds Yukon gold or russet potatoes,
   peeled, cut into 1-inch chunks
Salt to taste
1 to 2 tablespoons unsalted butter
1/2 cup (or more) milk
Kosher salt and pepper to taste
16 asparagus spears, trimmed
4 portobello mushroom caps, cleaned
1/4 cup balsamic vinegar
Paprika to taste

For the mashed potatoes, spray the garlic
with nonstick vegetable or olive oil cooking spray.
Arrange the garlic in a single layer on a double
thickness of foil. Fold the foil over the garlic and
seal the edges tightly. Bake at 400 degrees for
40 minutes or until very tender. Let cool and then
squeeze the cloves from their skins.

Boil the potatoes in salted water to cover in a
large saucepan for 10 to 12 minutes or until
tender; drain well. Mash the potatoes, garlic,
butter and milk in a bowl until smooth and
creamy. Season with kosher salt and pepper.

Brush the asparagus and mushroom caps with
vinegar. Let stand for 30 minutes to absorb the
flavors. Spray the vegetables with nonstick
cooking spray or brush with olive oil. Sprinkle
with kosher salt. Grill over hot coals for 5 to 7
minutes for the asparagus and 15 minutes for the
mushroom caps. Grill until the vegetables are
tender and grill marks appear.

Mound the mashed potatoes on upturned
mushroom caps. Arrange 4 asparagus spears in
spoke fashion on top of each serving. Sprinkle
lightly with paprika and garnish with fresh
thyme sprigs.

YIELD: 4 SERVINGS

Marilyn Horne's Holiday Dinner Onions

3 packages boiling onions, peeled
1/2 cup (1 stick) butter
1 teaspoon thyme, or to taste
1 teaspoon sugar
2 cups beef or chicken bouillon
Salt and pepper to taste

Sauté the onions in the butter in a skillet until
brown on all sides, turning frequently.

Add the thyme, sugar and bouillon to the
skillet. Simmer for 20 minutes or until the onions
are tender. Season with salt and pepper.

YIELD: 6 TO 8 SERVINGS

Potato Fans

6 baking potatoes, peeled
1/4 cup (1/2 stick) butter
1/4 cup olive oil
Paprika to taste
Salt and pepper to taste

Slice each potato at 1/3-inch intervals to within
1/2 inch of the bottom. Place the potatoes in a
nonstick baking dish sprayed with nonstick olive
oil cooking spray.

Melt the butter in a saucepan. Add the olive oil
and mix well. Drizzle over the potatoes.

Bake at 350 degrees for 50 minutes, basting
frequently with a bulb baster. The potatoes will
fan out as they bake. Remove from the oven and
sprinkle with paprika. Bake for 10 minutes longer.
Season with salt and pepper.

YIELD: 6 SERVINGS

Norwegian Temptation

28 anchovy fillets
12 large potatoes
4 large sweet onions, thinly
    sliced
5 garlic cloves, minced
¼ cup chopped fresh
    dillweed (optional)

⅓ cup butter
2 cups heavy cream
1 cup milk
½ teaspoon pepper

Rinse and drain the anchovies, reserving the oil. Scrub the unpeeled potatoes and cut into narrow strips as for French fries. Layer the potatoes, onions, garlic and anchovies in a buttered shallow baking dish. Sprinkle with the dillweed. Dot with the butter and reserved oil.

Bake at 350 degrees for 15 minutes. Remove from the oven. Mix the cream and milk in a 4-cup measuring cup. Pour ⅓ of the milk mixture over the baked layers. Bake for 15 minutes longer and add another ⅓ of the milk mixture. Repeat the process one more time, baking until the potatoes are tender. Place under the broiler to brown just before serving time.

YIELD: 8 TO 12 SERVINGS

Florentine Potatoes

1 (10-ounce) package frozen
    chopped spinach
6 cups mashed cooked
    potatoes
½ cup grated Parmesan
    cheese

1 cup sour cream
½ teaspoon salt
½ teaspoon pepper
3 egg yolks, beaten
5 egg whites, beaten
Grated Parmesan cheese

Cook the spinach using the package directions and drain well. Combine the spinach, mashed potatoes, ½ cup cheese, sour cream, salt and pepper in a bowl and mix well. Add the egg yolks and mix well. Fold in the egg whites.

Spoon the mixture into a soufflé dish. Bake at 350 degrees for 1 hour. Sprinkle with additional cheese.

YIELD: 8 SERVINGS

173

Marilyn Horne

"When people think of fall in Ann Arbor," one dedicated concert-goer says, "they think football. I love the games, too—the crowds, the tailgates, the band, all the trimmings. But fall means the start of the concert season, too. For me, nothing beats the thrill of heading toward Hill Auditorium on a beautiful, clear October or November evening—crisp leaves underfoot, lights twinkling in the windows of the League and the Alumni Center. Coming closer, you glimpse orchestra members milling around outside the stage doors. With the crowd, you go inside and take your seat in that gorgeous space and just wait for the magic to begin."

Potato, Onion and Goat Cheese Gratin

2 tablespoons olive oil
2 pounds medium onions (about 7), cut into
    halves lengthwise, thinly sliced crosswise
2 teaspoons minced fresh thyme, or
    1/4 teaspoon crumbled dried thyme
Salt and pepper to taste
2 1/2 pounds large red potatoes, peeled, cut
    crosswise into 1/4-inch slices
8 ounces chilled soft mild goat cheese,
    crumbled
1 1/2 tablespoons cold unsalted butter,
    cut into pieces
1 cup whole milk or skim milk

Heat the olive oil in a heavy 5- or 6-quart stockpot over medium heat until hot but not smoking. Add the onions, thyme, salt and pepper. Cook for 15 minutes or until golden brown, stirring frequently; reduce the heat if needed so that the onions don't burn.

Combine the potatoes with boiling salted water to cover in a saucepan. Boil for 5 minutes; drain well.

Arrange half the potato slices in a slightly overlapping layer in a lightly oiled 2 1/2-quart gratin dish or shallow baking dish. Season generously with salt and pepper. Cover with the onions and spread the goat cheese over the top. Arrange the remaining potatoes over the onions. At this point, the dish may be set aside and kept at room temperature for up to 2 hours. Dot with the butter. Pour the milk over the top.

Bake at 425 degrees for 35 minutes or until the potatoes are tender and the top is golden brown.

YIELD: 8 SERVINGS AS A SIDE DISH
4 TO 6 SERVINGS AS AN ENTRÉE

James Galway's Colcannon

This traditional Irish dish is sometimes called Bubble and Squeak.

2 pounds white potatoes, peeled, cut into
    1 1/2-inch pieces
2 bunches scallions, white parts only
1 small green cabbage, cored, cut into
    1-inch chunks
1/2 cup heated milk or half-and-half
1/4 to 1/2 cup (1/2 to 1 stick) butter, softened
Salt and pepper to taste

Combine the potatoes with cold water to cover in a saucepan. Top with the scallions and cabbage. Simmer, covered, until the potatoes are tender; drain well.

Return the potato mixture to the saucepan. Cook over low heat, mashing with a potato masher until coarse. Add the milk and butter and mix well. Season with salt and pepper.

YIELD: 6 TO 8 SERVINGS

Grilled Potato Planks

4 medium potatoes (about 1½ pounds), scrubbed
Salt to taste
6 tablespoons extra-virgin olive oil
1½ tablespoons white wine vinegar
2 garlic cloves, peeled, minced
1 teaspoon marjoram, oregano or dillweed
½ teaspoon hot pepper sauce, or to taste
½ teaspoon kosher salt, or to taste
Freshly ground pepper to taste

Cut the potatoes lengthwise into ⅓-inch slices. Combine the potato slices with lightly salted water to cover in a saucepan. Cover and bring to a boil. Boil for 5 minutes or until almost tender. Remove the potatoes to a shallow baking dish.

Combine the olive oil, vinegar, garlic, marjoram, hot pepper sauce, kosher salt and pepper in a small bowl or glass measuring cup and mix well. Pour over the potato slices, turning to coat well. Marinate, covered, at room temperature for 30 minutes.

Remove the potatoes from the marinade and brush with some of the remaining marinade. Be sure to include bits of the garlic and herbs. Place the potatoes on a lightly oiled grill 4 to 6 inches from medium-hot coals. Grill for 6 to 7 minutes per side or until light brown. Serve with additional hot pepper sauce and catsup.

YIELD: 4 SERVINGS

Flutist James Galway made his Ann Arbor debut in 1978 in the intimate Rackham Auditorium with the New Irish Chamber Orchestra. One audience member recalls Galway's roguishness that evening. "If you hadn't been struck by how pretty the concertmistress of the New Irish Chamber Orchestra was, you couldn't help noticing when Galway, during long rests, turned away from the conductor to stare at her."

Like all performers at Rackham, Galway had to cope with a peculiarity of the auditorium: to leave the stage, an artist uses a nearly invisible knobless door in the back wall, which must be opened from the other side by an alert staff member. Galway waited a few moments before the closed door. When nothing happened, "he rapped on it, as if trying to gain admittance to an after-hours club."

Moroccan Sweet Potatoes

1/8 teaspoon saffron
2 tablespoons hot water
2 (1-pound) sweet potatoes
1/4 cup (1/2 stick) unsalted butter
1 tablespoon vegetable oil
1 tablespoon minced fresh gingerroot
1/2 teaspoon cinnamon
Salt and pepper to taste
1 tablespoon minced parsley

Soak the saffron in the hot water. Peel the sweet potatoes and cut each into 8 pieces.

Combine the sweet potatoes, undrained saffron, butter, oil, gingerroot, cinnamon, salt and pepper in a saucepan. Cook over medium heat until the butter is melted, stirring frequently. Reduce the heat to low. Simmer, covered, for 20 minutes, stirring occasionally. Simmer, uncovered, until the sweet potatoes begin to fall apart and the sauce is syrupy. Spoon into a serving dish and sprinkle with the parsley.

YIELD: 4 SERVINGS

Tomato, Basil and Mozzarella Kabobs

1 thick loaf dry French or Italian bread
1 pound semi-firm mozzarella cheese
6 firm plum tomatoes
1 bunch fresh basil
5 tablespoons olive oil
Sea salt and freshly ground pepper to taste
1/2 cup (1 stick) unsalted butter
2 garlic cloves, minced
1 (2-ounce) can anchovies, drained, minced

Cut the bread into sixteen 1/2-inch-thick rounds. Cut the cheese into twelve 1/2-inch-thick slices. Cut the tomatoes into halves lengthwise. Separate the basil leaves from the stems, reserving 24 of the largest leaves for the kabobs. Discard the remaining basil or reserve for another use.

Thread 1 slice of bread, 1 basil leaf, 1 cheese slice, 1 basil leaf and 1 tomato half onto each of four 12-inch metal skewers, pressing the ingredients together firmly. Repeat the process until each kabob contains 4 bread slices, 6 basil leaves, 3 slices mozzarella and 3 tomato halves. Drizzle each with 1 tablespoon of the olive oil. Season with salt and pepper.

Heat the butter and remaining 1 tablespoon olive oil in a small skillet over medium heat until the butter is melted. Add the garlic and sauté for 1 minute or until fragrant. Add the anchovies and sauté for 1 minute. Keep warm over very low heat.

Place the kabobs in the center of the grill rack. Grill for 3 minutes per side or until the bread is toasted and the cheese is somewhat melted.

Place the kabobs on serving plates and drizzle generously with the warm anchovy mixture. Serve immediately.

YIELD: 4 SERVINGS

Baked Cherry Tomatoes with Herbs

2 pints small cherry tomatoes
¼ cup minced onion
2 garlic cloves, minced
½ cup chopped parsley
¼ teaspoon thyme
½ cup soft bread crumbs
½ teaspoon salt
Pepper to taste
¼ cup olive oil

Arrange the tomatoes in a single layer in a flat baking dish. Mix the onion, garlic, parsley, thyme, bread crumbs, salt, pepper and olive oil in a bowl. Sprinkle over the tomatoes.

Bake at 425 degrees for 6 to 8 minutes or until the tomatoes are tender.

YIELD: 6 TO 8 SERVINGS

Minted Zucchini

6 small zucchini
½ cup olive oil
2 garlic cloves, minced
2 teaspoons coarsely chopped mint leaves
Salt and freshly ground pepper to taste
½ cup red wine vinegar

Cut the zucchini lengthwise into ¼-inch-thick slices. Cook the zucchini slices in the olive oil in a skillet until browned. Remove from the skillet and drain on paper towels.

Place the drained zucchini in a shallow serving dish. Sprinkle with garlic and mint. Season with salt and pepper.

Bring the vinegar to a boil in a saucepan. Pour over the zucchini. Let stand until cool. Chill, covered, overnight. Serve at room temperature.

YIELD: 6 SERVINGS

"Food is extremely important to most musicians," says British cellist Steven Isserlis. His day-of-concert routine: "At lunch time I generally stuff myself with a steak or some lamb. This makes me feel quite slow and heavy, and I fall into a slumber, emerging (theoretically, at least) fit and fighting for the evening (fit for nothing and fighting for breath, that is). Then after the concert (usually after an anxious search for a restaurant that is still serving), I tend to eat chicken, pasta, or fish, the spicier the better. Sometimes it will be accompanied with some red wine or, on very special occasions, a margarita. Mmm."

177

Vegetable Gratin

2 medium onions, chopped
Salt and pepper to taste
2 teaspoons olive oil
1 large red bell pepper, cut into 1-inch pieces
1 (1-pound) eggplant, cut into 1-inch pieces
3/4 teaspoon herbes de Provence, or to taste
1 (14-ounce) can tomatoes, drained, chopped
3 garlic cloves, minced
2 teaspoons minced fresh basil
1 teaspoon tomato paste
1 pound fresh tomatoes, seeded, cut into
    1/8-inch slices
1 1/2 pounds zucchini, cut diagonally into
    1/8-inch slices
2 teaspoons olive oil
3/4 teaspoon herbes de Provence, or to taste
2 teaspoons freshly grated Parmesan cheese,
    or to taste

Combine the onions, salt, pepper and
2 teaspoons olive oil in a saucepan. Cook until
golden brown. Add the red pepper, eggplant and
3/4 teaspoon herbes de Provence. Cook until the
vegetables are tender, stirring occasionally.

Add the canned tomatoes and garlic. Simmer
for 5 minutes. Increase the heat to medium-high.
Cook until the liquid has evaporated, stirring
constantly. Stir in the basil and tomato paste.
Spoon into a shallow 9x13-inch baking dish.
Arrange the fresh tomato and zucchini slices
in alternate rows over the top. Brush with
2 teaspoons olive oil. Sprinkle with 3/4 teaspoon
herbes de Provence and the cheese.

Bake at 400 degrees for 30 minutes or until the
zucchini is tender. Broil 4 inches from the heat
source until golden brown.

YIELD: 6 SERVINGS

Warm Vegetable Salad

2 tablespoons olive oil
1 tablespoon lemon juice
1 teaspoon fresh oregano, or 1/2 teaspoon
    dried oregano
Salt and freshly ground pepper to taste
3 large potatoes, peeled or unpeeled, cut into
    1-inch chunks
4 large carrots, peeled, cut diagonally into
    1/4-inch slices
Florets of 1 3/4 pounds broccoli, cut into
    bite-size pieces
2 tablespoons chopped parsley

For the dressing, combine the olive oil, lemon
juice, oregano, salt and pepper in a bowl. Mix well
and set aside.

Combine the potatoes with lightly salted water
to cover in a saucepan. Bring to a boil. Cook,
covered, over medium-low heat for 5 minutes. Add
the carrots and return to a boil. Cook, covered,
over medium heat for 15 minutes. Add the
broccoli. Add additional hot water if needed and
return to a boil. Cook, uncovered, for 4 minutes or
until the vegetables are tender; drain well.

Spoon the vegetables into a bowl. Add the
dressing and mix gently. Adjust the seasonings.
Sprinkle with the parsley just before serving time.
Serve warm or at room temperature.

YIELD: 4 SERVINGS

Grilled Herb-Marinated Vegetables

5 tablespoons balsamic vinegar
1 tablespoon Dijon mustard
¼ cup olive oil
3 tablespoons minced fresh thyme
2 teaspoons salt
Freshly ground pepper to taste
2 medium red potatoes, sliced
1 medium onion, cut into ½-inch slices
6 to 7 scallions, trimmed
6 carrots, trimmed
3 small or medium eggplant, cut into halves lengthwise
1 red bell pepper, seeded, cut into quarters
1 green bell pepper, seeded, cut into quarters
2 to 3 green or yellow zucchini, cut into halves lengthwise

For the marinade, combine the vinegar and Dijon mustard in a small bowl and whisk until blended. Add the olive oil gradually, whisking constantly until emulsified. Season with the thyme, salt and pepper and set aside.

Combine the potatoes with boiling water to cover in a saucepan. Boil briefly, then plunge into cold water. Drain well. Combine the potatoes, onion, scallions, carrots, eggplant, bell peppers and zucchini in a large glass or ceramic bowl and toss well. Add the marinade and mix well. Marinate, covered, for 15 to 60 minutes, stirring several times.

Place the vegetables on a grill rack sprayed with nonstick cooking spray. Grill for 20 to 30 minutes or until tender, turning 1 to 2 times. Serve hot or at room temperature. The vegetables can instead be baked at 350 degrees for 30 to 40 minutes.

YIELD: 4 TO 6 SERVINGS

Yo-Yo Ma

University Musical Society president Ken Fischer and his wife, Penny, invited some music students to their home. "We were chatting about musicians," recalls Nancy Skinner-Oclander, a student mentor at the time. "Ken asked us for suggestions about which artists he should invite to perform. When her turn came, a student shyly suggested Yo-Yo Ma.

"Ken said, 'Great idea! I'll call him right now!' He went to the phone and dialed, and we heard him say, 'Hey, Yo, my man, what's up?'

"Everyone there believed he was talking to Yo-Yo Ma. In reality, he had signed the formidable cellist many weeks before. It was announced the next day. But for one wonderful day, we all thought that Ken had called Yo-Yo Ma and invited him just for us."

Accompaniments

1991

Tuesday, April 30, 1991, 8 p.m.

Hill Auditorium

A Benefit Concert for the University Musical Society

Metropolitan Opera Orchestra
James Levine   *Artistic Director and Conductor*
Jessye Norman   *Soprano*

Three Pieces for Orchestra, Op. 6   Berg
*Präludum: Langsam
Reigen: Anfangs etwas zögernd—
Leicht beschwingt
Marsch: Mässiges Marschtempo*

La Mort de Cléopâtre   Berlioz
*scène lyrique for Soprano
and Orchestra*

*Allegro vivace con impeto—Recitativo
Lento cantabile—Recitativo—Meditation
Largo misterioso—Allegro assai agitato
Moderato—Recitativo misurato*
Jessye Norman

A Siegfried Idyll   Wagner

*Immolation Scene,
from* **Götterdämmerung   Wagner**
Miss Norman

James Levine and Jessye Norman

JESSYE Norman and James Levine are linked as friends and as musical soul-mates. The celebrated soprano has written of Levine, conductor and artistic director of the Metropolitan Opera Orchestra, that he "lifts music-making far beyond the carelessness of routine to a plane where art, creativity, and soul meet and intertwine. I love him."

In the same book (*Dialogues and Discoveries*, a 1998 biography of Levine by Robert C. Marsh), the conductor says, "I'm surrounded with people who are literally indispensable to my artistic life and vision. Jessye Norman arrived [at the Met] in 1983. How could I live without her today?"

Until the benefit concert on April 30, 1991, Levine had not appeared elbow-to-elbow with Norman and the Metropolitan Opera Orchestra outside New York City. This was the very first concert of the orchestra's first tour on the stage rather than beneath it. Opera orchestras are "pit orchestras," rarely expected to achieve the level of perfection required of the national concert stage. Although the Met Orchestra's history of concerts at home goes back to the early 1900s, it was on this April night that Levine confirmed the Metropolitan Opera Orchestra as the equal of the world's great orchestras with a national concert tour that has since become an annual event.

Levine's touring premiere was also a Jessye Norman homecoming. In the late 1960s, she was a voice student in the University of Michigan master's program. From there she was whisked away to stardom, first in Europe, then in the United States. But she has retained her ties to Ann Arbor, returning to perform, to receive an honorary university doctorate, and to be presented with the Distinguished Artist Award at the 1997 Ford Honors Program.

"She has a special relationship with Hill Auditorium and with Ann Arbor," says Michael Kondziolka, UMS programming director. "She gives that extra something special. [For this concert] she wore a lilac, floor-length, silk jacquard, jewel-encrusted caftan. She was magnificent. She sang 'La Mort de Cléopâtre' by Berlioz and the Immolation Scene from 'Götterdämmerung.' It transcended expectation."

Norman's bearing, dress, and emotive force are counterparts to a powerful voice of great range and sensitivity. Glowing adjectives are applied to her like jewels to her gowns: character adjectives like regal and dramatic; texture adjectives like velvety, creamy, and satiny; and color adjectives like ruby-red, golden, and richly hued. The sum is vocal grandeur. Yet despite the glorious scale, says Kondziolka, she made every-one at the 1991 concert feel that she sang only to them. "It by-passed my mind," one concert-goer recalls. "It went straight to my heart."

What was cooking?

For the first time, salsa outsold catsup, as "ethnic" foods became increasingly commonplace. Raymond Sokolov, in his book Why We Eat What We Eat, *says of this trend, "The manipulation of local ingredients with culinary ideas inherited from many national pasts is a sensible extension of the notion of the melting pot— and an intrinsically American way to go."*

Apple Cilantro Chutney

2 apples, peeled, cored, chopped
3 tablespoons olive oil
3 cups loosely packed cilantro, chopped
1/3 cup sliced almonds, toasted
Juice and grated zest of 1 orange
Juice and grated zest of 1 lemon
2 tablespoons grated fresh gingerroot
1/8 teaspoon salt, or to taste
1/8 teaspoon pepper, or to taste

Sauté the apples in the olive oil in a heavy stainless steel skillet. Add the cilantro, almonds, orange juice, orange zest, lemon juice, lemon zest, gingerroot, salt and pepper and mix well. Simmer, covered, over low heat for 15 minutes or until the apples are tender. Add a small amount of water if the mixture becomes too dry.

YIELD: 2 TO 3 CUPS

Dried Cherry Chutney

4 cups dried cherries
4 cups water
1 cup red wine vinegar
1/2 cup packed brown sugar
1/2 cup molasses
1/4 cup chopped garlic
1 bay leaf
2 whole cloves, ground
1/2 teaspoon hot chile pods
1 tablespoon green peppercorns
1 teaspoon cinnamon
1/2 teaspoon nutmeg
1 teaspoon salt
1/2 teaspoon freshly ground white pepper

Combine the cherries, water, vinegar, brown sugar, molasses, garlic, bay leaf, cloves, chile pods, peppercorns, cinnamon, nutmeg, salt and white pepper in a heavy 2-quart saucepan. Cook, covered, for 30 minutes, stirring every 10 minutes. Cook, uncovered, for 30 minutes or until the mixture is the consistency of a light jam. Remove and discard the bay leaf.

YIELD: 1 QUART

Red Cabbage and Beet Relish

1 tablespoon olive oil
4 cups finely shredded cabbage
1/4 cup water
8 to 10 medium beets, cooked, grated
3 garlic cloves, minced
1/2 cup white vinegar or lemon juice, or
    to taste
1/4 cup sugar
6 tablespoons currant jelly
1 teaspoon salt
1/2 teaspoon coarsely ground pepper
1/4 cup golden raisins (optional)

Heat the olive oil in a 3-quart saucepan. Add the cabbage and cook until wilted, adding the water if needed. Add the beets and garlic and cook for several minutes. Add the vinegar and cook for 1 to 2 minutes. Add the sugar and jelly, stirring until the sugar is dissolved and the jelly is melted. Add the salt, pepper and raisins. Adjust the seasonings. Serve hot or cold. Serve with game, roast pork or grilled chicken.

YIELD: 6 SERVINGS

Gremolata

Grated zest of ½ lemon
1 garlic clove, finely chopped
1 cup loosely packed chopped fresh parsley

Combine the lemon zest, garlic and parsley in a bowl and mix well. Sprinkle over dishes such as Osso Buco (page 130) or use as a topping with fish or pasta.

YIELD: 1 CUP

Fig Relish

1 (8-ounce) Anjou or Bartlett pear, peeled, cored, finely chopped
⅓ cup packed brown sugar
⅓ cup red wine vinegar
1½ cups dried figs, stems removed, cut into quarters
¾ cup dried cranberries or raisins
¾ cup vegetable broth
⅛ teaspoon pepper
⅛ teaspoon cinnamon
⅛ teaspoon freshly ground nutmeg
4 teaspoons marsala
¼ cup thinly sliced green onions

Combine the pear, brown sugar and vinegar in a wide nonstick skillet. Add the figs, cranberries, vegetable broth, pepper, cinnamon and nutmeg and mix well. Bring to a boil over medium heat. Cook for 20 minutes or until the mixture has thickened and most of the liquid has evaporated, stirring frequently. Remove from the heat. Stir in the wine and green onions.

YIELD: 4 CUPS

Music archivist Richard LeSueur still remembers the date: July 10, 1967. Then a student in the University of Michigan music school, he was walking the hallway looking for an empty practice room when he heard a soprano voice that stopped him in place. "It was like no faculty or student voice I had heard at the university," recalls LeSueur. "I knocked on the door and said to the woman who opened it, 'Hello, I'm Richard LeSueur, and I have to get to know you.'" The student singer who opened the door was Jessye Norman, and thirty-some years later, the two are still friends.

Pesto Italiano

3 garlic cloves
1/2 cup pine nuts
6 bunches fresh basil, leaves only
3/4 to 1 cup olive oil
8 ounces Parmesan cheese, finely grated

Mince the garlic in a food processor. Add the pine nuts and process until coarsely chopped. Add the basil and process briefly. Stir in 6 to 8 tablespoons of the olive oil. Stir in the cheese and enough of the remaining olive oil to make of the desired consistency. Serve immediately over hot pasta or gnocchi. This pesto can be prepared ahead up through adding the basil. Pour into an airtight jar and cover completely with olive oil before sealing the jar. Stir in the cheese and remaining olive oil at serving time.

YIELD: 1⅛ CUPS

Marinated Artichoke and Roasted Red Pepper Pesto

1/2 cup marinated artichoke hearts, drained,
    coarsely chopped
1/2 cup coarsely chopped roasted red pepper
    (see page 39)
1/4 cup olive oil
2 cups Great Northern beans, cooked, drained
1/3 cup capers, rinsed, drained
4 garlic cloves, peeled, trimmed, coarsely
    chopped
1/4 cup packed minced fresh flat-leaf parsley
    or cilantro
1 teaspoon lemon juice
1 teaspoon salt, or to taste
1 teaspoon freshly ground pepper, or to taste

Combine the artichoke hearts, red pepper, olive oil, beans, capers, garlic, parsley, lemon juice, salt and pepper in a food processor container fitted with a metal blade or in a bowl and mix well. Adjust the seasonings. This pesto can be stored, covered, in the refrigerator for up to 5 days or frozen for 6 months. Serve with crackers or thinly sliced baguettes.

YIELD: 2 CUPS

Quick Choron Sauce

2 cups mayonnaise
1/4 cup tomato paste
1/4 cup (about) white wine
1 teaspoon salt
1/2 teaspoon freshly ground pepper
1 tablespoon chopped fresh tarragon, or
    1/2 teaspoon dried tarragon
2 garlic cloves, minced or pressed (optional)

Combine the mayonnaise, tomato paste, wine, salt, pepper, tarragon and garlic in a bowl and mix well. If the sauce is too thick, add 1 tablespoonful of wine at a time until of the desired consistency.

YIELD: 2 CUPS

Dill Sauce

1 cup yogurt
1 tablespoon Dijon mustard
1 cup mayonnaise
1 tablespoon fresh lemon juice
½ cup chopped fresh dillweed

Combine the yogurt, Dijon mustard, mayonnaise, lemon juice and dillweed in a bowl and mix well.

YIELD: 2 CUPS

Aïoli

1 thick slice French bread or
    other hearty bread, crust
    trimmed
3 tablespoons milk
4 to 6 garlic cloves, peeled
2 egg yolks (see Note)
1 cup olive oil
2 tablespoons (or more) fresh
    lemon juice
Salt and pepper to taste

Soak the bread in the milk in a bowl for 10 minutes; drain well. Wrap the bread in a clean towel and squeeze to remove the excess moisture.

Combine the bread and garlic in a blender and process for 10 seconds or until of a paste consistency. Add the egg yolks with the food processor running. Process for 10 seconds or until thick. Add the olive oil very gradually with the food processor running. Process until all the olive oil has been added and the mixture is thick and creamy. Add the lemon juice and process for several seconds or until mixed. Spoon into a bowl and add salt and pepper. Add additional lemon juice if desired.

Note: Some recipes call for using raw egg yolks, which is inadvisable from a health standpoint. The following method will allow the yolk to reach a temperature of 200 degrees without fully cooking it. Combine 1 egg yolk with 1 tablespoon lemon juice or vinegar and 1 tablespoon water in a bowl and whisk until mixed. Microwave, covered, on High for 30 seconds or until the mixture begins to rise. Microwave for 5 seconds longer and beat with a clean whisk until smooth. Microwave for 10 seconds longer or until the mixture rises a second time. Beat well. The mixture should be at 200 degrees at this point. Let stand, covered, for 1 minute before using.

YIELD: 1½ CUPS

In the first "Guitar Summit" a few years ago, Paco Peña (flamenco), Pepe Romero (classical), and Leo Kottke (folk) came together in a rare joint concert. The self-taught Kottke remarked that he felt insecure onstage with two of the world's greatest guitarists. But, he said, he could do one thing better than they: play slide guitar. He demonstrated with breathtaking slide work.

For the final encore of the evening, the three guitarists returned to play together. While Leo Kottke's head was turned, Romero whipped two guitar slides out of his sock (Peña wasn't wearing socks), and the two began playing slide guitar, quite badly. Kottke and a surprised audience loved it.

Rémoulade Sauce

1 cup mayonnaise
2 tablespoons Dijon mustard
1 tablespoon small capers, drained
1 tablespoon chopped gherkins
2 anchovies, drained, minced
1 tablespoon chopped fresh tarragon

Combine the mayonnaise, Dijon mustard, capers, pickles, anchovies and tarragon in a bowl and mix well. Other fresh herbs can be substituted for the tarragon.

YIELD: 1½ CUPS

Wasabi Sauce

2 tablespoons (or more) powdered wasabi
   (see Note)
2 tablespoons (or more) water
1 cup mayonnaise or yogurt
½ teaspoon salt
Chopped fresh cilantro

Blend the wasabi powder and water in a small bowl. Combine the mayonnaise, wasabi mixture, salt and cilantro in a large bowl and mix well. Add a few drops of green food coloring if desired.

Note: Wasabi is a Japanese horseradish. It is available in Japanese markets and in some supermarkets.

YIELD: 1 CUP

Salsa del Sol

1 large onion, cut into 8 wedges
1 tablespoon olive oil
1 teaspoon sugar
Salt and pepper to taste
2 cups chopped seeded tomatoes
⅓ cup chopped pitted green olives
⅓ cup chopped pitted Greek olives,
   such as kalamata
3 tablespoons chopped fresh basil
1 tablespoon capers, drained
2 teaspoons red wine vinegar
1 teaspoon anchovy paste
1 tablespoon olive oil

Place the onion wedges on a baking sheet. Brush with 1 tablespoon olive oil. Sprinkle with the sugar and season with salt and pepper. Bake at 450 degrees for 30 minutes or until golden brown, turning occasionally.

Combine the tomatoes, all the olives, basil, capers, vinegar and anchovy paste in a large bowl and mix well. Chop the baked onion. Stir the onion and 1 tablespoon olive oil into the tomato mixture. Adjust the seasonings. This salsa can be prepared 1 day ahead and stored, covered, in the refrigerator. Bring to room temperature before using. Serve with grilled halibut steaks, pork chops or sliced eggplant.

YIELD: 3 TO 4 CUPS

Island Salsa

1 cup chopped peeled pineapple
1 cup chopped peeled mango
1 cup chopped yellow or red bell pepper
⅔ cup chopped peeled kiwifruit
½ cup finely chopped red onion
¼ cup finely chopped fresh cilantro
1 teaspoon fresh lime juice
½ teaspoon minced serrano chile with seeds
Salt and white pepper to taste

Combine the pineapple, mango, bell pepper, kiwifruit, onion, cilantro, lime juice and serrano chile in a bowl and mix well. Season with salt and white pepper. This salsa can be prepared up to 3 hours ahead. Serve with lavash crackers or over grilled chicken.

YIELD: 4 CUPS

Roasted Red Pepper and Garlic Salsa

2 red bell peppers
2 large garlic cloves
Olive oil
1 pound tomatoes, peeled
1 jalapeño chile
1 hot banana chile
1 small red onion
1 teaspoon salt
½ teaspoon cumin

Place the bell peppers and garlic on a baking sheet. Cover the garlic lightly with olive oil. Bake at 400 degrees for 30 minutes or until the peppers are very tender. Let stand until cool. Remove the stems and seeds from the peppers. Squeeze the garlic from its skin.

Combine the bell peppers, garlic, tomatoes, jalapeño chile, banana chile, onion, salt and cumin in a food processor container. Process until of the desired consistency.

YIELD: 2 CUPS

189

Béarnaise Sauce

3 tablespoons white wine vinegar
3 tablespoons tarragon vinegar
2 shallots, finely chopped
½ tablespoon chopped parsley
1 tablespoon chopped fresh tarragon
3 egg yolks (see Note, page 187)
2 tablespoons water
1 cup hot clarified butter (see Note, below)
Coarse salt and freshly ground pepper to taste
1 teaspoon lemon juice

Combine all the vinegar and shallots in a small saucepan. Boil until the liquid is reduced by ½. Add the parsley and tarragon and keep warm. Mix the egg yolks and water in a heatproof bowl. Cook over simmering water until the mixture is lukewarm. Remove from the heat and beat until thick and creamy. Add the butter very gradually, whisking constantly. Season with salt, pepper and lemon juice. Add the vinegar mixture and stir gently. Keep warm over warm water. Serve lukewarm with beef or fish.

Note: For clarified butter, melt unsalted butter slowly to allow most of the water to evaporate. Skim off any foam from the top. Then pour off the clear butter, leaving behind the milky residue. This clear (clarified) butter is especially good for frying because it has a higher smoke point.

YIELD: 1½ CUPS

Tamarind Peanut Sauce

1 tablespoon tamarind concentrate (see Note)
½ cup water
1 teaspoon cornstarch
1 fresh or dried red chile, seeded
3 garlic cloves, peeled
1 tablespoon brown sugar
½ teaspoon salt
1 cup coconut milk
1 teaspoon shrimp paste
1 tablespoon fish sauce
¼ cup peanut butter
1 (1x1-inch) piece lemon zest

Dissolve the tamarind concentrate in the water. Combine with the cornstarch, red chile, garlic, brown sugar, salt, coconut milk, shrimp paste, fish sauce and peanut butter in a food processor or blender container. Process until blended and smooth. Pour into a small saucepan and add the lemon zest. Simmer for 15 minutes or until thickened, adding a small amount of water if too thick.

Note: Tamarind concentrate can be found in East Indian markets and in some Asian markets and supermarkets.

YIELD: 1½ CUPS

Rossini Sauce

½ cup (1 stick) butter
3 tablespoons flour
1 cup beef stock
5 peppercorns
1 bay leaf
1 whole clove
2 tablespoons brandy
2 tablespoons red wine

Melt the butter in a medium saucepan. Whisk in the flour. Bring to a gentle simmer and cook until light brown, whisking constantly. Stir in the beef stock. Add the peppercorns, bay leaf, clove, brandy and wine and simmer for 5 minutes. Remove and discard the bay leaf and clove. Serve with tenderloin or beef Wellington.

YIELD: 1 TO 1¼ CUPS

Shotgun Sauce

½ cup (1 stick) butter
1 cup red currant jelly
⅛ teaspoon Worcestershire sauce, or to taste

Bring the butter and jelly to a boil in a saucepan. Stir in the Worcestershire sauce. Skim off any foam. Serve hot over game.

YIELD: 1½ CUPS

André Previn and Hei-Kyung Hong

Musicians who come to Ann Arbor to perform usually find their way to SKR Classical, a campus record store. James Levine and André Previn have both stopped in, according to owner Jim Leonard. " Levine bought nothing but historical conductors and huge bound copies of Strauss operas," Leonard says. "Previn bought only pianists who were big before the Second World War. He asked for Alfred Cortot." Musicians often "buy the people they measure themselves against," says Leonard. "Except for the Russians, who buy everything." Even before the Soviet Union fell apart, "every time a Soviet orchestra came to town, the store filled up with Russian musicians, clutching American dollars and buying everything in sight."

Watercress Sauce

1 cup white wine
½ cup clamato juice
1 cup sour cream
¼ cup minced watercress
2 tablespoons lime juice
1 tablespoon Dijon mustard
4 drops of hot pepper sauce

Boil the wine and clamato juice in a small saucepan until reduced to ¼ cup. Let stand until cool. Stir in the sour cream, watercress, lime juice, Dijon mustard and hot pepper sauce. Chill thoroughly. Garnish with watercress leaves or sprigs. Serve with fish.

YIELD: 1½ CUPS

Mustard Vinaigrette

1 tablespoon Dijon mustard
1 teaspoon dry mustard
¼ cup olive oil
3 tablespoons red wine vinegar
1 teaspoon lemon juice
Salt and freshly ground pepper to taste

Combine the Dijon mustard, dry mustard, olive oil, vinegar, lemon juice, salt and pepper in a jar with a tight-fitting lid. Seal the jar and shake vigorously. The vinaigrette should be emulsified and look a bit cloudy.

YIELD: ½ CUP

Mustard Aspic

¾ cup sugar
1 teaspoon salt
1 tablespoon dry mustard
1 envelope unflavored gelatin
3 eggs, lightly beaten
½ cup each vinegar and boiling water
1 cup whipped cream

Mix the first 4 ingredients in a double boiler. Add the eggs, vinegar and water; mix well. Cook until thick, stirring constantly. Let stand until cool. Fold in the whipped cream. Spoon into 3-cup mold; chill until set. Serve with ham or beef.

YIELD: 3 CUPS (ABOUT 6 TO 8 SERVINGS)

Cranberry Port Wine Mold

3 cups fresh cranberries
½ cup cold water
1½ tablespoons unflavored gelatin
¼ cup port
½ cup sugar
1 tablespoon grated orange zest
1½ tablespoons chutney
¾ teaspoon curry powder
½ cup chopped walnuts

Cook the cranberries in the water in a saucepan until they pop. Soften the gelatin in the port. Add the gelatin mixture, sugar and orange zest to the cranberry mixture; stir until the gelatin is dissolved. Add the chutney, curry powder and walnuts. Set over ice; stir until partially set. Spoon into 4-cup mold. Chill until set. Unmold and garnish with parsley and lemon twists. Serve with poultry.

YIELD: 4 CUPS (ABOUT 6 TO 8 SERVINGS)

Onion Marmalade

2 tablespoons olive oil
8 ounces red onions, peeled, minced
2 bunches green onions, chopped
1 cup sliced leeks
¼ cup peeled sliced shallots
⅓ cup chardonnay
1 tablespoon sugar
Salt to taste

Heat the olive oil in a saucepan. Add all the onions, leeks and shallots. Cook over low heat until tender. Increase the heat. Add the wine and sugar and cook until the wine has evaporated. Season with salt.

YIELD: 3 CUPS

Pickled Ginger

1 (2-inch) piece fresh gingerroot, peeled, thinly sliced
1 teaspoon sugar
½ teaspoon salt
Juice of 1 lemon, or ¼ cup vinegar

Combine the gingerroot, sugar, salt and lemon juice in a bowl and mix well. The ginger will turn pink. Serve with rare tuna and wasabi.

Note: To store peeled fresh gingerroot in the refrigerator, combine the ginger with sherry to cover in a jar with a tight-fitting lid. The gingerroot will keep for several months and the sherry can then be reused for cooking.

YIELD: ENOUGH TO GARNISH 4 TO 6 SERVINGS TUNA

Desserts

1994

Sunday, October 23, through
Sunday, October 30, 1994

Rackham Auditorium
The Power Center for the Performing Arts

In the American Grain:
The Martha Graham
Centenary Festival

Martha Graham Dance Company
Ann Arbor Symphony Orchestra
Stanley Sussman   *Guest Conductor*
The Michigan Chamber Players
CHS Dance Body of
Community High School, Ann Arbor

Program I

Satyric Festival Song
Lamentation
Panorama (Excerpts)
Cave of the Heart
Acts of Light

Family Performance

Appalachian Spring
(Ballet for Martha) (Excerpt)
Lamentation
Satyric Festival Song
Tjanang Sari (A Short Study)
Maple Leaf Rag

Program II

El Penitente
Panorama (Excerpts)
Dark Meadow
Maple Leaf Rag

Program III

Fanfare for the Common Man
Long Time Ago
"Promise of Living" from The Tender Land
Reflections from the Original Cast Members
Appalachian Spring (Ballet for Martha)

Martha Graham

MARTHA Graham is considered, with Picasso and Stravinsky, a primal artistic force of the twentieth century. University of Michigan dance professor Peter Sparling describes her as "an anthropologist, an archaeologist, a supreme interpreter of myth, a dramatist, and a champion of American music."

These 1994 performances capped a three-week celebration of the hundredth anniversary of Graham's birth and the fiftieth anniversary of her ballet "Appalachian Spring." The Martha Graham Centenary Festival included a four-day residency of the Martha Graham Dance Company, master classes and open rehearsals, lectures and panels, performance videos, concerts, and art exhibits.

Martha Graham first performed in Ann Arbor in 1932 at the Lydia Mendelssohn Theater. Dancing solo, she premiered three original works. Graham and her company returned often; this residency was the company's eighth appearance under the auspices of the University Musical Society.

Sparling was a dance student at Juilliard when Graham saw him perform in 1973 and invited him to join her company. He was a principal dancer in her company from 1973 to 1987, and their professional and personal association lasted until her death in 1991. After she died, he began to consider how "to create new forms of presenting Martha's legacy." With the centenary of her birth approaching, he proposed the residency to UMS in 1992. It would also celebrate "Appalachian Spring," her signature ballet, set to an Aaron Copland score commissioned for her.

UMS was enthusiastic. With funding help from the Lila Wallace–Reader's Digest Fund, "In the American Grain: The Martha Graham Centenary Festival" became a huge collaborative endeavor. Participants included the Library of Congress (where the premiere of "Appalachian Spring" had been presented fifty years earlier) and the University's dance department, music school, and art museum. From the larger community, the Ann Arbor Symphony, the community college, and the public schools participated. And twenty-four university dance students, chosen by audition, performed with a professional company.

Ten of Graham's seminal and most celebrated works were performed in four sold-out concerts in the Power Center. In the final program celebrating "Appalachian Spring," two members of the ballet's original cast, Pearl Lang and Erick Hawkins, reminisced onstage. And in an unanticipated tribute to Sparling, the company invited him to reprise the role of the Revivalist.

It was a celebration of modern dance, Sparling says, that realized "the ideal of partnership, collaboration, and community outreach." For Sparling personally, "In the American Grain" was an opportunity to continue to honor his debt to Martha Graham. "I am translating Martha to another generation," he says, "extending her dream."

Among the other dance troupes to have completed Ann Arbor residencies are the Bill T. Jones/Arnie Zane, Merce Cunningham, Alvin Ailey, Mark Morris, Donald Byrd, and Twyla Tharp companies.

What was cooking?

Traditionally, the White House had served French foods, prepared with French ingredients by French chefs and presented by menus written in French. In 1992, a coalition of American chefs wrote to President-elect Bill Clinton, urging him to recognize American cuisine. In 1994, an American chef was appointed to head the White House kitchen.

Barbara Bonney's Carrot Cake

2 cups sugar
4 eggs
1½ cups corn oil
2 cups flour
1½ teaspoons baking soda
2 teaspoons baking powder
1 teaspoon salt
2 teaspoons cinnamon
½ cup raisins
1 cup chopped walnuts
5 cups grated carrots (about 6 large carrots)
8 ounces cream cheese, softened
½ cup (1 stick) butter, softened
2 teaspoons vanilla extract
Chopped walnuts (optional)

For the cake, mix the sugar, eggs and corn oil in a medium bowl. Mix the flour, baking soda, baking powder, salt and cinnamon in a large bowl. Add the egg mixture and mix well. Stir in the raisins, 1 cup walnuts and carrots. Spoon into 3 greased 8-inch round cake pans. Bake at 350 degrees for 1 hour. Cool in the pans for several minutes. Remove to a wire rack to cool completely.

For the frosting, beat the cream cheese, butter and vanilla in a mixer bowl for 3 minutes or until light and fluffy. Spread the frosting between the layers and over the top and side of the cake. Sprinkle with additional walnuts.

YIELD: 12 SERVINGS

Veronika Hagen's Gugelhupf

"Gugelhupf is the Austrian's cake for Sundays," says Veronika Hagen, violist for the Hagen Quartet.

1 cup plus 2 tablespoons (2¼ sticks) butter, softened
1¾ cups sugar
1½ teaspoons vanilla extract
4 eggs
3⅓ cups flour
3⅓ teaspoons baking powder
1 cup milk
3 tablespoons baking cocoa
3 tablespoons sugar
3 tablespoons milk
Whipped cream (optional)

Combine the butter, 1¾ cups sugar, vanilla, eggs, flour, baking powder and 1 cup milk in a large bowl and mix well. Mix the baking cocoa, 3 tablespoons sugar and 3 tablespoons milk in a medium bowl. Add ⅓ of the egg mixture to the cocoa mixture and mix well. Spoon the remaining egg mixture and then the cocoa mixture into a nonstick bundt pan.

Bake at 350 degrees for 1 hour. Top with whipped cream.

YIELD: 8 TO 10 SERVINGS

The King's Singers' Chocolate and Caramel Squares

½ cup (1 stick) butter, softened
¼ cup sugar
1 cup all-purpose flour
⅓ cup ground rice flour
⅛ teaspoon salt
½ cup (1 stick) butter
¼ cup sugar
2 teaspoons corn syrup
1 cup sweetened condensed milk
½ to ¾ cup (4 to 6 ounces) chocolate chips
3 to 4 tablespoons milk

For the base, cream ½ cup butter and ¼ cup sugar in a mixer bowl until light and fluffy. Add the all-purpose flour, rice flour and salt and stir until a soft dough forms. Knead on a floured surface until smooth. Press evenly into a shallow 9x11-inch baking dish. Prick the surface at close intervals with a fork. Bake at 350 degrees for 30 minutes or until light brown. Let stand until cool.

For the filling, combine ½ cup butter, ¼ cup sugar, corn syrup and condensed milk in a saucepan. Cook over low heat until the butter is melted and the sugar is dissolved, stirring constantly. Bring to a boil and simmer for 5 to 7 minutes or until golden brown, stirring constantly. Spread over the base and let stand until set.

For the topping, melt the chocolate chips in a small saucepan over low heat, thinning with the milk if needed. Spread over the filling and let stand until set. Cut into squares to serve.

Note: If rice flour is not available, all-purpose flour will work.

YIELD: 16 TO 24 SERVINGS

Veronika Hagen, violist of the Hagen Quartet, has toured the world. She loves pasta and Italian cuisine in general, but "can't wait for good burgers and pizza" when she comes to the United States. Her favorite post-concert snack, wherever she is: "Beer. After a performance, cool beer improves the quality of life tremendously."

Renowned clarinetist Richard Stoltzman would agree. His favorite post-concert treat is yaki soba (fried Japanese noodles)—and beer.

Susanne Mentzer's Sinful Brownies

1 cup (2 sticks) butter
4 (1-ounce) squares unsweetened chocolate
3 eggs
1 teaspoon vanilla extract
2 cups sugar
1½ cups flour

Melt the butter and chocolate in a double boiler. Beat the eggs in a mixer bowl until foamy. Add the vanilla and sugar to the eggs and mix well. Add the chocolate mixture and mix well. Add the flour gradually, mixing well after each addition. Spoon into a lightly greased 9x13-inch baking pan. Bake at 350 degrees for 25 to 35 minutes or until the brownies spring back when lightly touched but are still moist.

YIELD: 15 TO 18 SERVINGS

Chocolate Orange Shortbread

2 cups (4 sticks) unsalted butter, softened
1 cup confectioners' sugar
½ teaspoon orange extract
4¼ cups flour
1 teaspoon salt
2 tablespoons (or more) grated orange zest
1 cup miniature semisweet chocolate chips
Confectioners' sugar

Cream the butter and confectioners' sugar in a mixer bowl until light and fluffy. Beat in the orange extract. Add the flour, salt and orange zest gradually, mixing well after each addition until a soft dough forms. Stir in the chocolate chips. For larger cookies, divide the dough into 12 equal pieces. Shape into ¼-inch-thick circles or squares on an ungreased cookie sheet. Crimp the edges with a fork dipped in confectioners' sugar and score with a knife. For smaller cookies, shape into balls and place on an ungreased cookie sheet. Flatten with a glass. Crimp the edges with a fork dipped in confectioners' sugar. Bake at 350 degrees for 20 to 25 minutes or until very light brown. Let stand until cool. Watch these cookies carefully; they burn quickly.

YIELD: 1 DOZEN LARGER COOKIES
OR 4 DOZEN SMALLER COOKIES

Harbor House Caramels

1 cup sugar
1 cup dark corn syrup
1 cup (2 sticks) butter
1 (14-ounce) can sweetened condensed milk
1 teaspoon vanilla extract

Combine the sugar, corn syrup and butter in a medium saucepan. Bring to a boil over medium heat, stirring constantly. Boil for 7 minutes without stirring. Add the condensed milk and mix well. Return to a boil. Boil for 13 minutes, stirring constantly. Remove from the heat and stir in the vanilla. Spoon into a generously buttered 8x8-inch glass baking dish. Let stand overnight at room temperature. Cut into bite-size squares and wrap individually in colored plastic wrap.

YIELD: ABOUT 70 CARAMELS

Gingersnaps with Dried Cherries

¾ cup (1½ sticks) butter,
  softened
1 cup sugar
¼ cup molasses
1 egg
2 cups flour
2 teaspoons baking soda

1 teaspoon cinnamon
1 teaspoon ground cloves
1 teaspoon ground ginger
½ teaspoon salt
½ cup dried cherries
¼ cup chopped candied ginger
Sugar

Cream the butter and 1 cup sugar in a mixer bowl until light and fluffy. Add the molasses and egg and mix well. Add the flour, baking soda, cinnamon, cloves, ground ginger and salt and mix well. Stir in the cherries and candied ginger. Shape into ½-inch balls and roll in additional sugar. Place on a cookie sheet. Bake at 375 degrees for 8 to 10 minutes or until light brown.

YIELD: 3 TO 4 DOZEN

Pecan Triangles

1 cup (2 sticks) unsalted
  butter, softened
1 cup sugar
1 egg yolk
2 cups sifted flour

1½ tablespoons grated lemon
  zest
1 egg white, beaten
1 cup finely chopped pecans

Grease a 10x15-inch baking sheet with sides or spray with nonstick cooking spray. Cream the butter and sugar in a large mixer bowl until light and fluffy. Beat in the egg yolk. Add the flour and lemon zest and mix well. Spread evenly in the prepared pan. Brush with the egg white. Sprinkle the pecans over the top and press lightly into the dough. Bake at 275 degrees for 1¼ hours or until golden brown. Cut into 2½-inch squares while still hot. Cut each square diagonally into halves to form triangles. Cool on a wire rack. These cookies freeze well.

YIELD: 4 DOZEN

Iona Brown

In 1990, when the Academy of St. Martin in the Fields performed at Hill Auditorium, first violinist Iona Brown brought along her Stradivarius, which needed a repair. She left it with Joe Curtin and Gregg Alf, Ann Arbor violin makers. While they worked on the violin, Brown suggested, they could make a copy. Gratefully, the two artisans took the opportunity to replicate the priceless instrument.

They sold the Strad copy to violinist Elmar Oliveira, who later sold it at auction. The buyer was a young Maltese violinist, Carmine Lauri. Completing the circle, the Academy of St. Martin in the Fields returned, this time to Rackham Auditorium, with Carmine Lauri among its members. Not only was he playing Curtin and Alf's replica, but he was sitting alongside Iona Brown—who was playing the original Stradivarius.

Grand Marnier Marmalade Pie

1 (2-crust) pie pastry
2 medium oranges
1 cup sugar
Juice of ½ lemon
1 cup water
¼ cup sugar
2½ tablespoons cornstarch
¼ cup (½ stick) butter, softened
3 eggs
2 tablespoons Grand Marnier, Curaçao or
    Cointreau
1 teaspoon water
1 cup whipping cream, whipped
2 tablespoons confectioners' sugar
2 teaspoons grated orange zest

Fit 1 pastry into a pie plate. Cut the remaining pie pastry into thin strips and set aside. Peel the oranges and very finely chop the zest. Separate the oranges into sections and squeeze to extract the juice. Combine the orange zest, orange sections, orange juice, 1 cup sugar, lemon juice and 1 cup water in a saucepan and bring to a boil. Simmer for 15 minutes. Let stand until cool. Mix ¼ cup sugar and cornstarch in a mixer bowl. Add the butter and beat until smooth and fluffy. Reserve 1 teaspoon of an egg yolk. Beat the remaining eggs 1 at a time into the butter mixture. Fold in the juice mixture and liqueur. Spoon into the pie plate. Arrange the pastry strips lattice-fashion over the pie. Brush with a mixture of the reserved egg yolk and 1 teaspoon water. Bake at 425 degrees for 10 minutes. Reduce the oven temperature to 350 degrees. Bake for 35 minutes. Let stand until cool. Cut into small slices. Mix the whipped cream, confectioners' sugar and 2 teaspoons orange zest in a bowl and serve with the pie.

YIELD: 8 SERVINGS

Pine Nut Flan

2 cups flour
½ cup (1 stick) butter, softened
½ cup sugar
Ice water
4 egg yolks
⅓ cup sugar
½ cup packed brown sugar
½ cup light corn syrup
1 tablespoon flour
3 eggs
1 teaspoon vanilla extract, or 1 vanilla bean
2 teaspoons orange zest
1 cup pine nuts, lightly toasted

For the dough, combine the flour, butter and ½ cup sugar in a food processor container and process until crumbly. Add ice water 1 tablespoon at a time with the food processor running until the dough forms a ball. Let stand, covered, for 1 hour.

Roll the dough ¼ inch thick on a floured cloth. Place in a 9-inch flan pan with a removable bottom. Bake at 350 degrees for 8 minutes.

Combine the egg yolks, ⅓ cup sugar, brown sugar, corn syrup, flour, eggs, vanilla and orange zest in a food processor container and process until mixed. Pour into the partially baked pie crust. Top with the pine nuts. Bake for 30 to 40 minutes or until a knife inserted near the center comes out clean. Cover the top with foil if the pie browns too quickly.

Cut into small slices. Serve with whipped cream or ice cream.

YIELD: 10 TO 12 SERVINGS

Mango Tarts

2 cups macadamia nuts
1½ cups pistachios
1½ cups shredded
    sweetened coconut
½ cup packed brown sugar
Whites of 3 extra-large eggs
10 extra-large egg yolks
¾ cup fresh lime juice

1 cup sugar
½ cup (1 stick) butter,
    cut into pieces
¼ cup mango or passion fruit
    jelly (optional)
1 tablespoon dark rum
    (optional)
2 to 3 mangoes, peeled, sliced

For the crust, mix the macadamia nuts, pistachios, coconut and brown sugar in a bowl. Process in batches in a food processor until ground. Beat the egg whites in a mixer bowl until soft peaks form. Fold into the nut mixture. Let stand for 5 to 10 minutes so that the nuts can absorb some of the egg whites. Spray 10 to 12 individual tart pans with removable bottoms with nonstick baking spray. Press nut mixture onto the bottom and up the side of each tart pan, evening the surface to form a smooth thin crust. Place each tart pan on a baking sheet as it is finished. Bake at 350 degrees for 8 to 12 minutes or until medium brown, rotating the baking sheet to ensure even browning. Let stand until cool. The crusts can be stored for a few days in an airtight container or frozen if not being used immediately.

For the filling, bring 2 to 3 inches of water to a boil in a medium saucepan or double boiler. Place a stainless steel bowl over the saucepan. Whisk the egg yolks, lime juice and sugar in the bowl. Cook until the mixture is the consistency of mayonnaise, stirring frequently. Remove the bowl from the heat and whisk in the butter gradually. Spoon into a plastic container. Place plastic wrap directly on the surface of the filling and chill until needed. The filling will keep in the refrigerator for up to 1 week.

For the glaze, melt the jelly in a small saucepan. Add the rum. Strain through a sieve.

Fill each tart shell with ⅓ cup of the filling. Arrange mango slices attractively over the filling. Brush with warm glaze. Chill for 1 hour or longer.

YIELD: 10 TO 12 SERVINGS

Klezmer Conservatory Band

"When we went to hear Itzhak Perlman fiddle with four klezmer bands [December 1997], our seats were at the very top of the very highest balcony in Hill Auditorium," a concert-goer recalls. "The klezmer revival celebrates the Eastern European Yiddish-speaking culture that has survived so bravely for so long—aspects of daily life, the coarse as well as the mystic. Perlman and the bands so totally entered its exuberant spirit that they played on and on. Audience members were lifted out of their seats and into the aisles, linking arms and dancing. Seen from way up high, the dancers near the front edge of the balcony were silhouetted against the bright stage like a string of jiggling dark paper cutouts. The whole auditorium became a work of art."

Linzertorte à la Richard Stoltzman

*Clarinetist Richard Stoltzman says, "I made this tart for the
Marlboro Musical Festival International Night. I watched with great
trepidation as Irene Serkin, a fantastic cook, sampled it. To my delight,
she pronounced it acceptable, and her husband, Rudolf, had me
prepare it for all 100 musicians the next summer."*

1 cup almonds
1½ cups flour
½ cup sugar
2½ tablespoons baking cocoa
¼ teaspoon cinnamon
1 cup (2 sticks) unsalted butter, chopped
½ teaspoon lemon juice
1 teaspoon vanilla extract
2 extra-large egg yolks
2 cups raspberry jam, preferably homemade freezer jam
Confectioners' sugar

Process the almonds in a food processor until almost ground.
Add the flour, sugar, baking cocoa and cinnamon and process briefly.
Add the butter and process until crumbly. Add the lemon juice,
vanilla and egg yolks and process just until a smooth dough forms.
Shape the dough into a ball and wrap in plastic wrap. Chill in the
refrigerator for 30 minutes. Press ½ to ⅔ of the dough into a fluted
springform tart pan.

Place the remaining dough between sheets of waxed paper. Roll
into a 9x12-inch rectangle. Chill in the refrigerator for 30 minutes or
until firm enough to handle.

Spoon the jam over the dough in the tart pan. Peel the waxed
paper carefully from the chilled dough. Cut the dough into ½-inch
strips. Arrange the strips in a lattice pattern over the top of the tart,
piecing the strips together if needed.

Place the tart pan on a baking sheet. Bake at 350 degrees for
40 to 50 minutes or until brown and bubbly. Let stand until cool.
Remove the side of the pan. Sprinkle confectioners' sugar over the
tart just before serving.

YIELD: 8 SERVINGS

Frozen Soufflé Viola

1 mango, peeled
2 teaspoons lime juice
2 teaspoons orange juice
$\frac{1}{2}$ teaspoon unflavored gelatin
2 cups whipping cream
5 egg yolks, beaten
$\frac{1}{3}$ cup sugar
$\frac{1}{8}$ teaspoon (or less) salt
2 egg whites, stiffly beaten

Purée the mango, lime juice and orange juice in a food processor. Pour into a heatproof bowl and sprinkle with the gelatin. Set aside.

Beat the whipping cream in a mixer bowl until soft peaks form. Store in the refrigerator until needed.

Cook the mango purée in the heatproof bowl over barely simmering water. Beat the egg yolks, sugar and salt in a mixer bowl at high speed with a whisk attachment until very thick and pale yellow. Spoon into a large bowl and fold in the egg whites. Stir the whipped cream into the mango purée very gradually. Add to the egg mixture.

Spoon the egg mixture into 8 ramekins and freeze for 2 to 4 hours. To unmold, dip each ramekin in hot water until the soufflé slips out. Place on individual plates and serve with sugar cookies.

YIELD: 8 SERVINGS

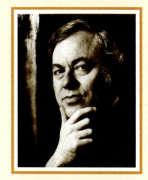

Richard Goode

Pianist Richard Goode, who often accompanies singers, gave a stunning recital of Bach, Brahms, and Beethoven piano works in March 1997. "Making this dense, brooding, gorgeous music," an Ann Arbor Observer writer said of some short Brahms pieces, "Richard Goode sometimes pounds his right heel as he works the pedal, leans into the keyboard as his fingers fly, and raises his bent leg slightly, bringing the foot down with the beat. A few times he even rises from his seat, as if he can barely contain the music pouring through his fingers." After Beethoven's sublimely beautiful last piano sonata, "he slumps slightly, his still hands on the keyboard, and the emotional release of the quiet ending brings involuntary sighs from the audience."

Mrs. Sink's Frozen Maple Mousse

1½ cups maple syrup
5 egg yolks, lightly beaten
1 quart whipping cream, whipped
Toasted pecans (optional)

Heat the maple syrup in a double boiler. Stir a small amount of the hot syrup into the egg yolks; stir the egg yolks into the hot syrup. Simmer until thickened, beating constantly. Let stand until cool. This mixture may be prepared up to 1 day ahead and stored in the refrigerator.

Combine the syrup mixture with the whipped cream in a large bowl. Pour into an ice cream freezer container. Freeze using the manufacturer's directions. Process the frozen mousse in a food processor until smooth. Refreeze until firm, then let stand to soften slightly. Spoon into serving dishes and sprinkle with toasted pecans. Serve with brown sugar meringues.

YIELD: 10 TO 12 SERVINGS

White Chocolate Mousse with Raspberry Sauce

¼ cup half-and-half
2 tablespoons white crème de cacao
9 ounces white chocolate, coarsely chopped
3 egg whites
⅛ teaspoon cream of tartar
1½ cups whipping cream, whipped
1 teaspoon vanilla extract
Fresh raspberries
Sugar to taste
Lemon juice to taste
Club soda to taste

Combine the half-and-half, liqueur and white chocolate in a double boiler. Cook over boiling water just until the chocolate is melted, stirring constantly. Remove from the heat and stir until cool.

Beat the egg whites and cream of tartar in a mixer bowl until soft peaks form. Fold into the white chocolate mixture. Fold in the whipped cream and vanilla.

Spoon the mousse into 8 serving dishes. Purée the raspberries in a food processor and strain into a bowl. Season with sugar, lemon juice and club soda. Top each serving with a spoonful of the raspberry purée.

YIELD: 8 SERVINGS

Arnold Steinhardt's Baked Rice Pudding

Arnold Steinhardt is the first violinist of the Guarneri Quartet. His recommendation is to "serve this pudding with espresso, whipped cream, and Fritz Kreisler violin music in the background."

4½ cups milk
¾ cup sugar
⅔ cup medium grain
    rice
½ cup raisins
2 large eggs

1 tablespoon rum, brandy or
    orange juice
1 teaspoon grated orange zest
1 teaspoon vanilla extract
Cinnamon to taste (optional)

Bring the milk to a simmer in a heavy saucepan, stirring occasionally to prevent scorching. Add the sugar and rice. Simmer over low heat for 40 minutes or until the rice is tender, stirring occasionally. Stir in the raisins. Pour into a bowl and let stand until cool, stirring occasionally.

Lightly coat eight 6-ounce custard cups or ramekins with butter. Whisk the eggs, rum, orange zest and vanilla in a small bowl until blended. Stir the egg mixture into the cooked rice. Spoon into the prepared custard cups.

Bake at 325 degrees for 25 to 30 minutes or until set. Cool on a wire rack for 10 minutes. Loosen the pudding from the side of the ramekins by running a knife around the pudding. Invert onto dessert plates. Sprinkle with cinnamon. Serve warm.

YIELD: 8 SERVINGS

Guarneri String Quartet

In 1992, David Daniels, a tenor studying vocal performance at the University of Michigan music school, underwent a dazzling musical transformation. He brought his teacher, George Shirley, a tape recording of mezzo-soprano arias, identifying the singer as a friend. Shirley, a former Metropolitan opera tenor, listened carefully, pronounced the voice wonderful, and astutely guessed it to be Daniels' own.

Since then, Daniels has been a countertenor—a male who sings in the mezzo-soprano range. He has performed across the country to growing acclaim for his muscular coloratura and his expressiveness. In 1997, he was astonishing as contralto soloist in the University Musical Society's annual "Messiah" concerts. His Ann Arbor performances seem to resonate with a special brilliance, emanating from ties of friendship and memory.

Cassata alla Siciliana

2 pounds ricotta cheese
2 tablespoons heavy cream
⅓ cup sugar
⅓ cup Grand Marnier or other orange-
*   flavored liqueur*
⅓ cup semisweet chocolate chips
½ cup candied mixed fruit
1 pound cake made with butter
2 cups semisweet chocolate chips
¾ cup brewed espresso or double-strength
*   coffee*
1 cup (2 sticks) unsalted butter,
*   cut into pieces*

For the filling, blend the ricotta cheese, cream, sugar and liqueur in a food processor. Add ⅓ cup chocolate chips and process until chopped. Add the candied fruit and process until finely chopped.

Slice the cake into 5 equal layers with a long serrated knife. Slice off the rounded top to make a flat surface. Place 1 layer on a serving plate and top with ¼ of the filling. Repeat the process with the remaining layers and filling, ending with a cake layer. Cover with plastic wrap and gently press top and side together. Chill for 2 to 3 hours.

For the frosting, heat 2 cups chocolate chips and espresso in a saucepan until the chocolate is melted, stirring frequently. Whisk in 1 tablespoon of the butter at a time until of the desired consistency. Spread thickly over the top and side of the cake.

Chill, uncovered, until the chocolate is firm. Cover with plastic wrap and chill for 8 to 24 hours. Cut into ½- to ⅓-inch pieces.

YIELD: 10 TO 12 SERVINGS

Michala Petri's Filled Almond Meringue

5 egg whites
1¼ cups confectioners' sugar
1⅓ cups finely chopped blanched almonds,
*   lightly toasted*
¼ cup bread crumbs
½ cup chopped dark chocolate
2 to 4 egg yolks (see Note, page 187)
A few spoonfuls confectioners' sugar
1 cup whipping cream, whipped
Fresh fruit

For the meringue, beat the egg whites in a mixer bowl until stiff peaks form. Add 1¼ cups confectioners' sugar and beat briefly. Fold in the almonds.

Sprinkle the bread crumbs in a buttered shallow round mold. Spoon the meringue into the mold. Bake at 200 degrees for 35 to 45 minutes or until the meringue feels dry when lightly touched. Turn off the oven. Let the meringue stand in the closed oven for several minutes.

Melt the chocolate in a double boiler. Brush the melted chocolate over the meringue.

Beat the egg yolks and a few spoonfuls of confectioners' sugar in a mixer bowl until light and fluffy. Fold in the whipped cream. Spread over the chocolate and top with fresh fruit.

YIELD: 8 SERVINGS

Sarah Walker's English Trifle

1 sponge cake, or 1 package
    trifle sponges
1 package ladyfingers
1 large can crushed
    pineapple
½ cup strawberry jam
1 package ratafia biscuits or
    macaroon-type cookies

½ cup sweet sherry
English Pastry Cream (below)
1 cup whipping cream, whipped
Toasted almond halves
Small fresh strawberries, or
    1 cherry

Line the bottom of a trifle bowl with slices of sponge cake. Cover with as many ladyfingers as possible. Spoon the undrained pineapple over the top; spread evenly. Spread the jam over the top. Cover the jam with ratafia biscuits. Sprinkle the sherry over the top very gradually. Chill in the refrigerator overnight so that the sherry can be absorbed. Spoon the English Pastry Cream over the trifle. Spread thickly with the whipped cream. Sprinkle with the almonds. Dot with strawberries or top with a cherry.

YIELD: 6 TO 12 SERVINGS

English Pastry Cream

2 cups milk
¼ cup flour
2 teaspoons cornstarch
½ cup sugar

4 egg yolks, lightly beaten
Cream or milk
1 teaspoon vanilla extract,
    whiskey or liqueur

Bring 1½ cups of the milk to a simmer in a small saucepan. Blend the remaining ½ cup milk, flour, cornstarch and sugar in a bowl. Add the egg yolks. Add a small amount of the hot milk to the egg yolk mixture; add the egg yolk mixture to the hot milk. Cook over low heat for 5 minutes or until thickened, stirring constantly. Add a small amount of cream if the mixture becomes too thick. Strain into a small bowl. Add the vanilla and let cool.

YIELD: 2 CUPS

Nadja Salerno-Sonnenberg

"She's one of the most expressive violinists I have ever heard," says a frequent concert-goer, describing Nadja Salerno-Sonnenberg. "As a musician I know how hard it is to play pianissimo, to play the notes softly yet distinctly, and still with feeling. She finds the meaning in every note. She does look pained when she plays, though. And she used to look like a New York street kid. She had a short haircut and wore black trousers and a red shirt. She dresses more conventionally now, but back then it was fun to eavesdrop in the lobby during intermission, to hear people discuss her startling appearance."

Chocolate Paradise Pâte

9 ounces bittersweet chocolate, grated
½ cup sugar
¾ cup (1½ sticks) butter, softened
5 egg yolks
5 egg whites
⅛ teaspoon salt
¼ cup sugar
2 cups pastry cream
¼ cup whipping cream, whipped
Rum to taste
1 teaspoon praline powder
¾ to 1 cup raspberry purée

Line a 3x3x12-inch mold with parchment paper or plastic wrap.

Melt the chocolate in a saucepan over low heat. Add ½ cup sugar and butter and beat until smooth. Add the egg yolks and mix well. Keep warm over low heat.

Beat the egg whites and salt in a mixer bowl until stiff peaks form. Add ¼ cup sugar, beating constantly until very stiff and glossy. Fold in the egg whites ⅓ at a time into the chocolate mixture. Spoon into the prepared mold. Chill for 24 hours.

Unmold the pâte onto a plate and cut into thin slices. Thin some pastry cream with a small amount of whipped cream and rum. Stir in some praline powder. Spoon some of this mixture onto chilled dessert plates. Place 1 or 2 slices of chocolate pâte in the center of each plate. Pipe a border of raspberry purée around the chocolate. Spread the purée into a swirling pattern. Garnish each serving with fresh berries or an orange slice.

YIELD: 10 TO 12 SERVINGS

Grilled Peppered Pineapple with Tequila Orange Sauce

1 large pineapple
1½ teaspoons green peppercorns, minced
¼ cup honey
1½ cups orange juice
½ cup tequila
1 pint vanilla ice cream

Cut the top and bottom from the pineapple with a large knife. Cut away the outside of the pineapple. Cut crosswise into ½- to ¾-inch slices. Remove the core with a round cutter. Rub each side of the pineapple slices with the peppercorns.

For the sauce, combine the honey, orange juice and tequila in a small heavy saucepan. Cook over medium heat until slightly thick and reduced by ¾. Set aside and keep warm.

Place the pineapple slices on a grill rack. Grill for 4 to 5 minutes or until both sides are well browned. Divide among 6 dessert plates. Drizzle each serving with 1 tablespoon of the orange sauce. Top each serving with ice cream. Serve immediately.

YIELD: 6 SERVINGS

Gingered Strawberry Shortcake

1 tablespoon finely chopped
   candied ginger
1¼ cups flour
3 tablespoons sugar
½ teaspoon baking powder
½ teaspoon baking soda
⅛ teaspoon salt
1 tablespoon chilled
   shortening, cut into
   pieces

1 tablespoon chilled unsalted
   butter, cut into pieces
½ cup low-fat buttermilk
2 cups chilled whipping cream
2 tablespoons sugar
2 teaspoons vanilla extract
2 pints fresh strawberries,
   hulled
¼ cup sugar
4 whole strawberries

Chill a mixer bowl and beaters in the freezer for 30 minutes before preparing the whipped cream.

For the shortcake, mix the ginger, flour, 3 tablespoons sugar, baking powder, baking soda and ⅛ teaspoon salt in a large bowl. Cut in the shortening and butter until crumbly. Add the buttermilk and stir until a soft dough forms. Knead on a lightly floured surface 4 to 5 times or until smooth.

Place 4 palm-size mounds of dough on a heavy baking sheet sprayed with nonstick cooking spray. Bake at 425 degrees for 15 minutes or until puffed and golden brown.

For the whipped cream, beat the whipping cream, 2 tablespoons sugar and vanilla at high speed in the chilled mixer bowl until stiff peaks form. Store in the refrigerator until needed.

Slice 12 of the hulled strawberries lengthwise and set aside. Crush the remaining hulled strawberries with a potato masher or fork. Mix the crushed berries and ¼ cup sugar in a medium bowl, stirring occasionally until needed.

Spread ½ cup of the whipped cream on each of 4 dessert plates. Cut each shortcake into halves. Center 1 bottom piece on each plate and surround with 6 of the reserved strawberry halves. Spoon 2 tablespoons of whipped cream onto each shortcake bottom. Cover with crushed strawberries, shortcake top and a dollop of whipped cream. Cut slits at regular intervals in the 4 whole strawberries; fan out and place on top of each serving. Garnish with mint sprigs and serve immediately.

YIELD: 4 SERVINGS

When the Russian National Orchestra traveled to Ann Arbor for a concert in March 1998, they were delayed at Finnish customs and missed a connecting flight. Players were parceled out among five different planes that arrived throughout the morning and afternoon. A small group of them ended up in a motel on the south edge of town, just off the interstate highway. One needed medicine, and when they inquired, the desk clerk naturally assumed they were driving, so directed them to a pharmacy several miles away. Not long afterward, a state policewoman spotted the musicians trudging along the interstate. She drove them to a pharmacy, waited while they bought what they needed, then delivered them to Hill Auditorium in time for their performance.

A Harbinger of the Future

December 18, 19, 20, and 21, 1996

The Power Center for the Performing Arts

The Harlem Nutcracker
(World-Première Season)

Donald Byrd
Choreographer/Director

Peter Ilyich Tchaikovsky
Composer

Music Arranged by
Duke Ellington with Billy Strayhorn
David Berger

Donald Byrd/The Group,
with Guest Artists
The Harlem Nutcracker Band
The Willis Patterson Our Own Thing Chorale

Act I
Clara's Home in Harlem
Scene 1. Empty House Blues
Scene 2. Clara Dances with Her Two Children
Later That Evening
Scene 3. Glimpse of Death
Scene 4. Walking Through Snow
Scene 5. Outside Club Sweets

Act II
Club Sweets
Scene 1. Inside Club Sweets
Scene 2. Passing Through Time
Clara's Home in Harlem
Scene 3. Christmas Morning

Scene from "The Harlem Nutcracker"

WHILE the University Musical Society has commissioned works in the past, "The Harlem Nutcracker," a two-act dance piece, came to life because several groups—including UMS—had faith enough to commit to it before it was finished. And during three holiday seasons, it has been performed, in both Ann Arbor and Detroit, with unprecedented levels of community participation.

In "The Harlem Nutcracker" choreographer Donald Byrd transforms the traditional fairy-tale ballet into a story of life, love, and death set in New York City's Harlem. Instead of a beautiful young girl, the heroine is a beautiful old woman. And Harlem's brassy, neon-bright Club Sweets is the setting for Act Two's divertissements, witty nightclub take-offs on the traditional solos and romantic *pas de deux*. The music is Duke Ellington and Billy Strayhorn's witty jazz take on Tchaikovsky's score, with additional music in the same spirit by David Berger.

The brilliant collaborative work graced the Power Center stage on its premiere tour in 1996. Many of its abundant riches were local: Detroit-area children danced as family members in Act One, local gospel groups sang, and the excellent jazz musicians were also from the area.

The Ann Arbor performances represented a bold new direction for UMS. In 1994, UMS president Ken Fischer learned of "The Harlem Nutcracker" while it was being created. He had been searching for an exciting new show, one he hoped might become as much a holiday tradition as the original "Nutcracker." Moreover, Byrd's piece seemed to mesh perfectly with the growing UMS commitment to present works that reflect the cultural and ethnic diversity of the southeastern Michigan community.

In collaboration with presenting organizations in five other communities around the country, UMS provided money and committed its presenting expertise to support the creation of this new work. Among the sweetest prospects for the collaborators was the certainty that "The Harlem Nutcracker" would be performed on their own stages. The piece has enjoyed a splendid success. In three seasons, it has traveled to New York, Chicago, Minneapolis, Washington, D.C., and Los Angeles.

Beyond the week-long residency of Byrd's dance company, UMS' community outreach was unprecedented in scope. To celebrate African-American culture, particularly the Harlem Renaissance, there were art and photography exhibits, readings, and storytelling by African-American seniors. Youth choirs sang before performances and at intermissions.

In 1998, UMS took the show to Detroit, collaborating with the Detroit Opera House and the Arts League of Michigan and presenting thirteen performances before a total audience of 24,000.

"UMS is pleased to have played a part in creating a new holiday tradition," says Ken Fischer. But beyond the enjoyment of helping a unique dance piece come to life, the "greatest satisfaction has come from sustaining this work of art we helped to create."

What was cooking?

Jell-O celebrated its hundredth birthday. But in The New Elegant But Easy, a redo of her 1978 book, Marian Burros left out the Jell-O recipes in favor of more sophisticated fusion dishes like sea bass with sake marinade. On the last day of 1998, New York Times food writers Ruth Reichl (who attended the University of Michigan) and Amanda Hesser, like Burros, predicted continuing creativity and innovation, but in less complicated dishes that use ingredients of the finest quality.

Acknowledgments

The cookbook Steering Committee gratefully acknowledges the contributions of the many volunteers whose gifts of time, effort, and expertise over the past two years have helped to make this book a success.

Our thanks to Kenneth C. Fischer, President of the University Musical Society, and his staff, who shared photographs, memories, expertise, and statistics: Catherine S. Arcure, Sara Billman, Sally Cushing, Elaine Economou, Susan Fitzpatrick, Michael Gowing, Susan Halloran, Elizabeth Jahn, Mark Jacobson, Ben Johnson, Michael Kondziolka, Gus Malmgren, Lisa Murray, J. Thad Schork, and Anne Griffin Sloan.

Special thanks to Gail Rector, president emeritus of UMS, who compiled a helpful booklet for us, *Artists and Associates Remembered and Recounted,* recalling his long tenure with the Society, and who was a gracious correspondent throughout the project.

Thanks also to the Bentley Historical Society of the University of Michigan, custodian of the UMS archives, Director Francis Blouin, and to his helpful staff; Richard LeSueur, music programmer, archivist, and patient fount of wisdom and information;

Charles Albert Sink, who for more than fifty years lived and breathed UMS and who, long after his death, informed and delighted us through his letters and memoirs;

John Woodford, editor of *Michigan Today,* who allowed us to use material he has published;

Jim Leonard, Paul Schwankl, and Bernice Lamey;

The artists who sent memories, anecdotes, and recipes:

Cecilia Bartoli	Skitch Henderson	Zubin Mehta	David Shifrin
Silvana Bazzoni	Wolfgang Holzmair	Susanne Mentzer	Arnold Steinhardt
Beaux Arts Trio	Marilyn Horne	Meredith Monk	Isaac Stern
Barbara Bonney	David Hurley	Joan Morris	Richard Stoltzman
Joshua Bell	Steven Isserlis	Jessye Norman	Richard Tognetti
William Bolcom	Michael Jaffee	Garrick Ohlsson	Benita Valente
Chamber Music	Bill T. Jones	Christopher	Frederica von Stade
Society of	Leila Josefowicz	Parkening	Sarah Walker
Lincoln Center	Martin Katz	Itzhak Perlman	Dale Warland
James Galway	Ida Kavafian	Michala Petri	
Horacio Gutierrez	The King's Singers	Menahem Pressler	
Veronika Hagen,	Evgeny Kissin	Leontyne Price	
Hagen String	Jaime Laredo	Bernice Johnson	
Quartet	Phillip Lawson	Reagon	

And to the music lovers who shared knowledge and memories:

Gregg Alf	Alice Dobson	Michael Malley	Herbert Sloan
Edith Leavis Bookstein	Kathy Duquette	Marilyn Mason	Peter Sparling
Allen Britton	Rosalie Edwards	Paul McCracken	Lois Stegeman
Donald Bryant	Nancy Elder	Robert MacGregor	Edward Surovell
Penelope Crawford	Don Faber	Charlotte McGeoch	Betty Thieme
Richard Crawford	Anne Glendon	Piotr Michalowski	Estelle Titiev
Ronnie Cresswell	Harold Haugh	Marguerite Oliver	Martin Tittle
Joseph Curtin	Elaine Heiserman	Mary Palmer	John Van Bolt
Sally Cushing	Norman Herbert	Lana Pollack	John Wagner
Mary Ann Daane	Elizabeth Hume	Bob Pratt	Carolin Wargelin
James Dapogny	Martin Katz	Deanna Relyea	Eileen Weiser
Bob Dascola	James Kibbie	Nancy Skinner-	Steven Whiting
Elizabeth Dexter	Jim Leonard	Oclander	

Chairs:
Mary Ann Daane
Anne E. Glendon

Editor:
Mary M. Matthews

Recipes:
Raquel Agranoff
Ann S. Schriber

Artwork:
Lois A. Baru
Mary F. VandenBelt

Promotions:
Debbie Herbert
Maya Savarino
Elizabeth Yhouse

Marketing:
Norma Davis
Jeanne Harrison
Andi McDonnell
Jeanne Merlanti
Robert Morris
Sue Schroeder
Maria Simonte

UMS Staff:
Catherine S. Arcure
John Kennard
Lisa M. Murray
J. Thad Schork

Credits:
Steve Maggio,
The Maggio Line,
Designer

Robert Foran,
Photographer

Peter Matthews,
Photographer

FRP Staff:
Steve Newman,
Art Director

Jim Scott,
Book Design

Mary Cummings,
Managing Editor

Judy Jackson,
Project Manager

Dean Tilton,
Associate Vice-President

Artwork and Photography:

Co-Chairs: Lois Baru, Mary VandenBelt

Our thanks to those who provided ideas, props, and musical instruments, and who helped gather and select archival photos:

Carty's Music, Inc.	Laurel Federbush,	Patrick Power	Benjamin VandenBelt
Mark Clague,	harpist	Pamela Rutledge	Suzanne Van
musicologist	Joni Muskovitz	J. Thad Schork	Appeldorn
Joseph Curtin,	King's Keyboard	Anne Griffin Sloan	
violin maker	House	Carol Spaly	

Non-Recipe Text:

Editor:	Mary M. Matthews		
Writers:	Jennifer Dix	Lois Kane	Penny Schreiber
	Annette Hodesh	Bonnie Paxton	Grace Shackman

Promotion, Special Events, and Artist Relations:
Co-Chairs: Maya Savarino, Elizabeth Yhouse

Barbara Busch	Debbie Herbert	Ingrid Merikoski	Sally Stegeman
Linda Greene	Beth Lavoie	Mary Pittman	Andrea Van Houweling
Karen Gunderson	Stephanie Lord	Sue Schroeder	

Marketing and Development:

Jeannine Buchanan	Maureen Isaac	John Mulcrone	Kathleen Treciak
Peter A. Davis	Stephanie Lord	Sue Schroeder	Van Dam
Norma Kircher	Doni Lystra	Maya Savarino	Andrea Van Houweling
Davis	Andi McDonnell	Maria Simonte	Elizabeth Yhouse
Rosalie Edwards	Jeanne Merlanti	Susan Ullrich	UMS Advisory Chairs:
Jeanne Harrison	Candice Mitchell	Bryan Ungard	Debbie Herbert
Paul Hysen	Robert Morris	Suzette Ungard	Len Niehoff

Recipes:

Co-Chairs: Raquel Agranoff, Ann Schriber
Chapter Coordination:

Raquel Agranoff	Jeannie Davis	Pat Pooley	Louise Townley
Norma Kircher Davis	Liz McLeary	Ann Schriber	

We are especially grateful to Catherine S. Arcure, UMS Director of Development, for her tireless support and guidance, and to her UMS staff for their administrative assistance in typing and compiling the recipes: Susan Fitzpatrick, Ann Hunter Greene, Lisa M. Murray, J. Thad Schork, and Anne Griffin Sloan.

Many thanks also to the renowned Michigan chefs and restaurants who contributed their hallmark specialties:

Antoinette Benjamin, Food for All Seasons	Dan Huntsbarger, The Moveable Feast	Marguerite Oliver, Pastabilities
Reid Ashton, The Golden Mushroom	Edward Janos, Merchant of Vino	Pike Street Restaurant
Misty and Todd Callies, Zanzibar	Brian J. Karam, Michigan League	Lorraine Platman, Sweet Lorraine's
Peggy de Parry and Maggie Long, Back Alley Gourmet	Andrew Kile, Heavenly Gourmet, Northville	Brian Polcyn, Five Lakes Grill
Katherine Farrell, Katherine's Catering	Jim Lark, The Lark	Matthew Prentice, Morels
Angelo and Sheila Graziano	David Loesel, Café Marie	Peachy Retenbach, La Becasse
Shelly Gruszczynski	Cheryl MacKrell	Lucien Robert, Maison Robert
Rick Halberg, Emily's Restaurant	John Metzger, Metzger's Restaurant	Marcia Sikarskie-Rhodes
Harbor House Inn, Grand Haven	Mike Monahan, Monahan's Seafood	Robert Sutch, UM Executive Chef
		Greg Upshur, Too Chez

We extend our heartfelt thanks to Dr. Herbert Sloan for his continuing encouragement and support of this project.

We wish to thank all those who made this a true community cookbook. The following people generously contributed their best recipes and spent hours in the kitchen testing and tasting:

Beatrice Adler
Patricia Adler
Raquel Agranoff
Catherine S. Arcure
Jennifer Arcure
Paulett Banks
Peter Banks
Lois Baru
Pauline Reisner
    Bernhard
Marge Biancke
Linda Binkow
Janice Stevens
    Botsford
Barbara Bryant
Barbara Busch
Bun Cristen
Mary Ann Daane
Roderick Daane
Martin Daffner
MariCarmen Davies
Norma Kircher Davis

Jeannie Davis
Peter A. Davis
Mike DeBeck
John Duffendack
Katie Derezinski
Katherine Farrell
Ken Fischer
Penny Fischer
Beverley Geltner
Anne Genovese
Anne Glendon
Paul Glendon
Shirley Goddard
Nina E. Hauser
Mary Kahn
Shirley Kauper
Wilma M. Kircher
Bernice Lamey
Emeril Lagasse
Katherine Leidy
Kathy Long
Adrienne Malley

Carol La Mantia
Chandler Matthews
Mary M. Matthews
Joe Mattimoe
Marty McClatchey
Jesse Lee Marshall
Rebecca McGowan
Patty Monahan
Melinda Morris
Robert Morris
Lisa Murray
Hillary Murt
Jan Barney Newman
Bonnie Paxton
Bruce Paxton
Jennifer Phillips
Bev Pooley
Pat Pooley
Linda Powell
Hank Prebys
Mary Price
Diane Quinn

Ieva Rasmussen
Anne Rubin
Maya Savarino
Grace Shackman
Penny Schreiber
Ann Schriber
Tom Schriber
Helen Siedel
Camille Severance
Meg Kennedy Shaw
Alva Gordon Sink
Anne Griffin Sloan
Mary VandenBelt
Shirley Van den
    Broek
Andrea Van
    Houweling
Casey Wilhelm
Michael Whiting
Bob Whitman
Elizabeth Yhouse

We wish to thank members of the UMS Advisory Committee and those who served as at-large members of the Cookbook Committee:

Jennifer Arcure
Martha Ause
Paulett Banks
Marge Biancke
Martha Bloom
Jeannine Buchanan
Letitia Byrd
Betty Byrne
Phil Cole
Peter A. Davis
Jeannine Davis
Lori Director
Betty Edman

Rosalie Edwards
H. Michael Endres
Don Faber
Katherine Farrell
Penny Fischer
Sara Frank
Joyce Ginsberg
Maryanna Graves
Linda Greene
Nina E. Hauser
Debbie Herbert
Maureen Isaac
Mercy Kasle

Maxine Larrouy
Beth Lavoie
Esther Martin
Jeanne Merlanti
Scott Merz
Candice Mitchell
Robert Morris
John Mulcrone
Len Niehoff
Nancy Niehoff
Karen Koykka O'Neal
Marysia Ostafin
Mary Pittman

Ieva Rasmussen
Anne Rubin
Jim Rudolph
Sue Schroeder
Meg Kennedy Shaw
Loretta Skewes
Cynny Spencer
Susan B. Ullrich
Bryan Ungard
Suzette Ungard
Kathleen Treciak
    Van Dam
Dody Viola

Finally, we wish to acknowledge the support of the UMS Board of Trustees:

Recipe Index

218

219

Artist Index

Photography Index

For more information, or for additional copies of *BRAVO!*, please contact:

University Musical Society
881 North University Avenue
Ann Arbor, Michigan 48109-1011
phone: (877) 238-0503 (toll free)
fax: (734) 936-0430
Online: www.ums.org